CW01084276

DEBATING SELF-KNOWLEDGE

Language users ordinarily suppose that they know what thoughts their own utterances express. We can call this supposed knowledge *minimal self-knowledge*. But what does it come to? And do we actually have it? *Anti-individualism* implies that the thoughts which a person's utterances express are partly determined by facts about their social and physical environments. If anti-individualism is true, then there are some apparently coherent skeptical hypotheses that conflict with our supposition that we have minimal self-knowledge. In this book, Anthony Brueckner and Gary Ebbs debate how to characterize this problem and develop opposing views of what it shows. Their discussion is the only sustained, in-depth debate about anti-individualism, skepticism, and knowledge of one's own thoughts, and will interest both scholars and graduate students in philosophy of language, philosophy of mind, and epistemology.

ANTHONY BRUECKNER is Professor of Philosophy at the University of California, Santa Barbara. He is author of *Essays on Skepticism* (2010).

GARY EBBS is Professor of Philosophy at Indiana University, Bloomington. He is the author of *Rule-Following and Realism* (1997) and *Truth and Words* (2009).

DEBATING
SELF-KNOWLEDGE

ANTHONY BRUECKNER

University of California, Santa Barbara

and

GARY EBBS

Indiana University, Bloomington

CAMBRIDGE
UNIVERSITY PRESS

CAMBRIDGE UNIVERSITY PRESS
Cambridge, New York, Melbourne, Madrid, Cape Town,
Singapore, São Paulo, Delhi, Mexico City

Cambridge University Press
The Edinburgh Building, Cambridge CB2 8RU, UK

Published in the United States of America by Cambridge University Press, New York

www.cambridge.org
Information on this title: www.cambridge.org/9781107017139

First published 2012

Printed in the United Kingdom at the University Press, Cambridge

A catalog record for this publication is available from the British Library

Library of Congress Cataloging in Publication data

ISBN 978-1-107-01713-9 Hardback

*Anthony Brueckner dedicates this book to his father,
Keith Brueckner, the King of Mt. Woodson*

*Gary Ebbs dedicates this book to his parents,
John and Josette Ebbs*

Contents

Acknowledgements

We acknowledge our intellectual debts to philosophical works, colleagues, and friends in footnotes to the chapters. The Introduction, and Chapters 4, 12, and 13 were written just for this volume. Chapters 1–3, and 5–11, were originally published in journals, as follows:

Chapter 1, Anthony Brueckner, "Brains in a vat," *Journal of Philosophy* 83/3 (March 1986): 148–167.

Chapter 2, Gary Ebbs, "Skepticism, objectivity, and brains in vats," *Pacific Philosophical Quarterly* 73/3 (1992): 239–266.

Chapter 3, Anthony Brueckner, "Ebbs on skepticism, objectivity, and brains in vats," *Pacific Philosophical Quarterly* 75 (1994): 77–87.

Chapter 5, Anthony Brueckner, "Trying to get outside your own skin," *Philosophical Topics* 23/1 (Spring 1995): 79–111.

Chapter 6, Gary Ebbs, "Can we take our words at face value?" *Philosophy and Phenomenological Research* 56/3 (September 1996): 499–530.

Chapter 7, Anthony Brueckner, "Is scepticism about self-knowledge incoherent?" *Analysis* 57/4 (October 1997): 287–290.

Chapter 8, Gary Ebbs, "Is skepticism about self-knowledge coherent?" *Philosophical Studies* 105 (2001): 43–58.

Chapter 9, Anthony Brueckner, "The coherence of scepticism about self-Knowledge," *Analysis* 63/1 (January 2003): 41–48.

Chapter 10, Gary Ebbs, "Why skepticism about self-knowledge is self-undermining," *Analysis* 65/3 (July 2005): 237–244.

Chapter 11, Anthony Brueckner, "Scepticism about self-knowledge redux," *Analysis* 67/4 (October 2007): 311–315.

We thank the respective journals, university presses, and editors for granting us permission to reprint these articles. We also thank Hilary Gaskin for her interest in this project, and her prompt, efficient oversight of the review and contracting for the book, and Anna Lowe and Jodie Hodgson for their supervision of its production.

Introduction

Anthony Brueckner and Gary Ebbs

Language users ordinarily suppose that they know without empirical investigation what thoughts their own utterances express. Call this supposed knowledge *minimal self-knowledge*. What does it come to? And do we actually have it? These questions are puzzling on just about any view of meaning, reference, and the nature of mental states. They are puzzling in a special way, however, if one accepts *anti-individualism*, which implies that the thoughts that a person's utterances express are partly determined by facts about her social and physical environments. The problem is that if anti-individualism is true, then there are some apparently intelligible skeptical hypotheses that threaten to undermine our ordinary supposition that we have minimal self-knowledge.

In the essays collected in this volume, we debate how to characterize this problem and what it shows. One of us (Brueckner) argues that in some skeptical contexts, there is a coherent, powerful, prima facie worry that we lack minimal self-knowledge, given the assumption of anti-individualism, while the other (Ebbs) argues that the apparent intelligibility of the allegedly problematic skeptical hypotheses is illusory, and hence does not undermine our supposed minimal self-knowledge. In this introduction we sketch some of the essential background for our debate and present a brief overview of our essays.

I ARGUMENTS FOR ANTI-INDIVIDUALISM

The following argument illustrates a general pattern of arguments for anti-individualism (taken from Putnam 1975 and Burge 1979) that we presuppose in our debate:

Step one

We imagine that Oscar, an ordinary English speaker who is competent in the use of the English word 'water' but does not accept (or reject) the sentence 'Water is H$_2$O', utters a sentence containing the word 'water', for instance, the sentence 'Water is a liquid at room temperature'. Since Oscar is a competent English speaker, other English speakers take his word 'water' to be the same as their word 'water', hence they take him to have said that *water is a liquid at room temperature*. If, in addition, they think his utterance is sincere, they take him to believe this.

Step two

We stipulate that there is a planet called Twin Earth which is just like Earth except that wherever there is water on Earth there is twin-water, a liquid with an underlying chemical structure that is very different from the chemical structure of water, on Twin Earth. We suppose that on Twin Earth there lives a person we may call Twin-Oscar, who is a physical, phenomenological, and behavioral twin of Oscar. Twin-Oscar is a normal speaker of Twin-English, the Twin-Earth counterpart of English. When Twin Oscar utters the sentence 'Water is a liquid at room temperature', his fellow Twin-English speakers take his word 'water' to be the same as their word 'water', hence they take him to have said (when translated into English) that *twin-water is a liquid at room temperature*. If, in addition, they (and we) think his utterance is sincere, they (and we) take him to believe this.

These two steps together support anti-individualism. For, by hypothesis, Oscar and Twin-Oscar share all the same *individualistic properties*: those which concern their qualitative perceptual experience and stream of consciousness, their behavior and behavioral dispositions, and their functional states. Even so, Oscar's word 'water' differs in reference from Twin-Oscar's 'water', which correctly applies to all and only samples of XYZ, rather than to all and only samples of H$_2$O. Oscar's word 'water' and Twin-Oscar's word 'water' thus have different extensions and express different concepts. The truth conditions of Oscar's 'water'-sentences accordingly differ from those of Twin-Oscar's corresponding 'water'-sentences. When Oscar utters his sentence 'Water is a liquid at room temperature', he thinks *that water is a liquid at room temperature*, whereas Twin-Oscar, who simultaneously utters his sentence 'Water is a liquid at room temperature', thinks (as we express it) *that twin-water is a liquid at room temperature*. If we suppose that the content of a person's mental state is what is specified by what follows 'that' in a description of that mental state, then the thought that Oscar thinks by using his sentence 'Water is a liquid at room temperature' differs in *content* from Twin-Oscar's corresponding thought. These differences in content apparently derive from the differences between Oscar's and Twin-Oscar's external social and, especially, physical environments – Oscar's replete with water (H_2O), and Twin-Oscar's replete with twin-water (XYZ). The observations therefore support anti-individualism, according to which a thinker's external physical and social environment partly determines the semantic properties of his words and sentences, and the contents of his intentional mental states. (Following standard usage, we sometimes call anti-individualism about content *content externalism*, and anti-individualism about semantic properties, such as reference, *semantic externalism*.)

2 MENTAL CONTENT AND INCOMPLETE UNDERSTANDING

Gareth Evans (Evans 1982, Chapter 11) grants that speakers of a natural language typically take each other's utterances at face value in the way that is illustrated by the Twin-Earth thought experiments, but insists that a speaker cannot be credited with having a mental state with a given content unless he has accurate and complete beliefs about what that content is. On Evans's view, a speaker may utter a sentence that expresses a content which is not the content of any of the speaker's own mental states. In the situation described above, for instance, when Oscar utters the sentence 'Water is a liquid at room temperature', he thereby expresses the content *that water is liquid at room temperature*, but, according to Evans, he does not *also* thereby express or have any mental state, including any thought, with that content. Evans's view implies that in the cases that we focus on in this volume, speakers do not express thoughts whose contents match the contents of the public language sentences they utter, and hence the question about minimal self-knowledge that concerns us in this volume – the question of how a person can know without empirical investigation what thoughts her utterances express, assuming that the contents of her thoughts are the same as the contents of the sentences she utters – does not arise.

Unlike Evans, we take arguments for anti-individualism to show that in ordinary situations, at least, when skepticism is not in question, there is no distance between a speaker's sincere utterance of a sentence that expresses a particular content, such as the content that water is a liquid at room temperature, on the one hand, and the speaker's thereby expressing a mental state of his with that content, on the other. We take arguments for anti-individualism to show that even speakers who do not have a full understanding of the concepts expressed by the words that they utter ordinarily possess mental states with contents that contain those concepts.

Assuming anti-individualism, understood in this way, our debate focuses on the question of how one can take oneself to have minimal self-knowledge in contexts in which one entertains certain radical skeptical hypotheses.

Chapters 1–13 fall into three main groups, comprising Chapters 1–5, 6–11, and 12–13, respectively. In Chapters 1–5, we focus on questions about minimal self-knowledge that are raised by Putnam's argument that we are not brains in a vat, and we come to see that a central question for us is whether doubts about one's apparent knowledge of the contents of one's own mental states are coherent. In Chapters 6–11 we debate this question in detail, starting with an argument Ebbs presents in Chapter 6. In Chapters 12 and 13 we each summarize and further develop our different views of what Chapters 1–11 establish and where they lead.

Here is a bit more detail about the chapters in each of these groups.

Chapters 1–5

Chapter 1, Brueckner's "Brains in a vat," was the first extended analysis of Putnam's approach to the problem of skepticism in Chapter 1 of *Reason, Truth and History* (Putnam 1981), where Putnam sought to use the semantic externalist component of anti-individualism to construct an argument that would rule out the skeptical hypothesis that one has always been a massively deceived brain in a vat whose experiences are systematically caused by a complexly programmed supercomputer. The neo-Cartesian skeptic maintains that one does not know, for example, that one has hands, in virtue of one's inability to knowledgeably rule out the vat hypothesis. Putnam's starting point was the idea that due to the differences between the causal environments in which normal thinkers and brains in vats are ensconced, the semantic properties of the language of the brain in a vat (supposing that it thinks in a language) differ from those of the language spoken by his normal unenvatted counterpart. Putnam thought that this difference would enable one to argue that one is *not* a handless brain in a vat. In Chapter 1, Brueckner reconstructs an anti-skeptical argument from these Putnamian materials. Brueckner's main worry about the reconstructed argument is that given the dialectical situation between the skeptic and the Putnamian anti-skeptic, the semantic externalism that drives the argument also undercuts the argument. The worry is that if at the outset of the anti-skeptical argument, one does not know whether one is a normal human or, instead, a brain in a vat, then one does not know the meanings and associated truth conditions of one's sentences. If this worry is well-founded, then Putnam's argument does not enable one to establish that one is not a brain in a vat. The worry presupposes that there can be coherent skeptical doubts about one's apparent knowledge of the semantic properties of one's own language.

Chapter 2, Ebbs's "Skepticism, objectivity and brains in vats," argues, among other things, that such doubts, as well as corresponding doubts about one's apparent knowledge of the contents of one's own mental states, are incoherent. Ebbs argues that to understand and evaluate Putnam's argument that we are not always brains in vats, we must not simply grant the skeptic from the start that *we may actually be brains in vats from the beginning to the end of our lives*, as Brueckner does in his assessment of his reconstructed Putnamian argument. Instead, we must take seriously from the start that we might not be able to make sense of actually being brains in vats from the beginning to the end of our lives. Ebbs argues, in effect, that if we regard it as a genuine possibility that we cannot make sense of actually being brains in vats, then the main results of anti-individualism support Putnam's reasoning. Ebbs also aims to rehabilitate the Putnamian considerations by shifting from the use of semantic externalism to the use of anti-individualism about mental content in the construction of an anti-skeptical argument. Applying these two aspects of his reading of Putnam's argument, Ebbs argues that Thomas Nagel's well-known response to Putnam in *The View from Nowhere* (Nagel 1986) depends on a misunderstanding of anti-individualistic accounts of belief content.

Chapter 3, Brueckner's paper "Ebbs on skepticism, objectivity and brains in vats," responds to Ebbs's criticisms in Chapter 2, holding that an analogue to Brueckner's worry about his own semantic externalist argument arises for the Ebbs-style argument that is fueled by content externalism. Assuming again, as he does in Chapter 1, that there can be coherent skeptical doubts about one's apparent knowledge of the semantic properties of one's own language, Brueckner suggests that in the dialectical situation in play in the skeptic/anti-skeptic dispute, claims to know the contents of one's own thoughts are just as problematic as claims to know the semantic properties of one's own language. Brueckner also discusses the question of whether one can extend the anti-individualist approach to non-empirical concepts, a question that Ebbs raises in his discussion of Nagelian objectivity in Chapter 2.

In Chapter 4, a new essay written for this volume, Ebbs responds to Brueckner's criticisms in Chapter 3 by distinguishing between two different conceptions of the dialectical context of Putnam's argument. Ebbs grants that Putnam's argument must begin with an attitude of agnosticism about whether we are in a vat world or a normal world, but he does not accept Brueckner's understanding of the sense of agnosticism that is relevant to the dialectical context of Putnam's argument. Brueckner's understanding of the agnosticism rules out an important kind of response to a skeptical argument, one that begins by entertaining the possibility that a given skeptical hypothesis is coherent, and may actually be true, and ends by concluding that the hypothesis, while meaningful, is not coherent, and therefore cannot actually be true. According to Ebbs, it is this latter kind of response to skepticism that is relevant to the dialectical contexts of Putnam's argument and of Ebbs's related criticism in Chapter 2 of Thomas Nagel's conception of objectivity.

Chapters 2–4 highlight the central importance for both Brueckner and Ebbs of the question whether doubts about one's apparent knowledge of the contents of one's own mental states are incoherent. Chapter 5, Brueckner's "Trying to get outside your own skin," canvasses and criticizes several of the ways in which philosophers, including Ebbs, have tried to respond to the charge that externalist semantic views generate a coherent, powerful, prima facie worry that we lack minimal self-knowledge.

Chapters 6–11

The second main group of chapters begins with Chapter 6, Ebbs's "Can we take our words at face value?" which presents a new way of responding to the charge that externalist semantic views generate a coherent skeptical challenge to our ordinary assumption that we have minimal self-knowledge. Ebbs argues that we can't even try to raise a skeptical challenge to our ordinary beliefs about what thoughts our utterances express unless we take for granted that we are competent to use our words to raise the challenge, and this requires that we presuppose some background empirical beliefs. But if we presuppose background empirical beliefs that are sufficient for minimal competence, Ebbs argues, then we cannot make sense of the content skeptic's claim that we may actually be in a world in which our utterances express thoughts that are different from what we take them to express.

Chapter 7, Brueckner's paper "Is skepticism about self-knowledge incoherent?" replies to Chapter 6 by attempting to show that we can know we have presented a *sound* argument for content skepticism even if we do not presuppose any empirical beliefs, and hence don't know what thoughts we express when we utter the premises of the argument for content skepticism. Against this, Chapter 8, Ebbs's "Is skepticism about self-knowledge incoherent?," observes that Brueckner's reply in Chapter 7 depends on the assumption that we are not in any possible world in which the argument that we express by uttering the sentences of the skeptic's argument is unsound. Ebbs argues that the principles of anti-individualism imply that for each of us there are such weird possible worlds. Ebbs also points out that if Brueckner's account of what we can know without empirical investigation is correct, then we cannot know without empirical investigation that we are not in one of the weird possible worlds. Ebbs concludes that Brueckner's reply in Chapter 7 depends on an empirical assumption – the assumption that we are not in one of the weird worlds – that by his own standards we cannot be justified in accepting without empirical investigation. This observation prompted further objections and replies, developed in Chapters 8–11, which concern the difficult questions of whether one can be justified in accepting the premises of the argument for content skepticism, and, if not, whether that shows that content skepticism is incoherent. In addition to these central issues, Chapters 8–11 range over such related topics as the use of reductio arguments in philosophy and skepticism about reasoning itself.

Chapters 12–13

In Chapter 12 and Chapter 13, both of them new and written just for this volume, we each summarize and further develop our own views of what the debate has established and where it leads.

In Chapter 12, "Self-knowledge in doubt," Ebbs lays down three conditions on a successful skeptical argument of the sort that Brueckner aims to construct, and then summarizes and expands on his criticisms of Brueckner's attempts to raise a skeptical doubt about whether we have minimal self-knowledge. According to Ebbs, his criticisms show that we should reject the conception of minimal self-knowledge on which Brueckner's skeptical arguments rely. Ebbs argues that if we adopt instead the minimalist conception of minimal self-knowledge that he sketches in Chapters 6, 8, and 10, we simultaneously avoid the problems with Brueckner's reasoning, and commit ourselves to principles from which it follows that we cannot make sense of doubting that we have minimal self-knowledge. Ebbs ends the chapter by sketching a methodological framework within which our failure to be able to raise a coherent doubt about whether we have minimal self-knowledge helps us to see both what it is and that we have it.

In Chapter 13, "Looking back," Brueckner revisits the exchange with Ebbs in the first group of chapters regarding Putnam's brains in vats, commenting on Ebbs's new, previously unpublished Chapter 4. Brueckner then tries to summarize the exchange regarding skepticism about knowledge of thought-content embodied in Chapters 6–11, while trying to explicitly formulate principles about a stretch of reasoning's being *self-undermining*. A discussion of Descartes on the latter issue concludes the chapter.

Brains in a vat

Anthony Brueckner

In Chapter I of *Reason, Truth, and History*,[1] Hilary Putnam argues from some plausible assumptions about the nature of reference to the conclusion that it is not possible that all sentient creatures are brains in a vat. If this argument is successful, it seemingly refutes an updated form of Cartesian skepticism concerning knowledge of physical objects. In this chapter, I will state what I take to be the most promising interpretation of Putnam's argument. My reconstructed argument differs from an argument strongly suggested by Putnam's text. I will show that the latter argument obviously does not work. The more promising argument which I reconstruct on behalf of Putnam raises some interesting questions about the relation between the contents of one's beliefs and one's environment and about how this relation affects the evaluation of anti-skeptical arguments. I conclude that my reconstructed argument ultimately fails as a response to Cartesian skepticism: the argument engenders a skepticism about knowledge of meaning, or propositional content, which undercuts its anti-skeptical force.[2]

I.1

I will begin by stating a Cartesian skeptical argument about brains in a vat. Let us say that if Q is a logically possible proposition that is incompatible

I would like to thank the members of a seminar on epistemology at Yale University in fall, 1983, for helpful discussions of these issues. I have also benefited from conversations with John Fischer and Jonathan Wilwerding. I am especially indebted to Phillip Bricker for quite extensive criticisms and suggestions which greatly changed and improved this paper.

[1] Putnam 1981; parenthetical page references will be to this book, unless otherwise noted.

[2] The argument of Chapter I should be sharply distinguished from the "model-theoretic" argument against metaphysical realism which Putnam develops in Chapters 2 and 3 of his book (see also Putnam 1978 and Putnam 1980). His argument against metaphysical realism, if successful, would show, in a quite different way from Chapter I's argument, that the brains-in-a-vat "possibility" is incoherent. The argument of Chapter I indeed depends upon causal-theoretic assumptions about reference which Putnam explicitly rejects in Chapters 2 and 3. Putnam has indicated (in conversation) that it was in fact his intention to construct an argument in Chapter I quite different from the model-theoretic argument of the later chapters. For a criticism of that argument, see Brueckner 1984.

with *P* and *P* is a logically possible proposition, then *Q* is a *counterpossibility* to *P*. Let us also state a *counterpossibility principle*:

(CP) If I know that *P* and that *Q* is a counterpossibility to *P*, then I know that *Q* is not the case.[3]

The argument proceeds as follows.

(A) *That I am a brain in a vat inhabiting a world in which the only objects are brains in a vat and laboratories containing computers programmed to stimulate the brains* is a logically possible proposition.
(B) If I am a brain in a vat of the Putnamian sort just specified (hereafter a *BIV*), then I am not, for example, now sitting on a chair.
(C) The proposition that I am a BIV is a counterpossibility to the proposition that I am now sitting on a chair. [(A), (B)]
(D) If I know that I am now sitting on a chair and that the proposition that I am a BIV is a counterpossibility to the proposition that I am now sitting on a chair, then I know that I am not a BIV. [(CP)]
(E) I know that (C).
(F) I do not know that I am not a BIV.
(G) I do not know that I am now sitting on a chair. [(D), (E), (F)]

The same argument can be stated with respect to every proposition about physical objects which I claim to know, except the propositions that there are objects, that there are computers, that there are brains, that there are vats, and the like (propositions that would be true even if I were a BIV). Now if Putnam can show that it is *not* possible that all sentient creatures are BIVs, then he can block the foregoing argument by refuting premise (A). This is indeed the kind of anti-skeptical strategy which is suggested by many of Putnam's remarks, but later in this section I will show that it is not available to him.

Putnam's argument to show that (A) is false, that is, that it is not possible that I am a BIV, depends upon an analysis of the truth conditions for the sentence 'I am a BIV' as uttered (or thought) by a BIV.[4] It is natural to suppose that the sentence would be *true* as uttered by a BIV and that,

---

[3] (CP) is not importantly different from the principle that knowledge is closed under known logical implication:

If I know that *P* and that *P* logically implies *Q*, then I know that *Q*.

One might challenge the skeptical argument by challenging this sort of principle, but this is not Putnam's strategy.

[4] In speaking about BIVs, I will use 'utter' to mean, in effect, 'seem to utter', since a BIV cannot speak or write, but only seems to himself to be speaking or writing. Alternatively, one could take 'utter' to mean 'think a sentence token'.

correlatively, the sentence 'I am sitting on a chair' would be *false* as uttered by a BIV. The BIV's utterance of 'I am a BIV' would presumably be held to be true, though, by virtue of the supposed fact that a BIV's token of 'brain' would refer to brains and his token of 'vat' would refer to vats. However, Putnam argues that a proper understanding of the causal requirements for reference will show that the brain's token of 'BIV' does not refer to BIVs.

Suppose that there are no trees on Mars and that a Martian forms a mental image exactly resembling one of *my* tree images as a result of his perceiving a blob of paint that accidentally resembles a tree. Putnam's intuition is that the Martian's image is not a representation of a tree. Now if I were a BIV, then (a) my mental life would be qualitatively identical to my actual mental life ("from the inside"), (b) my mental life would be caused by a computer's electrical stimulation of my brain, (c) the same would be true of every other sentient creature, (d) the situation described in (a)–(c) would have arisen completely randomly, and (e) there would be no trees, since there would be no objects other than brains, a vat, and the computers that stimulate the brains. If I were a BIV, then, my mental image "of a tree" would no more be a representation of a tree than would the Martian's mental image. Neither of us would have the sort of causal contact with trees which is required for our images to refer to trees. The same reasoning applies to any tokens of 'tree' which might come to be uttered (or thought) by the Martian and by my BIV counterpart. (We assume that the Martian's token is just as randomly caused as is his "treelike" image – we assume that the token is not ultimately caused by, say, a conversation with a visiting Earthling.)

What does the BIV's token of 'tree' refer to, if not to trees? Putnam offers three possibilities: (i) to "trees-in-the-image" (I take it that by 'the image' Putnam means *the succession of sense impressions had by the BIV*), (ii) to the electrical impulses that stimulate the brain and thereby cause it to have sense impressions just like those I have when I see a tree, and (iii) to the program features that are causally responsible for the stimuli described in (ii). On the *natural* assignment of references which one would make in evaluating the truth value of a BIV's utterance of 'Here is a tree', one would hold that the brain's token of 'tree' refers to trees and, hence, that his sentence token is false (expresses a falsehood),[5] since he is not near a tree. On each of Putnam's proposed reference assignments, though, the brain's sentence

---

[5] It makes no difference to this chapter whether sentence tokens or propositions (or something else) are the truth-bearers. I will often speak of *utterances* as being true. One could regard this as shorthand for whichever account is deemed superior.

token comes out *true* (provided that the brain is indeed being stimulated so as to have sense impressions just like those I have when I see a tree and that the stimulation is caused by a computer's program features). On account (i), e.g., the brain's utterance of 'Here is a tree' is true iff the brain is having sense impressions as of being near a tree.[6]

On account (i), a BIV's token of 'BIV' refers to *BIVs-in-the-image*, and a BIV's utterance of 'I am a BIV' would be true iff he were a BIV-in-the-image. As I understand it, those truth conditions are equivalent to these: the BIV's utterance would be true iff he had sense impressions as of being a BIV. But by Putnam's hypothesis, a BIV never has such sense impressions. A BIV has only sense impressions as of being a normal, embodied human being moving through a richly varied world of physical objects. Thus, on account (i), a BIV's utterance of 'I am a BIV' would never be true, contrary to the deliverance of what I called the "natural" account of the utterance's truth conditions.[7]

Before considering the question of what actually follows from Putnam's claims about reference, we must note that these claims do not obviously hold for what one might call a *standard* brain-in-a-vat situation. The claims do not obviously hold for a situation in which I am a brain in a vat and am stimulated by evil neuroscientists who, e.g., stimulate my brain in exactly the way their brains are stimulated when they see a beech tree outside their laboratory, thereby causing me to have sense impressions just like their *veridical* sense impressions as of beeches. In such a standard brain-in-a-vat situation, a reasonable causal theorist of reference would surely hold that the brain's token of 'tree' is causally connected with trees by virtue of the token's causal connection with the evil neuroscientist and *his* tokens of 'tree'. Putnam's claims about reference, then, hold at best for worlds in

---

[6] More exactly, the truth conditions for a BIV's utterance of 'Here is a tree' are the would-be phenomenalist truth conditions for English utterances of the sentence. That is, a sophisticated phenomenalist would hold that, e.g., one need not have sense impressions as of a green tree in order for one's sentence 'Here is a green tree' to be true. This is because a sophisticated phenomenalist would want to allow for the drawing of an is/seems distinction within the phenomenalistic language, allowing one to say truly, "A green tree is before me, though I have sense impressions as of a red tree (though there seems to be a red tree before me)." The truth conditions for a BIV's utterance of 'I am a BIV' [on account (i)] accordingly concern more complex facts about sense impressions than those discussed in the text. However, please allow me the more simplistic formulation in the text in order to avoid excessive complication. I am indebted here to David Braun and Michael Thompson.

[7] On account (i), a person whom we would normally consider to be a victim of deception by a nonphysical Cartesian evil genius would say something true when he uttered 'Here is a tree', since 'tree' would refer to sense impressions as of trees. On the analogue to accounts (ii) and (iii), the victim's term would presumably refer to the states of the evil genius which are causally responsible for the aforementioned sense impressions, and the victim would again say something true. (So he would not really be a *victim of deception*.)

which there is nothing other than brains in a vat and their automatic tenders (innocent human bystanders causally unconnected with the computers would not affect Putnam's claims). So even if it follows from Putnam's remarks that it is not possible that I am in a vat of the latter sort, it does not follow that it is not possible that I am a brain in a vat of the standard sort. Hence Putnam's remarks have no force against a Cartesian skeptical argument built upon the (supposed) counterpossibility that I am a brain in a vat of the standard sort.

Do Putnam's remarks about reference even show that "it cannot possibly be true" that I am a BIV (a *Putnamian* brain in a vat)? Here is Putnam's own summary of his reasoning: "In short, if we are brains in a vat, then 'We are brains in a vat' is false. So it is (necessarily) false" (p. 15). This argument (which depends upon the claims about reference) does not show that the proposition that I am a BIV is not a logically possible proposition. It does not show that this proposition is necessarily false. The main point of Putnam's remarks about reference is that the sentence 'I am a BIV' as uttered by a BIV expresses a *different proposition* from the proposition it expresses as uttered by a non-BIV. In the latter case, the sentence expresses a proposition about BIVs, whereas in the former case, it expresses a proposition about sense impressions [on account (i)]. That is, the truth conditions for utterances of the sentence shift from the one case to the other (since the references of the parts of the sentence shift), and this means that the sentence expresses different propositions in the two cases. So we cannot reason from Putnam's claims about reference to the conclusion that a single proposition – that I am a BIV – is not a logically possible proposition (is necessarily false).

Putnam at times states his conclusion in a less misleading way. He says that the proposition that I am a BIV is, like the proposition that I do not exist, a *self-refuting supposition*, such that the entertaining or enunciating of the supposition entails its falsity (pp. 8–9). But this is not quite right either as an account of what Putnam has argued on the basis of his claims about reference. Being self-refuting, in the sense Putnam apparently has in mind, is a property not of suppositions or propositions, but rather of sentences. It is the following property: if a self-refuting sentence S of a given language is uttered or thought, then S expresses some false proposition or other. Some self-refuting sentences (such as 'I do not exist') express different propositions when different people utter them, so that in such cases, there is no *single* supposition or proposition that is false simply by virtue of being entertained. Now the proposition expressed by a particular utterance of a self-refuting sentence need not be a necessarily false (logically impossible) proposition.[8] The proposition expressed by a particular utterance of the English sentence 'I do not exist' is obviously not necessarily false. When I utter the sentence, I express a proposition that is true at some possible worlds (those in which I never come into existence).[9] Similarly, for all Putnam has shown, the proposition that I am a BIV is not necessarily false either. It is rather that, if I were a BIV, the proposition that my sentence 'I am a BIV' would express would be false, and, if I were not a BIV, the *different* proposition that my sentence 'I am a BIV' would express in that case would be false as well. It is not even quite right to say that, given all this, the sentence 'I am a BIV' is self-refuting in the way in which 'I do not exist' is. This is because when a non-BIV English speaker utters the sentence, it is apparently part of a different language from that of a BIV, since a BIV speaks vat-English, a language with a great number of semantical properties different from those of English. So there is in this case no sentence *of a given language* which expresses a false proposition when uttered by a non-BIV and expresses a *different* false proposition when uttered by a BIV.[10]

1.2

If Putnam cannot show that the proposition that I am a BIV is necessarily false, then he cannot refute the Cartesian skeptical argument considered above by way of refuting premise (A) in the envisaged manner. So the suggested anti-skeptical strategy seems to fail. If he is right, however, in holding that the sentence 'I am a BIV' has a property like that of being self-refuting (that it has some such property follows from the claims about reference), then Putnam apparently does have available another way of refuting the skeptical argument. Consider the following reasoning, in which I use account (i) of vat-English truth conditions.

---

[8] A sentence that expresses a necessarily false proposition will be a self-refuting sentence, on the present account.

[9] On certain views of the semantics of indexical expressions (e.g., Kaplan 1989), the whole story will not be told if we say that 'I do not exist' expresses different propositions when uttered by different people. This is because (on Kaplan's view, for example) the sentence has a uniform *character* across different speakers, though the *content* shifts. The content, though, is true at some worlds and false at others.

[10] One might hold that a BIV speaks the same language as an English-speaking non-BIV, though many of the BIV's terms have different references from the non-BIV's (just as my indexicals have different references from yours, even though we both speak English). Nothing in this chapter hinges upon whether we call the BIV's language English. All that is crucial is that many of the BIV's terms have different references from the non-BIV's, and that one does not know which set of references one's own terms have (the BIV set or the non-BIV set).

(1) Either I am a BIV (speaking vat-English) or I am a non-BIV (speaking English).
(2) If I am a BIV (speaking vat-English), then my utterances of 'I am a BIV' are true iff I have sense impressions as of being a BIV.
(3) If I am a BIV (speaking vat-English), then I do not have sense impressions as of being a BIV.
(4) If I am a BIV (speaking vat-English), then my utterances of 'I am a BIV' are false. [(2), (3)]
(5) If I am a non-BIV (speaking English), then my utterances of 'I am a BIV' are true iff I am a BIV.
(6) If I am a non-BIV (speaking English), then my utterances of 'I am a BIV' are false. [(5)]
(7) My utterances of 'I am a BIV' are false. [(1), (4), (6)]

The intuition behind the argument is that no matter whether or not I am a BIV – no matter whether I am speaking vat-English or English – when I utter 'I am a BIV', I say something false. So, by the argument, I know that whatever proposition is expressed by my utterances of 'I am a BIV' is a false proposition. How does this conclusion enable me to refute the Cartesian skeptical argument? Presumably the proposition expressed by my utterances of 'I am a BIV' is the proposition that I am a BIV. So if I know on the basis of the above argument that the proposition expressed by my utterances of 'I am a BIV' is false, then I know that it is false that I am a BIV. Hence, I have refuted premise (F) of the skeptical argument

(F) I do not know that I am not a BIV.

On this strategy, then, the anti-skeptic does not try to refute the skeptical argument by refuting premise (A), as in the strategy suggested by some of Putnam's remarks and rejected above.

Before proceeding to evaluate the above anti-skeptical argument, I will pause in order to point out the affinities between the reconstructed Putnamian position and an interesting position in the philosophy of mind. Suppose that one holds that in Putnam's famous Twin Earth example, the sentence 'Water is wet' expresses different propositions when my twin and I utter it, simply in virtue of the fact that the liquid on Twin Earth superficially indistinguishable from Earthly water has the chemical structure XYZ rather than H_2O. Anyone who holds this view has the makings of an anti-skeptical argument like that above at his disposal. Tyler Burge, for example, in "Other Bodies,"[11] maintains that "the contents of Adam and ... [Adam's twin's]

---

[11] Burge 1982b; see also Burge 1979.

beliefs and thoughts differ while every feature of their non-intentionally and individualistically described physical, behavioural, dispositional, and phenomenal histories remains the same." On Burge's "anti-individualistic" view, it would, for example, be incorrect for me to attribute to my twin the belief that water is wet. According to Burge, my twin's term 'water' does not mean the same thing as my term 'water' despite our exact similarity from the skin inward, given the difference in our physical environments. It would therefore be incorrect to use my term 'water' in oblique occurrence in a 'that'-clause which ascribes content to the belief that my twin expresses by using 'Water is wet'. It would be best to coin a word like 'twater' to use in such (de dicto) belief ascription.

Burge does not in fact use these claims about how one's physical environment can affect the content of one's thoughts and beliefs in the same anti-skeptical manner as that embodied in the foregoing argument. He does, however, think it would be incredible to claim that my twin would hold beliefs involving the notion of water in a solipsistic world in which no water exists, no twater exists, and no community of speakers exists to spin even deluded stories using the term 'water'. How would my twin have acquired the concept of water, as opposed to, say, the concept of twater in such a world, Burge wonders? Why would the beliefs expressed by his uses of 'water' in such a world be false when evaluated with respect to that world and yet (a) *true* when evaluated with respect to a world containing water, but (b) *false* when evaluated with respect to a world containing twater? Wouldn't it be just as reasonable to hold that the beliefs would be *false* when evaluated with respect to a world containing water, but *true* when evaluated with respect to a world containing twater?[12] Burge's point is apparently that there is no clearly correct choice to be made in the ascription of content to a solipsistic subject's "beliefs" expressed using 'water' and that there is hence something incoherent in the supposition that it is possible that I am a solipsistic subject holding the false belief that water is wet (and the false belief that I am sitting on a chair, etc.). This suggestion of an anti-skeptical strategy is echoed by Putnam's remark (p. 15) that a BIV might mean nothing at all when he utters 'I am a BIV'. That is, the suggestion seems to be that there is no clearly correct choice to be made in the ascription of content to a BIV's "beliefs." This sort of anti-skeptical move is importantly

---

[12] See Burge 1982b, pp. 114–118, for his remarks on skepticism. See also Burge 1982b, fn. 18, p. 120. Burge has indicated (in conversation) that he regarded a straightforward anti-individualist argument against skepticism as no more than a tantalizing possibility when he was writing "Other bodies" and is now dubious about the success of such reasoning.

different from that embodied in the reconstructed Putnamian argument, according to which there *is* a correct choice: the correct ascription of content to a BIV's beliefs is such as to make them *true*. The evaluation of the variant Burge-style strategy will have to wait upon the evaluation of the reconstructed Putnamian argument.[13]

I . 3

Let us from now on refer to the set of sentences (1)–(7), which express our anti-skeptical argument, as E. To begin to see how peculiar E is, consider the following apparent problem with premise (2). It seems that (2) does not correctly state the truth conditions that my utterances of 'I am a BIV' have on condition that I am a BIV. We are assuming that 'true' (and 'if', 'and', etc.) have the same semantical properties in their occurrences in vat-English that they have in their occurrences in English. Hence, even for a BIV, the following sentence would be true as uttered by him in vat-English:

(T) My utterances of 'I am a BIV' are true iff I am a BIV.

(T) is true so long as the metalanguage used in stating (T) is the same as (or contains) the language of the mentioned sentence. And this relation does hold for the relevant meta- and object languages: if (T) is uttered by a BIV, then vat-English will be both the meta- and the object language, and if (T) is uttered by a non-BIV, English will be both the meta- and the object language. It is not as if a speaker might be bilingual in English and vat-English (in which case the sentence mentioned in (T) could be in a different language from the language of the words used in (T)). In the light of these remarks, recall argument E's premise:

(5) If I am a non-BIV (speaking English), then my utterances of 'I am a BIV' are true iff I am a BIV.

Given that (T) would also be true as uttered by a BIV, we apparently also have

(8) If I am a BIV (speaking vat-English), then my utterances of 'I am a BIV' are true iff I am a BIV.

Compare (8) with

(9) If I am speaking a language in which 'tail' refers to legs, then horses have four tails.

---

[13] See Fodor unpublished for a conception of belief content according to which my twin and I express the same content by our utterances of 'Water is wet'. On this view, one cannot develop a Burge-style anti-skeptical strategy. See also Fodor 1982, together with Burge's rejoinder (1982a).

But the truth of (8) raises problems for the reconstructed argument. Given premise (3) in E:

(3) If I am a BIV (speaking vat-English), then I do not have sense impressions as of being a BIV.

it follows that (8) and premise (2) give incompatible truth conditions for my utterances of 'I am a BIV' on condition that I am a BIV. The truth conditions specified in

(2) If I am a BIV (speaking vat-English), then my utterances of 'I am a BIV' are true iff I have sense impressions as of being a BIV.

are incompatible with those given in (8) if premise (3) is true. Premise (2), then, seems problematic if (8) is true.

One might respond to the foregoing objection by maintaining that (8) is false for the same reason that (9) is false. That is, one could reasonably maintain that in evaluating the truth value of (9) at a world, we are *not* to (I) interpret its consequent in such a way that the condition specified in its antecedent is taken as applying to the language used in stating the consequent and (II) evaluate the latter's truth value accordingly. It is only if we did so interpret the consequent that it would come out true (holding the rest of English fixed) whenever the antecedent is true. If we did not interpret the consequent in this nonstandard manner, we would evaluate (9) at a world in which its antecedent is true (a world in which a variant of English is spoken) by determining whether in such a world, the *English* sentence 'Horses have four tails' would be true. On this view, (8) is no more plausible than (9) and hence presents no problem for (2). (8) seemed plausible only because it was mistakenly assumed that, since (T) would be true as uttered by a BIV speaking vat-English, (8) is thereby established. But this fact about (T) establishes (8) only if, in evaluating the truth value of (8) at a world in which its antecedent is true, we must interpret its consequent as being in vat-English and evaluate its truth value accordingly. This method of interpretation, however, is just as nonstandard for (8) as for (9).[14]

This response, of course, depends upon the assumption that, just as in (9) we interpret the consequent as being in English even when we are evaluating its truth value at a world in which a variant of English is spoken, so in (8) we interpret the consequent as being in English when we are evaluating its

---

[14] There is surely no temptation to suppose that this variant on (9) is true:

(9′) If I were speaking a language in which 'tail' refers to legs, then horses would have four tails.

(8) and (9), I am claiming in the text, are no more plausible than (9′).

truth value at a world in which vat-English is spoken – we interpret the consequent of (8) as being an English specification of the truth conditions that the mentioned sentence would have as uttered in vat-English. The idea is that the consequent of (2) gives the correct English specification of those truth conditions. The consequent of (8), *if understood as a piece of vat-English*, would give the correct specification of the mentioned sentence's vat-English truth conditions. But the language used throughout (8), we assume, is English. On this understanding, (8)'s consequent does *not* give the truth conditions that 'I am a BIV' would have as uttered by a BIV. (8) is false, then, because there are worlds at which its antecedent is true, yet its consequent false: worlds in which I am a BIV.

Now this is not an entirely legitimate response to the original objection. If I am allowed to assume that I am speaking English rather than vat-English, then I am allowed to assume that I am not a BIV. In that case, the argument E is of no interest. If I do not assume that the argument is being given in English, though, the problem of evaluating the argument becomes quite bizarre. Normally, when one evaluates an argument, one is allowed to assume that it is stated in a given language L, but this is not so in the case at hand. Consider the following question. Suppose a BIV were to consider the sentences comprising E [(1)–(7)]. Would he then be entertaining a set of propositions that constituted a sound argument? If not, then a problem for the current anti-Cartesian strategy would arise as follows. On Putnam's view (as interpreted in the current anti-skeptical strategy), there is a sense in which I do not know which propositions are expressed by the sentences in E when I utter them. Which proposition is expressed by my utterances of, say, 'I am a BIV' depends upon whether or not I am a BIV speaking vat-English, and I cannot claim to know that I am not a BIV until I can claim to know that E is a sound argument and that it somehow allows me to know that I am not a BIV. The tactic of the current strategy is to show, by means of E, that no matter which proposition is expressed by 'I am a BIV' when I utter it, what is expressed is false. But a condition for the success of the strategy is that I can at least claim to know that the sentences in E express propositions forming a sound argument when I utter them. Can I claim to know this without assuming that I am speaking English?

Before attempting to answer this question, let me explain why our most recent considerations show that the Burge-style anti-skeptical strategy (as I have construed it) is problematic. If I do not know whether I am speaking English or the "language" spoken by a BIV, and if the utterances of a BIV lack content (as Burge seemed to claim in the case of the solipsistic twin), then I do not know whether or not my own utterances have content. I think that they obviously do have content; yet I do not know this unless I know whether or not I am a BIV. So the Burge-style strategy engenders a skeptical problem about the very meaningfulness of my sentences. By contrast, on the reconstructed Putnamian view, my utterances have a determinate content even if I am a BIV speaking vat-English, and even in such a situation these utterances express truths (contrary to what the skeptic had thought). One's lack of knowledge as to whether one is speaking English or vat-English also raises a problem for yet a third strategy suggested by Putnam (which is distinct from both his suggested move on which a BIV means nothing by 'I am a BIV' and from the move embodied in E). Putnam at one point says, "although the people in . . . [the vat-world] can think and 'say' any words we can think or say, they cannot (I claim) *refer* to what we can refer to. In particular, they cannot think or say that they are brains in a vat (*even by thinking 'we are brains in a vat'*)" (p. 8). This remark might seem to contain the seeds of an anti-skeptical argument which is different from both the Burge-style "no-content" argument and the argument developed at some length above. Thus, Michael Williams (in a review of *Reason, Truth and History*[15]) says that Putnam adopts a "view of meaning and reference which precludes his taking seriously the skeptical problems which bedevil the metaphysical realist" (1984, p. 260), and Williams goes on to characterize Putnam's anti-skeptical reasoning as follows: "the words or thought-signs used by brains-in-vats, including 'brain', 'vat', etc., do not mean what they mean when used by normal human beings. Thus anyone who can think to himself, 'I may be a brain in a vat,' meaning by this what we would normally mean by it, is not a brain in a vat" (1984, p. 261). However, I can conclude from this that I am a normal human being rather than a BIV – and thereby lay the skeptical problem to rest – only if I can assume that I mean by 'I may be a BIV' what normal human beings mean by it. But I am entitled to that assumption only if I am entitled to assume that I am a normal human being speaking English rather than a BIV speaking vat-English. This must be *shown* by an anti-skeptical argument, not assumed in advance.

I.4

To return to our evaluation of the argument E, do the constituent sentences of E express propositions forming a sound argument if these sentences are in vat-English? In order to answer this question, I will try to express the propositions that would be expressed by the sentences in E as uttered by a BIV speaking

---

[15] Williams 1984.

vat-English. The point will then be to see whether the propositions expressed form a sound argument. Before we can begin to undertake this maneuver, the question arises, what would a BIV's token of 'sense impression' refer to? It seems absurd to say that just as his token of 'tree' would refer to sense impressions as of trees (on account (i)), so his token of 'sense impression' would refer to sense impressions as of sense impressions. It would probably be best for Putnam to say that a BIV's token of 'sense impression' would refer to sense impressions.[16] On this construal, then, according to account (i), a BIV's token of 'sense impression as of trees' would refer to sense impressions as of trees. Here, then, is the set E′ of sentences which (apparently) express the propositions that a BIV would be considering were he to consider the sentences in E (I use account (i) throughout):[17]

(1′) Either I have sense impressions as of being a BIV or I do not have sense impressions as of being a BIV.
(2′) If I have sense impressions as of being a BIV, then my utterances of 'I am a BIV' are true iff I have sense impressions as of being a BIV.
(3′) If I have sense impressions as of being a BIV, then I do not have sense impressions as of being a BIV.
(4′) If I have sense impressions as of being a BIV, then my utterances of 'I am a BIV' are false. [(2′), (3′)]
(5′) If I do not have sense impressions as of being a BIV, then my utterances of 'I am a BIV' are true iff I have sense impressions as of being a BIV.
(6′) If I do not have sense impressions as of being a BIV, then my utterances of 'I am a BIV' are false. [(5′)]
(7′) My utterances of 'I am a BIV' are false. [(1′), (4′), (6′)]

Call the set of sentences (1′)–(7′) E′. Does E′ express a sound argument? The argument is valid, and the question whether it is sound hinges upon the truth values of (2′), (3′), and (5′). Whether these premises are true depends upon whether any sense impression could possibly count as a *seeming to be a BIV*, in the way in which my current sense impression clearly counts as a

---

[16] Alternatively: just as 'Here is a tree' has as its vat-English truth conditions the would-be phenomenalist truth conditions for the English reading of the sentence 'Here is a tree', so 'It merely seems as if there is a tree here' has as its vat-English truth conditions the would-be phenomenalist truth conditions of that English sentence. These latter truth conditions, though, are apparently the same as the normal truth conditions of the English sentence about seeming. I am indebted to Michael Thompson here.

[17] On account (ii), the antecedent of the counterpart to premise (2) would be 'I have electrical impulses which cause me to have sense impressions as of being a BIV'. So we would have to ask what a BIV's token of 'electrical impulses which cause me to have sense impressions as of being a BIV' refers to. Presumably, it would refer to electrical impulses which cause me to have sense impressions as of electrical impulses which cause me to have sense impressions as of being a BIV.

seeming to be in a library room. A sense impression as of seeing a room containing a brain in a vat connected to a computer would not count as the former sort of seeming, even if the seeming to see were as if from a disembodied point of view. If such a sense impression would not count as a seeming to be a BIV, then it is hard to imagine which sort of sense impression *would.* If no sense impression could count as a seeming to be a BIV, then Putnam can maintain that (2′) and (3′) are both true by virtue of having a common necessarily false antecedent.[18]

What about (5′)? Its antecedent is not a necessary falsehood. Further, this premise will be false if the conditionals in the argument are read as being stronger than material conditionals (as we have in fact been reading them). This is because even the subjunctive reading of (5′) is false, since if I were a non-BIV who does not have sense impressions as of being a BIV, then the truth conditions for my utterances of 'I am a BIV' would *not* be those specified in (5′)'s consequent. Rather, they would be those specified in (5)'s consequent:

(5) If I am a non-BIV (speaking English), then my utterances of 'I am a BIV' are true iff I am a BIV.

However, even though the semantical premises of the original argument E were presumably supposed to follow from conceptual facts of some kind concerning reference (and hence the argument's conditionals were thought to be stronger than material conditionals), we need not insist on interpreting the conditionals in E′ as being stronger than material conditionals. So long as the sentences in E′ express a sound deductive argument of some kind regardless of whether they are interpreted as being in English or in vat-English, I can reason that the sentences in the original argument E express a sound deductive argument regardless of whether they are interpreted as being in English or in vat-English. The fact that the vat-English argument would be unsound if the conditionals were interpreted as subjunctive or strict conditionals seems irrelevant so long as the material conditional reading yields a sound argument.

(5′) is true when read as a material conditional and evaluated at a world in which its utterer is a BIV. In such a world, its antecedent is true because a BIV does not have sense impressions as of being a BIV. In a vat world, its consequent comes out true as well, since it is a correct specification

---

[18] The same point would hold if either account (ii) or (iii) were used in the foregoing argument. For example, on account (ii), the antecedent shared by the counterparts to (2′) and (3′) would apparently be necessarily false (see fn. 17).

(on Putnam's views about reference) of the vat-English truth conditions for 'I am a BIV'. Hence, when a BIV utters sentence (5) of the original set of sentences E, the sentence, read as a material conditional, expresses a true proposition. The same holds, we have seen, for the other premise sentences (since, on their vat-English readings, their common antecedent expresses a falsehood – indeed an apparently necessary falsehood). Further, the argument expressed is valid. So when a BIV utters the sentences in E, these sentences express propositions forming a sound argument (i.e., the sentences express the propositions expressed by the sentences in E', and these propositions, I have just argued, form a sound argument).[19] On the other hand, when an English-speaking non-BIV utters the sentences in E, we have seen, these sentences also express propositions forming a sound argument.[20]

---

[19] We are now in a position to see that, for both the BIV and the non-BIV, (2) and (8) are *compatible* so long as they are read as material conditionals. This is because (2) and (8) share a false antecedent on both their English and vat-English readings. When (2) and (8) are read as involving subjunctive or strict conditionals, they are incompatible, but (8) is false (I argued in the text) on its English reading.

[20] I have just reasoned that, no matter whether the sentences (1)–(7) expressing our anti-skeptical argument are in English or in vat-English, the sentences express propositions forming a sound argument. This reasoning was conducted in the metametalanguage in which the relevant part of the text of this paper is stated, i.e., the language used to discuss such metalinguistic sentences as (1)–(7). It might be objected that, in the course of that reasoning, I have tacitly assumed that this metametalanguage is English. In particular, one might object that I have in effect been arguing as follows:

(x)   The metalanguage in which the sentences in E [(1)–(7)] are stated is either English or vat-English.

(y)   If the metalanguage is English, then the sentences in E express propositions forming a sound argument, given that the sentences in E are to be read homophonically.

(z)   If the metalanguage is vat-English, then the sentences in E express propositions forming a sound argument, given that the sentences in E are not to be read homophonically but rather as expressing the propositions expressed by the sentences in E'.

(w)   The sentences in E express propositions forming a sound argument, [(x), (y), (z)]

Premises (y) and (z) depend upon the assumption that the metametalanguage in which the relevant part of this paper is stated is English. We need to ask, though, whether the reasoning that supports (y) and (z) is correct if the metametalanguage in which it is conducted is vat-English rather than English. For example, a defense of (y) would require the claim that if a non-BIV uttered

(5)   If I am a non-BIV (speaking English), then my utterances of 'I am a BIV' are true iff I am a BIV.

then his sentence would express a true proposition, since it would be read homophonically. This is the claim that:

(CL)   If one is a non-BIV, then the proposition that: *if one is a non-BIV, then one's utterances of 'I am a BIV' are true iff one is a BIV* is true.

Suppose that I am in fact speaking vat-English. Then we need to ask whether (CL), as uttered by me, expresses a true proposition. If it expresses a false proposition, then my reasoning in the text on the matter of our anti-skeptical argument's soundness rests upon a false claim. I leave it to the patient reader to verify that (CL) would express a true proposition as uttered by a BIV and that, more generally, the evaluation of our anti-skeptical argument's soundness is unproblematic, even given the assumption that the metametalanguage is vat-English.

The argument expressed by E (whether in English or in vat-English) does not directly refute premise (F) of the Cartesian skeptical argument:

(F) I do not know that I am not a BIV.

The problem is whether I can argue from my knowledge of E's conclusion:

(7) My utterances of 'I am a BIV' are false.

to the further conclusion that I *do* know that I am not a BIV. Let us recall that, whether or not I am a BIV, the following sentence is true as uttered by me:

(T) My utterances of 'I am a BIV' are true iff I am a BIV.

(7) and (T) entail

(10) It is not the case that I am a BIV.

Since I know that my utterances of 'I am a BIV' are false and that these utterances are true iff I am a BIV (I know these things on the basis of the argument of this paper and my knowledge of the disquotational principle (T)), it follows that I know that I am not a BIV.[21] Hence, premise (F) of the skeptical argument is false.[22]

1.5

Given the presuppositions of our anti-skeptical argument, it is difficult to avoid an uneasy feeling that there is some trick involved in the reasoning of the last paragraph. To see that there *is* a trick and that there is thus a severe limit to the anti-skeptical force of our argument, note that we move from that argument's conclusion – (7) – to (10) only by invoking (T). But we

---

[21] This inference requires that knowledge is closed under known logical implication, which we are assuming to be true for the purposes of the present paper.

[22] Jane McIntyre (1984) interprets Putnam's argument as follows:

(1) If we are brains in a vat, then the sentence 'we are brains in a vat' says something false.

(2) If the sentence 'we are brains in a vat' says something false, then we are not brains in a vat.

(3) Therefore, if we are brains in a vat, then we are not brains in a vat (from (1) and (2)).

(4) Therefore, we are not brains in a vat (from (3)).

McIntyre criticizes this reconstruction of Putnam's argument (p. 60) by saying that in premise (1) the purported falsity of the mentioned sentence "derives from its status as a sentence of vat-English, and its . . . [consequent] reference to brain images and vat images." However, she argues, "the falsity of 'I am a brain in a vat' in *vat-English* does not entail that I am not a brain in a vat." Thus, "the argument that supports premise (1) . . . defeats premise (2) and Putnam's argument is therefore unsound." The text's discussion of my own reconstructed argument shows that McIntyre's reconstruction falls short through lack of consideration of the *English* truth conditions for 'I am a brain in a vat'. Such a consideration leads one to propound an argument – E – which is more complex than McIntyre's and which is sound (I have argued) no matter which language it is expressed in.

have already seen that disquotational principles like (T) must be used quite carefully in contexts such as this. For example, if I do not know whether *S* is speaking English or vat-English, then I cannot apply a disquotational principle analogous to (T) to *S*'s utterances of '*S* is a BIV' and conclude that those utterances are true iff *S* is a BIV. Similarly, if I do not know whether *I* am speaking English or vat-English, then I cannot apply (T) to my own utterances of 'I am a BIV' as a step toward the conclusion that I know that I am not a BIV and hence am speaking English. Another way to see the point is to note that since I do not know whether I am speaking English or vat-English, I do not know whether the truth conditions of my utterances of 'I am a BIV' are the strange ones specified in premise (2) or rather the disquotational ones specified in premise (5) (those given by (T)). Even on this assumption, our argument ran, I can still know that my utterances of 'I am a BIV' are false. Using (T) in aid of our anti-skeptical argument is thus inconsistent with one of the assumptions behind the argument. And if that assumption is dropped (if I claim to know that I am speaking English rather than vat-English), then there is no longer any need for the anti-skeptical argument.

To see even more clearly that our anti-skeptical argument grinds to a halt at (7) – at the level of sentences, not propositions – consider a case in which a trustworthy set theorist tells me that the sentence 'Omega is not a regular cardinal' expresses a true proposition. Knowing very little about set theory, I do not understand the technical terminology in the sentence. So, even though I can claim to know that the sentence expresses a true proposition, I do not know *which* proposition. Hence I cannot claim to know *that omega is not a regular cardinal*, given only my metalinguistic knowledge that the relevant sentence is true. Suppose you say that surely I know that 'Omega is not a regular cardinal' is true iff omega is not a regular cardinal, and that I therefore know that omega is not a regular cardinal, given my knowledge that the relevant sentence is true. However, isn't it rather that I know only that the following sentence is true: "'Omega is not a regular cardinal' is true iff omega is not a regular cardinal?" This seems to be what I know in virtue of my knowledge of what 'true' means, given the fact that I do not (by hypothesis) understand the sentence 'Omega is not a regular cardinal'. Hence I cannot claim to know that omega is not a regular cardinal, given only my metalinguistic knowledge that these two sentences are true: 'Omega is not a regular cardinal', "'Omega is not a regular cardinal' is true iff omega is not a regular cardinal."

The current problem facing our anti-skeptical argument, then, is that it at best affords knowledge that a certain sentence expresses a false proposition, whereas the intended sort of refutation of skepticism depends upon the availability of knowledge that a certain proposition is false – the proposition that I am a BIV. It is useful to compare the result of our Putnamian anti-skeptical argument with the anti-skeptical result afforded by verificationism. In each case, the skeptic is reduced to silence: he cannot succeed in asserting any proposition that is a counterpossibility to our ordinary knowledge claims and not known by us to be false. When the skeptic tries to assert such a proposition, according to the two strategies, he inevitably ends up asserting some *other* unproblematic proposition which *is* known by us to be false. A difference between the two strategies is that verificationism, but not our Putnamian strategy, has it that there is *no* genuine proposition that is (1) susceptible of confirmation (or infirmation) by sensory evidence, (2) a counterpossibility to our ordinary knowledge claims, and (3) not known by us to be false. This is not a contention of the reconstructed Putnamian strategy, and it might seem that this strategy is therefore preferable to verificationism (since it might seem implausible to hold that the skeptic has not even succeeded in stating an epistemological problem that is at least superficially interesting). According to the Putnamian strategy, there *is* a genuine counterpossibility proposition such that (i) if I am not a BIV, then my sentence 'I am a BIV' expresses that proposition, and (ii) if I am a BIV, then even though the proposition is true, it neither is expressed by my sentence 'I am a BIV' nor constitutes a counterpossibility to anything I claim to know (any proposition expressed by a sentence I assent to). The skeptic's problematic proposition exists, according to the reconstructed Putnamian strategy, yet is not what a BIV knows to be false when he knows that the proposition expressed by his sentence 'I am a BIV' is false. A BIV knows some *other* proposition to be false, i.e., the proposition expressed by his utterances of 'I am a BIV'.

The fact that our reconstructed anti-skeptical strategy, unlike verificationism, countenances the skeptic's supposedly problematic proposition does not in the end constitute a ground for preferring our strategy to verificationism. Countenancing the apparently genuine counterpossibility proposition is one thing, but it is quite another to go on to acknowledge that even though I know that my sentence 'I am a BIV' expresses a false proposition, I do not know whether or not it expresses the skeptic's counterpossibility proposition. If I do not know whether or not the sentence expresses that problematic proposition, then our anti-skeptical argument has not enabled me to conclude that I know that I am not a BIV.

The anti-skeptical strategy reconstructed herein fails in the end because it engenders a sort of skepticism about meaning or propositional content.

According to the presuppositions of this strategy, the sentence 'I am a BIV' has different truth conditions in vat-English from those it has in English, and therefore the sentence expresses a different proposition in vat-English from that which it expresses in English. So if I do not know whether I am speaking vat-English or English, then I do not know which proposition my utterance of 'I am a BIV' expresses.[23] Though this kind of lack of knowledge (I have argued) does not affect my claim to know that our anti-skeptical argument is sound, it clearly does place a limit on what I can claim to know by virtue of knowing that argument's conclusion. All I can claim is the metalinguistic knowledge that a certain sentence expresses a false proposition, rather than the object-language knowledge that I am not a brain in a vat.[24] Since the latter knowledge was required in order to refute the skeptical argument in the envisaged manner, the present anti-skeptical strategy fails.[25]

[23] Whereas the Putnamian anti-skeptical strategy is severely limited by the fact that it engenders skepticism about what my sentences mean, the Burge-style anti-skeptical strategy, as noted above, is severely limited by the fact that it engenders skepticism about whether my sentences mean anything at all (about whether they express any determinate propositional content at all).

[24] One might hold that, even if 'I am a BIV' has different truth conditions in vat-English from those it has in English, it does not follow that there is a difference in propositional content between the beliefs expressed by vat-English and English utterances of the sentence. Fodor, for example, would hold that, despite the difference in truth conditions, a vat-English speaker and an English speaker who both uttered 'I am a BIV' should both be ascribed the same (de dicto) belief content (this would be his position according to Fodor 1982 motivated by his methodological solipsism with respect to cognitive science). Though such a view would block the objection in the text to the Putnamian argument, it would at the same time contradict the main assumption behind the argument: in virtue of the difference in (causal-theoretically determined) truth conditions, vat-English and English utterers of 'I am a BIV' believe different propositions, and in each case a *true* proposition is believed.

[25] There is a strong similarity between the Putnamian anti-skeptical strategy discussed here and that espoused by Paul Horwich (1982, see especially pp. 75–76; Hartry Field called my attention to this similarity). The problems discussed in the text, I would argue, equally afflict Horwich's strategy. It is worth noting that the formulation of our normal theory of the external world and the formulation of the BIV theory are not *potential notational variants* of the sort Horwich discusses in arguing for his claim that we can know a priori that a potential notational variant S_2 of "the actual formulation of our beliefs" S_1 is false. In that discussion (1982, p. 66), it is crucial that a potential notational variant S_2 of S_1 will differ from S_1 only in the following way: S_2, when interpreted homophonically, says that, e.g., some entities other than *trees* satisfy all the beliefs expressed in S_1 using 'tree'. In that case, Horwich claims, we know a priori that S_2 (interpreted homophonically) is false. This is because, if anything satisfies all the aforementioned beliefs, trees do. This reasoning, though, cannot be straightforwardly extended to the BIV case, since a formulation of the BIV theory will not say that some entities other than trees are green, leafy, etc. The BIV theory's formulation, when interpreted homophonically, will say that *nothing* is leafy, green, etc.

CHAPTER 2

Skepticism, objectivity, and brains in vats

Gary Ebbs

2.1 PUTNAM'S ARGUMENT

Imagine a world in which a duplicate of your brain is kept alive in a vat of nutrients, connected to a machine which produces electro-chemical stimulations of its neural receptors. If the pattern of stimulations produced by the machine is just like the pattern of stimulations that your brain receives, it is tempting to think that you and your twin brain in the vat would have the same experiences and thoughts. In particular, since you don't believe that you are a brain in a vat, your twin wouldn't either. So your twin would have radically false beliefs. This well-worn path leads to familiar skeptical questions. If all your experiences and thoughts are the same as those you would have if you were a brain in a vat, then what reasons do you have for believing that you *aren't* a brain in a vat? And if you can never be sure that you aren't a brain in a vat, how can you ever attain an objective understanding of yourself and the world?

In Chapter 1 of *Reason, Truth and History*,[1] Hilary Putnam considers the situation in which duplicates of our brains remain in vats throughout their existence, and both they and the machines which stimulate them came into existence by accident. Putnam argues that if we can raise the question of whether we are in this situation, then we are not. Here is a preliminary reconstruction of his reasoning:[2]

(i) I can raise the question: *Am I always a brain in a vat?*
(ii) If I were always a brain in a vat, I could not raise this question.
(iii) So I am not always a brain in a vat.

For comments on earlier drafts I am grateful to Steve Engstrom, Brian Loar, Fred Neuhouser, Charles Parsons, Julian Pears, Hilary Putnam, Miriam Solomon, and especially Thomas Ricketts. For lively discussions which helped me to develop my first thoughts on these issues, I am also grateful to the participants in my seminar at Harvard University in fall term, 1989.
[1] Putnam 1981.
[2] This elegant version of Putnam's argument is due in essentials to Thomas Tymoczko (1989).

(i) is obviously true (though it has been questioned, as we will see below). (ii) is the heart of Putnam's argument.

In support of (ii) Putnam reasons as follows. We know from reflecting on more ordinary contexts that what a person believes depends partly on the nature of the things with which she is causally related. In particular, if a person is not causally related in an appropriate way with trees or brains or vats, then we can't interpret her words as applying to trees or brains or vats. Now suppose we want to interpret the sentence 'I am always a brain in a vat,' as uttered by a brain in a vat. We must consider the kinds of things with which the brain is causally related, and the typical salient causes of the brain's uses of the words 'brain', and 'vat'. Since the brain is not causally related in the appropriate way with brains and vats, the typical salient causes of its uses of the words 'brain' and 'vat' aren't brains or vats. So if the brain's utterance of 'I am always a brain in a vat' means anything at all, it isn't what *we* mean when *we* use the sentence 'I am always a brain in a vat'.[3] This shows that if I were always a brain in a vat, I would not be able to ask the question: *Am I always a brain in a vat?* Given that I can ask that question, it follows that I am not always a brain in a vat.

My aim here is to develop a more detailed understanding of Putnam's argument, and to clarify what I take to be its deepest consequences. The story of the brain in a vat is often used to support the intuition that we can conceive of a radically detached perspective on the world, a perspective completely external to our beliefs. In the process of developing an interpretation and reconstruction of Putnam's reasoning, I shall argue that this intuition is based in a misunderstanding of the relationship between our thoughts and the language we use to express them.

2.2 MEANING AND LINGUISTIC PRACTICE

Before considering the details of Putnam's argument, it will help to consider a very basic objection. In its most general form, the objection is this:

Any view of meaning which has as a consequence that we are not always brains in a vat must be based in assumptions which beg the question, and which are

---

[3] As we will see in Sections 2.5 and 2.6, according to Putnam, 'I am always a brain in a vat', when uttered by a brain which is always in a vat, will state something false, and the brain's utterance of 'I am not always a brain in a vat' will be true. But this is not essential to the argument (i)–(iii). It is consistent with (i)–(iii) that a brain which is always in a vat has no thoughts and means nothing at all by its "words."

less convincing than the intuition that for all we know we are always brains in a vat.[4]

Aimed specifically at Putnam's argument, it might be expressed as follows:

According to Putnam's theory of meaning, one can't have thoughts about brains and vats unless one is causally related with brains and vats. And Putnam assumes that we can have thoughts about brains and vats. So he *presupposes* that we are causally related with brains and vats. But this begs the question against the skeptic, who has the intuition that for all we know we are always brains in a vat.

It is important to see that this objection is not as powerful as it first appears. In order to establish that Putnam's argument begs the question against skepticism, it is not enough to point out that Putnam's view of meaning has a consequence which many skeptics are reluctant to accept. One must also show that this consequence flows from an assumption which skeptics are entitled to question. But that is not an easy thing to show. It is not in general true that a skeptic is entitled to question assumptions which we make about meaning. A skepticism which consists solely in challenges to particular assumptions we make is uninteresting. Interesting skeptical challenges purport to yield deeply troubling *discoveries* about the consequences of our ordinary concepts of truth, justification, meaning, and thought. If our ordinary concepts of meaning and thought have the consequence that we can't have thoughts about brains and vats unless we are causally related with brains and vats, the charge that Putnam is begging the question is out of place. The real issue, then, is whether this causal constraint is implicit in our ordinary concepts of meaning and thought.

Putnam's arguments for the causal constraint are based in our ordinary judgments about how we would interpret people in a wide range of situations. In "The Meaning of 'Meaning'"[5] and elsewhere, Putnam uses a series of thought experiments to investigate our ordinary judgments about what people mean and think in various actual and counterfactual situations. In the best-known of these, we imagine that there exists a planet called Twin Earth which is the same as Earth in all ordinarily observable ways. But Twin

---

[4] Here is Nagel's way of expressing a similar objection:

> Critics of skepticism bring against it various theories of how the language works – theories of verifiability, causal theories of reference, principles of charity. I believe the argument goes in the opposite direction. Such theories are refuted by the evident possibility and intelligibility of skepticism, which reveals that by "tree" I don't mean just anything that is causally responsible for my impressions of trees, or anything that looks and feels like a tree, or even anything of the sort that I and others have traditionally called trees. Since those things could conceivably not be trees, any theory that says they have to be is wrong. (Nagel 1986, p. 73)

[5] Putnam 1975.

Earth is different from Earth in one crucial respect: where there is water on Earth, there is another substance, twin-water, on Twin Earth. Twin-water is in all ordinary contexts qualitatively indistinguishable from water. But it has a radically different molecular structure. On Twin Earth lives my twin, a molecule-for-molecule duplicate of me, who has had the same kind of linguistic conditioning, and whose neuro-physiological dispositions are just like mine. Putnam judges that when my twin uses the word 'water', he is speaking about twin-water, not water, for he typically applies his word 'water' to samples of twin-water, and he is not causally related with water. This and similar thought experiments support the general conclusion that what one means and believes is partly determined by the nature of the things with which one is causally related.[6]

The Twin-Earth thought experiments are tools for investigating our ordinary concepts of meaning and thought. They enable us to make *discoveries* about the way our thoughts are related to our social and physical environments. This use of the thought experiments depends on the assumption that our understanding of the concepts of meaning and thought is grounded in linguistic practice. When we use the thought experiments in this way, we presuppose that our understanding of these concepts is rooted in our ordinary judgments about what a person's utterances mean, and what thoughts she expresses with them. In mastering a language, we develop the ability to interpret the utterances of others. This ability is not restricted to utterances of our own language. Given sufficient exposure to the linguistic behavior of speakers of an alien tongue, we can correctly interpret their utterances. Our ability to interpret is sophisticated and versatile. Although this ability does not result from an explicit adherence to any

---

[6] In a series of papers beginning with Burge 1979, Tyler Burge has used Twin-Earth style thought experiments to deepen Putnam's conclusions. Burge (1986) argues that individualism is not true even for basic kinds of perceptual representations:

> Most perceptual representations are formed and obtain their content through regular interaction with the environment. They represent what, in some complex sense of 'normally', they normally stem from and are applied to. (Burge 1986, p. 131)

I agree, and it seems clear to me that the *basis* for this conclusion is our ordinary intuitions about meaning, grounded in our linguistic practice. Burge has expressed this as follows:

> The empirical character of perceptual representation formation is evinced in our common methods of interpreting a creature's perceptual experience. . . . It makes no sense to attribute systematic perceptual error to a being whose perceptual representations can be explained as the results of regular interaction with a physical environment and whose discriminative activity is reasonably well adapted to that environment. (Burge 1986, p. 130)

This passage draws on a principle of charity in interpretation. Donald Davidson argues similarly in Davidson 1984 and 1986.

rules or principles, it does *exemplify* or *embody* certain basic principles of interpretation.

The Twin-Earth thought experiments show that there is a connection between what thoughts we are able to express and the things with which we are causally related. Through these thought experiments we discover that *there are some thoughts which we would not attribute to an individual if she were not causally related with the appropriate types of things.* If our ordinary judgments about how to interpret an individual's utterances in actual and counterfactual situations are *constitutive* of our concepts of meaning and thought, this discovery shows that *there are some thoughts which an individual could not express if she were not causally related with the appropriate types of things.* If we accept this view of the thought experiments, and we share Putnam's judgments about what the subjects of the thought experiments mean and believe, we should conclude that Putnam's causal constraint on meaning and thought is implicit in our ordinary concept of meaning.[7]

Some philosophers disagree with this conclusion. They say that we can make sense of certain kinds of skeptical doubts which would be meaningless if Putnam's causal constraint on meaning were correct. This kind of reply reflects a disagreement about the nature of our ordinary concepts of meaning and thought. Such disagreements must be taken seriously; we should try to understand and resolve them. But we will not make any progress toward these goals if we accept the facile charge that Putnam's causal constraint on meaning and thought begs the question against skepticism.

2.3 SKEPTICISM ABOUT JUSTIFICATION

Two kinds of skepticism are fueled by the familiar view that if we were brains in vats, then our beliefs about the world would be massively mistaken. The possibility of massive error naturally raises a question about *justification*: if everything would seem exactly the same if you were a brain in a vat, then what reasons do you have for believing that you are not a brain in a vat? And it raises a question about *objectivity*: if you can never be sure that

---

[7] Moreover, if we accept the view of the thought experiments sketched here, we will not be tempted to think of Putnam's causal constraint on meaning as a proto causal theory of reference. I assume that a causal theory of reference is a non-circular statement of necessary and sufficient conditions for words to refer to things, given in terms of causal connections between speakers, the words they use, and things in their environments. Given my understanding of how Putnam's causal constraint is introduced, I see no reason to think that we can specify the appropriate causal connections in a non-circular way. Hence I see no reason to think that a causal theory of reference is possible. Our understanding of Putnam's causal constraint cannot be separated from our judgments about what individual speakers are talking about in particular contexts.

you aren't a brain in a vat, how can you ever attain an objective understanding of yourself and the world? In the context of the standard assumption that if we were brains in vats, then our beliefs about the world would be
massively mistaken, these questions point toward *skepticism about justification*, and *skepticism about objectivity*, respectively.

The possibility of massive error is often combined with assumptions
about the nature of justification to yield the skeptical conclusion that we
can't have justified beliefs. Skeptics lay down requirements on justification,
and argue that the requirements cannot be met, given the possibility of
massive error. Thus the possibility of massive error is not sufficient to
generate such doubts. One must also make assumptions about what it
takes to possess *justification* for a belief.

Some philosophers have taken Putnam to be trying to undermine
skepticism about justification by arguing that massive error is not really
possible. The implicit reasoning goes something like this: The possibility of
massive error is a necessary condition for skepticism about justification. So
Putnam can undermine skepticism about justification if he can show that
massive error is not really possible. The argument in Chapter 1 of *Reason,
Truth, and History*, if sound, shows that massive error is not possible.[8] So it
is natural to think that Putnam is trying to undermine skepticism about
justification.

There are several problems with this interpretation. First, it is not
obvious that skepticism about justification can arise only if massive error
is possible. For suppose we have reason to believe that massive error isn't
possible. It follows that most of our beliefs are true. But which ones? What
reasons do we have for holding any *particular* belief to be true? There may be
no satisfactory answer to this question. So even if massive error isn't
possible, there may still be a skeptical problem about justification.[9]

Second, Putnam's argument can't rule out all sources of serious cognitive
error. His argument only works against a very specific version of the familiar
worry about whether we are brains in vats, the version in which the brains
remain in vats throughout their existence. The argument has no force
against cases in which our brains are removed without our knowledge,
placed in vats, and stimulated by a machine in just the way they would

---

[8] Putnam does not *explicitly* draw this conclusion in Chapter 1 of *Reason, Truth, and History* (Putnam
1981), although it is clear that he endorses it. In a recent discussion of the argument, however, he says
that brains in vats "are *not* deceived – not thinking anything radically false." See Putnam 1989, p. 67.

[9] These skeptical problems may depend on misunderstandings of our ordinary conception of justification. If so, and we can see why, then they would not be particularly troubling. But this is a potential
problem for all forms of skepticism about justification, as J. L. Austin (1979) shows.

have been stimulated had they not been removed. For in this kind of case, the necessary causal interactions with brains and vats is in place.[10] Even if the meanings of the brain's utterances slowly change, there will be a time during which the brain's beliefs about its immediate situation are unchanged and mostly false.[11]

One might think that these cases are not a threat to justification, since we have reason to believe that the medical technology necessary for making the brain transfer is not now available.[12] But our technological capabilities may develop to the point where we can make such transfers. Raised in those circumstances, doubts about whether or not we are brains in vats would be particularly troubling: our own beliefs about the technologies available would give us reason to doubt that any of our current beliefs about the world are justified. So even if Putnam is right about the situation in which our brains are always in vats, this does not show that serious skeptical doubts about whether our beliefs are justified could not arise.

2.4 SKEPTICISM ABOUT OBJECTIVITY

In addition to doubts about whether one's beliefs are justified, one might also have doubts about whether it is possible to overcome the limitations built into one's own cognitive perspective on the world. This would lead to skepticism about objectivity: the claim that no matter how hard we try, we may never have fully objective beliefs and thoughts about the world.

---

[10] Tymoczko (1989, pp. 294–295) also discusses this possibility. But he believes that such situations do not pose any skeptical problems. I question this below. In Chapter 1, Anthony Brueckner makes the same sort of point, but uses an example which is much less intuitive than mine. He argues as follows:

> [Putnam's] . . . claims do not obviously hold for a situation in which I am a brain in a vat and am stimulated by evil neuroscientists who, e.g., stimulate my brain in exactly the way their brains are stimulated when they see a beech tree outside their laboratory, thereby causing me to have sense impressions just like their *veridical* sense impressions as of beeches. In such a standard brain-in-a-vat situation, a reasonable causal theorist of reference would surely hold that the brain's token of 'tree' is causally connected with trees by virtue of the token's causal connection with the evil neuroscientist and *his* tokens of 'tree'. Putnam's claims about reference, then, hold at best for worlds in which there is nothing other than brains in a vat and their automatic tenders (innocent bystanders causally unconnected with the computers would not affect Putnam's claims). (pp. 12–13)

[11] So the fundamental intuition that, at any given time, it could be that we are brains in a vat, is unaffected by Putnam's argument. In fact, his view of meaning offers an *explanation* of how it would be possible to have the true thought that one is a brain in a vat: the expression of the thought is made possible by our previous *causal interaction* with brains and vats.

[12] Tymoczko (1989, pp. 294–295) argues this way and I have heard this view expressed informally several times. For present purposes I leave open the question of whether we have reason to believe that the medical technology necessary for making the brain transfer is not now available. This question, as I argued above, is not settled by the present considerations. My argument here is an *ad hominem* against anyone who believes that brain transfer cases are not a threat to justification.

Skepticism about objectivity is not necessarily linked to the worry that our beliefs are *false*. As we will see, Thomas Nagel believes that even if Putnam is right to conclude that a brain in a vat has mostly true beliefs, it still has reason to be skeptical about the *objectivity* of its conception of the world. The reason is that the brain's understanding of the world is seriously limited: it doesn't possess and can't acquire the concepts necessary to express the true thought that it is a brain in a vat.

Skepticism about objectivity is linked with the idea of an absolutely objective representation of the world. This idea apparently arises in the following way. We naturally think that our beliefs result from interactions with an independently existing world. But we accept that our perceptual perspective on the world might systematically limit or distort our beliefs and thoughts about it. To accept this is to conceive of a more encompassing representation of the world, one which includes an account of how our interactions with the world affect the judgments that we make. But this more encompassing representation might *also* systematically limit or distort the judgments made from it. And to accept this is to conceive of an even more encompassing representation of the world, one which includes an understanding of the subjective features of the first two representations. And so on. At the limit, it seems that this dialectic leads to the idea of an absolutely objective representation of the world, without any subjective elements, from which all other representations of the world can be understood. Let us call this the *absolute conception* of the world.[13]

In its most general form, skepticism about objectivity is the view that, no matter how much one tries, one can't arrive at an absolutely objective representation of the world. Nagel expresses the worry as follows:

The aim is to form a conception of reality which includes ourselves and our view of things among its objects, but it seems that whatever forms the conception will not be included by it. It seems to follow that the most objective view we can achieve will have to rest on an unexamined subjective base, and that since we can never abandon our own point of view, but can only alter it, the idea that we are coming closer to the reality outside it with each successive step has no foundation.[14]

This might suggest that the very *idea* of an absolute conception of the world is incoherent. But Nagel does not go that far. He apparently believes that the idea of an absolute conception of the world is one which does have content for us, even if there are serious doubts about whether we can

---

[13] This is a streamlined version of the description of the absolute conception of reality given by Bernard Williams (1978, pp. 64–65), and by Thomas Nagel (1986, Chapters II and V).

[14] Nagel 1986, p. 68.

overcome our own point of view. This attitude is made clear in a passage where he responds to Putnam's conclusion that, if we were brains in a vat, we could not think that we were. Nagel believes this conclusion leads to skepticism:

> If I accept the argument, I must conclude that a brain in a vat can't think truly that it is a brain in a vat, even though others can think this about it. What follows? Only that I can't express my skepticism by saying "Perhaps I am a brain in a vat." Instead I must say, "Perhaps I can't even *think* the truth about what I am, because I lack the necessary concepts and my circumstances make it impossible for me to acquire them!" If this doesn't qualify as skepticism, I don't know what does.[15]

What troubles Nagel is that, assuming that Putnam is right, a brain in a vat would be unable to describe a *radical* way in which its perspective on the world is limited. Thus there are certain cognitive perspectives whose radical limits can't be overcome. Nagel believes that, for all we know, ours is one of them.

Nagel doesn't believe that Putnam's argument undermines the idea of an absolute conception. He believes that somehow we can have this conception in spite of the essential limits on our cognitive perspectives suggested by Putnam's argument. Thus Nagel does not seem to accept (or perhaps even to see) the most radical consequence of Putnam's argument. By casting doubts on the *possibility* of entertaining certain thoughts about one's own cognitive perspective, Putnam's reflections raise doubts about the *intelligibility* of the absolute conception. In order to see how this is so, we must look more closely at Putnam's argument. In Sections 2.5 to 2.9, I will explain why Anthony Brueckner's reconstruction of Putnam's argument can't be right. In the process, a more systematic and compelling interpretation of Putnam's reasoning will emerge. In Sections 2.10 to 2.12, I will return to Nagel's objection.

2.5 BRUECKNER'S RECONSTRUCTION

As I presented the argument above, it turns on the central premise that if I were always a brain in a vat, I could not ask the question: *Am I always a brain in a vat?* The central argument for this premise is that, if I *were* always a brain in a vat, then I would not be causally related with brains and vats. But, according to Putnam's view of meaning, I can't have thoughts about brains and vats unless I am causally related with them. Since I *can* ask the

---

[15] Nagel 1986, p. 73.

question of whether I am always a brain in a vat, this shows that I am not always a brain in a vat. This version of the argument is basically correct, but it leaves out some puzzling features of Putnam's presentation. These features have led critics astray. A proper understanding of them, however, will put us in a position to see that Putnam's conclusion raises serious doubts about the intelligibility of an absolute conception of the world.

Before we can discuss these further features of Putnam's argument, we must say more about what the brain in a vat means by its words. The reason is not that Putnam's argument depends essentially on assumptions about what the brain's utterances mean, but that for dialectical purposes it is interesting to reflect on this question, and see why some philosophers view it as essential to Putnam's reasoning. My own view is that we have no reason to believe that a brain which is always in a vat could have any thoughts at all. The usual description of the situation of a brain which is always in a vat does not support any firm judgments about what it believes and thinks. Even if we had a much more detailed description of the brain's situation, it is not clear that we would find any attributions of beliefs and thoughts which make sense of the brain's utterances in that situation. Moreover, the argument (i)–(iii) presented above does not depend on the assumption that a brain which is always in a vat has any thoughts at all. (ii) is the central premise: if I were always a brain in a vat I would not be able to ask the question: *Am I always a brain in a vat?* This premise may be true even if the brain in a vat has no beliefs or thoughts at all. Nevertheless, Putnam assumes that a brain which is always in a vat has thoughts. And Anthony Brueckner's reconstruction of Putnam's reasoning depends on this assumption. In order to develop a deeper understanding of Putnam's reasoning, I will in the next few sections assume that a brain which is always in a vat does have thoughts, and can mean things by its utterances. The assumption can be dropped once it has served its dialectical purpose.

Putnam supposes that a brain in a vat is causally related with the *appearances* or *images* which result from the pattern of neural stimulation produced by the machine, from which it follows that the typical causes of the brain's use of the words 'brain' and 'vat' are the images of brains and the images of vats. Thus he supposes that the utterances of a brain in a vat are (in a sense) about images. I have misgivings about this, since it seems that these images would be essentially *private*, but interpretation requires *public* objects of belief.[16] But for

---

[16] It is not clear *what* we would take to be the typical causes of the brain's uses of these words. A more plausible suggestion, because it does not invoke private mental items like images, is that the words

present purposes, I will assume that the brain's utterances are (in a sense) about images.

In order to interpret any of the brain's utterances, we must somehow construct an English sentence which has the same meaning. But it is not at all clear how to do this. Even if the brain's utterances are about images in some sense, it is not obvious what the correct interpretations of the brain's utterances would be. The problem can be put to the side if we represent the interpretations of the brain's utterances without really stating them. Putnam does this by offering a very loose interpretation of the brain's utterances. For example, Putnam suggests that if a brain which is always in a vat utters 'I am always a brain in a vat', it means something like *I am always a brain in a vat in the image*. Here we are aided by the assumption that the brain uses a language which is syntactically identical to English. Let's continue making this assumption. In what follows, I will represent the content of the brain's utterance of a sentence S with ⌐(S) in the image⌐[17]. By using the resulting English sentence, I will *pretend* to interpret the brain's utterances. Thus, if the brain utters 'I am always a brain in a vat', I will say it means that *(I am always a brain in a vat) in the image*.[18]

At one point Putnam seems to reason as follows. Suppose you are always a brain in a vat. When you utter 'I am always a brain in a vat', you must mean something like *(I am always a brain in a vat) in the image*. But this statement will be false, if you are always a brain in a vat, for reasons I will discuss in the next section. Now suppose that you aren't always a brain in a vat. Then when you say 'I am always a brain in a vat', you express the thought that you are always a brain in a vat. But this thought is false, by supposition. So either way, when you utter 'I am always a brain in a vat', you utter something false. Here is the passage which suggests this:

if their 'possible world' [the world of the brains in vats] . . . is really the actual one, and we are really the brains in a vat, then what we now mean by 'we are brains in a vat' is that we are brains in a vat in the image or something of that kind (if we mean anything at all). But part of the hypothesis that we are brains in a vat is that we aren't brains in a vat in the image (i.e., what we are 'hallucinating' isn't that we are brains in a vat). So, if we are brains in a vat, then the sentence 'We are brains in a

---

'brain' and 'vat' are correctly applied when certain patterns of neural stimulation occur. An even better suggestion is that they correctly apply to the distal causes of the patterns of sensory stimulation which typically accompany the brain's use of the words 'brain' and 'vat'. These distal causes would most likely be states of the stimulation machine itself. Putnam considers these and other possibilities in Putnam 1981, p. 14.

[17] I use the corner quotation marks as Quine does in Quine 1940.

[18] Of course, the brain's utterance is not about *me*, as the indexical 'I', if used strictly, would imply. But this complication may be safely ignored for present purposes.

vat' says something false (if it says anything). In short, if we are brains in a vat, then 'We are brains in a vat' is false.[19]

In this version of the argument, we are asked to consider the possibility that, for all we know, we really are always brains in a vat. We are told that if we are brains in a vat, the meanings of our words are such that the utterance of 'I am always a brain in a vat' is false – but in *vat-English*, the language which we actually speak if we are always brains in a vat. This seems quite different from just noting that brains in vats cannot express the thought that they are brains in vats; it seems to go further in asking us to imagine that we are in fact *in* that situation, and that the meanings of our words are partly determined by the causal relations we bear to things in the world in which we *are* brains in vats. This introduces a potential for a kind of *meaning vertigo*, an uncertainty that the meanings of our utterances can be taken for granted.

This meaning vertigo is implicitly coupled with an otherwise unobjectionable semantic principle: since one is in a position to *use* the sentences of one's own language, one can employ a disquotational truth predicate to give the truth-conditions of sentences of one's own language. Specifically, we should accept (T):

(T) My utterances of 'I am a brain in a vat' are true iff I am a brain in a vat.[20]

Given the argument that whether or not we are always brains in a vat, our utterances of 'I am a brain in a vat' are false, (T) enables us to conclude that we are not brains in a vat.

Anthony Brueckner's reconstruction of Putnam's argument features this disjunctive style of reasoning:[21]

(1) Either I am a brain in a vat (and I speak vat-English) or I am not a brain in a vat (and I speak English).
(2) Suppose I am a brain in a vat (and I speak vat-English).
(3) Then 'I am a brain in a vat' is true in my language (vat-English) if and only if (I am a brain in a vat) in the image. [(2), Theory of meaning]
(4) (I am not a brain in a vat) in the image. [Empirical fact(?)]
(5) So 'I am a brain in a vat' is not true in my language. [(3), (4)]
(6) Suppose I am not a brain in a vat (and I speak English).

---

[19] Putnam 1981, p. 15. The other side of the argument – that if we *aren't* brains in vats, then when we utter 'we are brains in vats' we say something false – is obvious, hence implicit in Putnam's remarks here.
[20] This is taken from Chapter 1, p. 17.
[21] This reconstruction is given by Brueckner in Chapter 1, p. 15. I am indebted to Brian Loar for this particular consolidation of Brueckner's reconstruction.

(7) Then 'I am a brain in a vat' is true in my language (English) if and only if I am a brain in a vat. [(T), (6)]

(8) Hence 'I am a brain in a vat' is not true in my language (English). [(6), (7)]

(9) 'I am a brain in a vat' is not true in my language. [(1)–(8), Disjunction elimination]

(10) 'I am a brain in a vat' is true in my language if and only if I am a brain in a vat. [(T)]

(11) Therefore, I am not a brain in a vat.

At first it may seem that (1)–(11) accurately formulate the extended version of the argument which is summarized in the Putnam quote above. But there are two serious problems with this reconstruction. The most interesting consequences of Putnam's argument become clear only once one sees why this reconstruction can't be right.

2.6 REMOVING HINTS OF VERIFICATIONISM

One problem with the reconstruction concerns (4), the premise that, supposing that I am always a brain in a vat, *(I am not a brain in a vat) in the image.*[22] As Brueckner understands it, this premise amounts to the claim that the sentence 'I am a brain in a vat', as used by a brain which is always in a vat, is false. Why is this premise supposed to be true, on Brueckner's reading? He reasons as follows (using 'BIV' as short for 'brain which is always in a vat'):

> a BIV's utterance of 'I am a BIV' would be true iff he were a BIV-in-the-image. As I understand it, those truth conditions are equivalent to these: the BIV's utterance would be true iff he had sense impressions as of being a BIV. But by Putnam's hypothesis, a BIV never has such sense impressions . . . Thus . . . a BIV's utterance of 'I am a BIV' would never be true . . .[23]

This captures what *seems* to be Putnam's reasoning in the paragraph quoted above. He argues that:

> part of the hypothesis that we are brains in a vat is that we aren't brains in a vat in the image (i.e., what we are 'hallucinating' isn't that we are brains in a vat). So, if we

---

[22] Strictly speaking, since I am not always a brain in a vat, the conditional 'If I am always a brain in a vat, then *I am not a brain in a vat in the image*' is true simply by virtue of having a false antecedent. Brueckner does not see it this way, since he believes that we do not know whether we are speaking English or vat-English. I will discuss this aspect of his position in the next two sections. For present purposes I want to focus on that part of the content of premise (4) which is independent of Brueckner's assumption that we do not know which language we are speaking.

[23] From Chapter 1, p. 12.

are brains in a vat, then the sentence 'We are brains in a vat' says something false (if it says anything).[24]

The parenthetical remark that if we are brains in a vat, "what we are 'hallucinating' isn't that we are brains in a vat," seems to suggest that the sentence 'we are brains in a vat' is false because we are not hallucinating the sense impressions which would verify that sentence: we do not have the sense impressions as of being in a vat.

But this *can't* be the reason why the sentence 'I am a brain in a vat', as used by a brain which is always in a vat, is false. It rests on a false verificationist account of the meaning of 'I am a brain in a vat', one which is not consistent with Putnam's causal constraint on meaning. I pointed out earlier that a person's brain might have been removed and placed in a vat *without her knowledge*. This is a possibility which Putnam's argument can't rule out, since it is compatible with the causal constraint on interpretation. But in that possible situation, her utterance of 'I am a brain in a vat' would be *true*, even though she would not have sense impressions as of being in a vat. Thus there is no way to read off from one's *sense impressions* whether or not one is a brain in a vat. Parallel reasoning suggests that a brain which is always in a vat can't conclude that *(I am not a brain in a vat) in the image* from the fact that it never has the sense-impressions as of being a brain in a vat in the image.[25]

So why is it true that, as used by a brain which is always in a vat, the sentence 'I am a brain in a vat' is false? First, recall that a brain which is always in a vat is not related with brains and vats in such a way that the typical salient causes of its uses of the words 'brain' and 'vat' are, respectively, brains and vats. So if the brain's utterances of 'I am always a brain in a vat' mean anything at all, they do not mean what I now mean when I use the sentence 'I am always a brain in a vat'. This follows from the causal

---

[24] Putnam 1981, p. 15.

[25] In Chapter 1, Brueckner acknowledges that his claim that "the BIV's utterance would be true iff he had sense impressions as of being a BIV" is strictly speaking false:

> This is because a sophisticated phenomenalist would want to allow for the drawing of an is/seems distinction within the phenomenalistic language, allowing one to say truly, "A green tree is before me, though I have sense impressions as of a red tree (though there seems to be a red tree before me)." The truth conditions for a BIV's utterance of 'I am a BIV' ... accordingly concern more complex facts about sense impressions than those discussed in the text. (footnote 6, p. 12)

> Presumably Brueckner thinks that this just complicates the phenomenalistic argument for (4), but does not undermine it. My point in the text is that phenomenalism is an unacceptable theory of meaning, and that anyone arguing against the brain in a vat hypothesis must not presuppose it. There is also no compelling reason to attribute a phenomenalistic premise to Putnam, aside from a few slips of the pen. As discussed in note 16 above, Putnam clearly accepts other alternatives for the references of the brain's utterances, and this implies that he does not believe that his argument depends on a verificationist premise.

constraints on interpretation. Second, we supposed earlier that a brain which is always in a vat is causally related (in a sense) with images. Thus, translated into English, the brain's utterances of 'I am always a brain in a vat' mean that *(I am always a brain in a vat) in the image*. This claim, made by the brain using the sentence 'I am always a brain in a vat', must be false.[26] For if the brain *were* always a brain in a vat in the image (whatever *that* means), then it would not be causally related with the images of brains and the images of vats, and so it could not claim that *(I am always a brain in a vat) in the image*. But we are assuming that it can claim that *(I am always a brain in a vat) in the image*. Given this assumption, we can see that the claim itself must be false.[27]

This argument is parallel in structure to the argument we can each run for ourselves, using (i)–(iii) of the introduction. Since we are not in a position to use the sentence 'I am always a brain in a vat' in the way the brain can, we are unable to say in any detail what the possibility that the brain is always a brain in a vat in the image amounts to. Nevertheless, if we assume that the brain's utterances are meaningful, we can see that the statement that the brain makes using the sentence 'I am always a brain in a vat' can't be true, for reasons parallel to those that convince us that we are not always brains in vats. We know that if we were always brains in vats, then none of us could raise the question *Am I always a brain in a vat?* Since each of us can raise this question, we are not always brains in vats. Thus I suggest that we interpret Putnam as follows. When he says that if we are brains in a vat, "what we are 'hallucinating' isn't that we are brains in a vat," he is saying in effect that when a brain which is always in a vat utters the sentence 'I am always a brain in a vat', it means that *(I am always a brain in a vat) in the image*. This can't be true, given the causal constraint on meaning, for reasons parallel to those we are each able to give for the conclusion that we are not always brains in a vat.

---

[26] For caveats about (i)–(iii), and the parallel argument for the brain in a vat, see the Appendix.

[27] This reasoning is hard to follow because we are unable to say what possibility is really in question. I believe that we can't really make sense of the assumption that the brain's utterances are meaningful. When Putnam tries to extend his reasoning to the case of a brain in a vat, we lose all understanding of the contents of the statements in question. I am indulgently trying to make sense of Putnam's argument for the claim that when a brain in a vat uses the sentence 'I am always a brain in a vat', it is making a meaningful, but false, claim. I believe that the assumption is important *dialectically*: it can lead us to a position where we are tempted to imagine a perspective from which it could be seen that we are always brains in vats. Reflecting on Putnam's argument can help us to see that this perspective is illusory. We can then take or leave the assumption that a brain which is always in a vat can have thoughts and make claims. I would argue that, without much more detail about the typical salient causes of the brain's utterances, we simply don't know how to make sense of this assumption.

2.7 BRUECKNER'S OBJECTION

There is another problem with Brueckner's understanding of the argument. He believes that even if it is valid it is compatible with a kind of skepticism about what we mean. Suppose that I am presented with the utterances of a subject S. All I know is that S is either a brain in a vat, or an ordinary person who exists outside a vat, and is causally related in the usual way with ordinary things. Brueckner reasons as follows:

if I do not know whether S is speaking English or vat-English, then I cannot apply a disquotational principle analogous to (T) to S's utterances of "S is a BIV" and conclude that those utterances are true iff S is a BIV.

On the reconstruction just given, it is assumed at the start that we do not know whether we are speaking English or vat-English. But, Brueckner points out,

if I do not know whether I am speaking English or vat English, then I cannot apply (T) as a step toward the conclusion that I know that I am not a BIV and hence am speaking English.[28]

Thus Brueckner argues that even if Putnam's argument is valid, it is compatible with skepticism about what one *means*. Brueckner claims that Putnam's reasoning should at best convince us that we can't know whether we are speaking English or vat-English.[29] And this means that we can't conclude that we are not brains in a vat.

2.8 AM I SPEAKING ENGLISH?

Do I know whether I am speaking English or vat-English? According to Brueckner, when I ask 'Am I always a brain in a vat?' I don't know whether I am asking *Am I always a brain in a vat?* or *(Am I always a brain in a vat) in the image?* In short, I don't know what my own utterances mean. If I do not know what my utterances mean, then even if Putnam's argument is valid, I can't conclude that I am not always a brain in a vat.

---

[28] Chapter 1, p. 27; previous quotation from p. 25.
[29] Brueckner puts his conclusion as follows:

> The anti-skeptical strategy reconstructed herein fails in the end because it engenders a sort of skepticism about meaning, or propositional content. ... if I do not know whether I am speaking vat-English or English, I do not know which proposition my utterance of 'I am a BIV' expresses ... All I can claim is the metalinguistic knowledge that a certain sentence expresses a false proposition, rather than the object-language knowledge that I am not a brain in a vat. (Chapter 1, pp. 26–27)

Premise (1) of Brueckner's reconstruction invites this objection. It seems to say that *either* one of these things might *actually* be true: I am a brain in a vat (and speak vat-English) or I am not a brain in a vat (and speak English). Now it is true that if I do not know whether I am a brain in a vat, then I do not know whether I speak English or vat-English. But it is not true that I do not know whether I speak English or vat-English.

The skepticism about which language I am speaking is undercut by the very fact that I represent the possibilities with a particular language. This language cannot be vat-English. Vat-English is *defined* as that language spoken by a brain which is always in a vat. It follows from Putnam's theory of meaning that if I were such a brain, I couldn't characterize the language it speaks as vat-English. For if I were such a brain, then I could not express the thoughts necessary to define vat-English. But the fact that I can state Brueckner's first premise shows that I can characterize the language of a brain in a vat as vat-English. This shows that I am not such a brain, and that I am not speaking vat-English.[30]

Here we see one of the deepest and most interesting features of Putnam's reasoning: we can't detach ourselves from the very facts on which the meaningful use of language depends. Beginning with our meaningful use of language, we can make discoveries about the necessary conditions for that use. We can't simply distance ourselves from these conditions, even if they surprise us.[31]

2.9 PUTNAM'S DISJUNCTION EXPLAINED

We have seen that the core of Putnam's argument is captured by (i)–(iii). But Putnam also argues that *whether or not I am always a brain in a vat, my utterance of 'I am always a brain in a vat' is false.* This claim goes *beyond* the

---

[30] Tymoczko (1989, pp. 284–285) makes a similar point. The crux of the reply is that "Vat-English is always something other than the language we are speaking." Brueckner's idea that we can somehow detach ourselves from the very facts which give our words their meaning, and wonder which of two very different languages we are actually speaking, is very odd. I agree with Tyler Burge, who has written that

> The idea that we can attempt to determine what our thoughts are from a vantage point that is neutral as to which of various alternative thoughts we are thinking seems to me to be not only deeply implausible but incoherent. (Burge 1988b, p. 93)

[31] Skepticism about meaning has been a common reaction to Putnam's causal constraint on meaning among philosophers wedded to a Cartesian picture of the epistemology of understanding. I believe that the Cartesian picture is false. We each have first-person authority about what we mean, even though what we mean is partly determined by the nature of our social and physical environments. We know what we mean because we know how to *use* our language. I can't defend this claim here. I am sympathetic with the account offered by Tyler Burge in Burge 1988a.

reasoning expressed by (i)–(iii), which does not depend on the assumption that a brain in a vat can express any thought at all, much less a *false* thought.[32] A satisfactory interpretation of Putnam's reasoning should explain why he goes beyond the reasoning formulated in (i)–(iii) to argue that *whatever situation I am in*, 'I am always a brain in a vat' is false.

I believe that Putnam is interested in this further conclusion because he wants to emphasize the radical *consequences* of the reasoning captured by (i)–(iii). He wants to underline the point that, if his reasoning is sound, it undercuts the illusion of an absolutely objective third-person perspective on our current situation, from which it would be possible to express the thought that we are always brains in vats. The reasoning shows, to put it paradoxically, that whether or not we are brains in vats, we can conclude that we are not brains in vats. A natural first reaction to Putnam's disjunctive reasoning is to try to take up a third-person perspective on one's situation, and to reason as follows:

How can we be sure that, when judged from an objective third-person perspective, we are not always brains in vats? If we are, then when we use Putnam's argument, we will be concluding that *(we are not always brains in vats) in the image*. This is quite different from saying that we are not brains in vats.

But this worry is unfounded, if Putnam's reasoning is sound. The fact that whether or not we are always brains in vats, we can conclude that we aren't always brains in vats, shows that we *aren't* always brains in vats, and hence that we aren't concluding thereby that *(we aren't always brains in vats) in the image*. This undermines the initial *third-person* point of view from which it *seemed* that we might be brains in vats who conclude that *(we aren't always brains in vats) in the image*. Thus Putnam's disjunctive style of reasoning emphasizes the priority of the meaningful use of language to a detached semantical perspective on it.

2.10 NAGEL'S OBJECTION AGAIN

Let us return to the question of whether Putnam's argument, once properly understood, leads to skepticism about objectivity, or in some way

---

[32] Putnam would not need to say anything at all about what the brain in the vat means by his "utterances" if he were not interested in the disjunctive style of reasoning, and its implications for our understanding of an "absolute" conception of reality. As I mentioned above, I doubt that our ordinary concept of meaning can be usefully extended to apply to the case of a brain which is always in a vat. But my argument here is an *ad hominem* against those like Nagel who believe that the absolute conception of reality makes sense, and that for all we know we might always be brains in a vat.

undermines the absolute conception of reality. Earlier I discussed Nagel's claim that the conclusion of Putnam's argument leads to a kind of skepticism about objectivity, and I suggested that Nagel does not see the most radical consequence of Putnam's reasoning. By casting doubts on the *possibility* of entertaining certain thoughts about one's own cognitive perspective, Putnam's reflections raise doubts about the *intelligibility* of the objective conception on which Nagel's skepticism depends.

Recall that Nagel reasons as follows about Putnam's argument:

> If I accept the argument, I must conclude that a brain in a vat can't think truly that it is a brain in a vat, even though others can think this about it. What follows? Only that I can't express my skepticism by saying "Perhaps I am a brain in a vat." Instead I must say, "Perhaps I can't even *think* the truth about what I am, because I lack the necessary concepts and my circumstances make it impossible for me to acquire them!" If this doesn't qualify as skepticism, I don't know what does.[33]

But why does Nagel believe that this qualifies as *skepticism*? I suggested above that what bothers Nagel is that if Putnam's argument is sound, then a brain which is always in a vat would be unable to describe the radical way in which its cognitive perspective is limited. And this seems to engender skepticism about the objectivity of *our* cognitive perspective. For it suggests that, for all we know, our cognitive perspective may be one whose limits can't be overcome. Let us see if we can make this worry more precise.

One way to raise a skeptical doubt about our actual cognitive perspective is to show that there is a situation *s* such that

(1) if we *were* in *s*, our conceptual perspective would be radically limited,

and

(2) for all we know, *s* may be the situation we are actually in.

But this attempt to raise a skeptical doubt about our cognitive perspective can't work for the situation of a brain that is always in a vat. We can accept that

(3) Brains which are always in vats can't think that they are always in vats.[34] So if our brains were always in vats, our cognitive perspective would be radically limited.

But we can't accept that

(4) For all we know, our brains are actually always in vats.

---

[33] Nagel 1986, p. 68.
[34] Strictly speaking, Putnam's conclusion does not establish this point, for reasons I explain below in the Appendix. But it is a plausible extension of the strictly established conclusion.

We can see that (4) is false by reflecting on what it says, in light of our discoveries about meaning. If we were brains that are always in vats, then we could not understand or express (4). But we *can* understand (4). And so (4) must be false. So this way of trying to raise a skeptical doubt about the objectivity of our cognitive perspective can't succeed. Nagel acknowledges this when he says "I can't express my skepticism by saying 'Perhaps I am a brain in a vat.'"

2.11 TRUE THOUGHTS WE CAN'T NOW EXPRESS

Nagel argues that if Putnam's conclusion is true, he must express his skepticism about the objectivity of his thoughts by saying "Perhaps I can't even think the truth about what I am, because I lack the necessary concepts and my circumstances make it impossible for me to acquire them!" Let us consider whether skepticism about objectivity follows from the assumption that there are true thoughts which we are currently unable to express, when it *is* possible for us to acquire the concepts necessary to express those thoughts. We will then be in a better position to understand Nagel's objection to Putnam's conclusion.

Suppose that:

(5) There are true thoughts about our present situation which we can't now express.

Is (5) *sufficient* to engender skepticism about the objectivity of our thoughts? We might be tempted to argue that if (5) is true, then for all we know some of the thoughts which we are currently unable to express are more encompassing and objective than ours. And this might lead us to be skeptical about the objectivity of our thoughts.

To see that (5) is *not* sufficient to engender skepticism about the objectivity of our thoughts, consider the following line of reasoning:

In learning English, I developed the ability to express thoughts which I couldn't previously express. I had new experiences and learned the use of words and expressions of English. There are many languages I don't now know, but which I could learn. This suggests that there are thoughts which I can't now express, but which I would be able to express, if I had the appropriate experiences and learned the uses of the relevant linguistic expressions. For example, it is likely that there are true thoughts about my current situation which I can't now express, but which are expressible in Chinese. If I learned Chinese, I would be able to express these thoughts.

This conclusion is compatible with the causal constraint on meaning, and it supports (5). But it does not lead to skepticism about the objectivity of our thoughts, because it is based in what we know about human languages. One thing we know about them is that we can *learn* them. So even though there are thoughts which we can't now think, we know that we *could* come to think any one (though probably not all) of them. In our circumstances it is possible for us to acquire the necessary concepts. Moreover, the speakers of these languages exist in the same world as ours, and about most mundane matters we can expect widespread agreement with them. It is unlikely that the new thoughts we might come to express as we learn these languages would so startle us that we lose confidence in the objectivity of all of our previous thoughts. The new thoughts might lead us to abandon some of our old familiar ways of thinking, but it is unlikely that they would undermine them all. And so the reasons I just sketched for (5) should not engender skepticism about the objectivity of our current thoughts. Nagel implicitly acknowledges this point when he writes

I can't express my skepticism by saying "Perhaps I am a brain in a vat." Instead I must say, "Perhaps I can't even think the truth about what I am, because I lack the necessary concepts *and my circumstances make it impossible for me to acquire them.*"[35]

2.12 NAGEL'S SKEPTICISM ABOUT OBJECTIVITY

We can now see that an adequate reconstruction of Nagel's argument for skepticism about objectivity must give us a reason for believing that, for all we know, there are true thoughts about our present situation which we can't now express, and that circumstances make it impossible for us to acquire the concepts necessary to express those thoughts.

Nagel's implicit argument is that even if Putnam's conclusion is correct, a careful consideration of the situation of a brain that is always in a vat should lead us to doubt the objectivity of all our beliefs about the world. Nagel is willing to assume, for the sake of the argument, that a brain which is always in a vat has mostly true beliefs. But we know that there are true thoughts about the brain's current situation which it can't express, and that the brain can't acquire the concepts necessary to express those thoughts. Thus even though its beliefs are mostly true, they are extremely limited. Because they leave out so much, the brain's beliefs and thoughts are not fully objective.

---

[35] Nagel 1986, p. 68, emphasis mine.

For all we know we are in an analogous situation, according to Nagel. Let's say that a subject's *representation* of the world consists in all her beliefs and thoughts about it. Nagel believes that the situation of the brain in the vat, and others like it, show that a subject's representation of the world may be seriously limited, even if what it says about the world is mostly true. Nagel applies this general moral to our own case, and concludes that even if our beliefs about the world are mostly true, our representation of the world may still be seriously limited. Just as the brain's representation is seriously limited, despite its internal coherence and truth, so for all we know *our* representation of the world is limited, despite *its* internal coherence and truth.

Our representation is more encompassing than the brain's, since it captures features of the brain's situation which the brain can't represent. To imagine that, for all we know, our representation of the world is limited, despite its internal coherence and truth, is to imagine that there is some representation (or other) which stands to our representation, as ours stands to the brain's representation. This is the central premise of my reconstruction of Nagel's argument:

(6) For all we know, there is some representation (or other) which is related to our representation as ours is related to the brain's representation.

Relative to such a representation, our representation of the world would look as limited as the brain's looks to us. Just as the brain is unable to acquire the concepts necessary to express the true thought that it is a brain in a vat, if (6) is true *we* are unable to acquire the concepts necessary to overcome the limits of *our* way of representing the world. So for all we know there are true thoughts about our present situation which we can't now express, and our situation makes it impossible for us to acquire the concepts necessary to express them. For this reason, Nagel concludes that even if Putnam's argument establishes that we are not always brains in vats, there remain considerations which lead to a general skepticism about the objectivity of our representation of the world.[36]

---

[36] One might object to this skeptical conclusion on the grounds that, even if it is *possible* that there be a representation which is related to our representation as ours is related to the brain's representation, we have no reason to believe that there is. But this reply is weak. For, assuming that we accept (6), we have no reason for believing that such a representation does *not* exist. And without such a reason, Nagel would insist, we aren't justified in believing that our representation of the world is not seriously limited. One might press further here, and urge that we give up the assumption that unless we can provide concrete evidence that *rules out* a skeptical possibility, we have no justification for believing that it doesn't obtain. But this is not the most interesting place at which to challenge the argument.

Nagel's argument depends on the assumption that we can conceive of a representation of the world which is radically detached from all of our substantive beliefs about the world. It is essential to Nagel's skeptical conclusion that we have no clue as to how the world is portrayed by a representation which stands to our representation as ours stands to the brain's. For if our cognitive situation is analogous to the brain's, then our beliefs and thoughts about the world, even if they are mostly true, are so seriously limited that we can never attain an objective understanding of our situation. We would have no way of finding out which truths our representation fails to include. We couldn't even speculate about this. For no speculation of *ours* could indicate truths which we don't have the conceptual resources to express. To understand the possibility that our conceptual resources are limited in this way, we must be able to conceive of a representation which portrays the world using concepts we don't possess and can't acquire. And so we must be able to conceive of a representation of the world which is radically detached from and independent of our substantive beliefs about the world.

The assumption that we can conceive of a representation of the world which is radically detached from all of our substantive beliefs about the world goes hand in hand with the idea of an absolute conception of the world. Nagel believes that we understand the absolute conception of the world as the limit of a dialectic which progresses through ever-widening circles of representations. The dialectic begins with the thought that our beliefs result from interactions with an independently existing world, and the observation that some of our beliefs are limited or distorted. The discovery and understanding of limits or distortions in our beliefs requires that we have a more objective representation of the world, which includes a more objective understanding of the cognitive processes which limited or distorted our beliefs. When this happens locally, *within* our commonsense representation of the world, it does not require that we conceive of a representation which is radically detached from and external to our substantive beliefs and thoughts. But Nagel maintains that we can extend our understanding of the dialectical overcoming of limitations or distortions in our beliefs far beyond the conceptual limits of our representation of the world. He believes that we can conceive of a representation of the world which encompasses ours completely, and shows us to be severely limited in our understanding of the world, even if most of our beliefs are true. The dialectic of representations can in principle continue, Nagel believes, until it reaches the *absolute conception* of the world: a representation of the world which has no subjective, limiting elements, from which all other representations can be understood. We can make sense of the idea of an absolute conception of the world only if we can understand the possibility of a representation which portrays the world using concepts we don't possess and can't acquire. So the idea of an absolute conception also depends on the assumption that we can conceive of a representation of the world which is radically detached from our substantive beliefs about the world.[37]

The problem with Nagel's argument, and with the related idea of an absolute conception of the world, is that we don't really understand the idea of a representation of the world which is radically detached from and independent of our substantive beliefs. As I argued in Section 2.2, a careful investigation of our ordinary concept of meaning reveals that our thoughts are partly determined by the things with which we are causally related. Thoughts and beliefs aren't individuated – their contents can't be fully characterized – independently of the natures of our social and physical environments. There is no way to conceive of a thought or belief unless we have some idea of the social and physical environment on which its individuation depends. This means that our understanding of a representation of the world and our thoughts about what the world is like are essentially interconnected. So we don't really understand the idea of a representation of the world which is radically detached from and independent of our ability to express its content.

Nagel's idea of a representation that portrays the world using concepts we don't possess and can't acquire is an illegitimate generalization of our conception of representation, which is essentially tied to the particular beliefs and thoughts whose contents we can (in principle) express. We can convince ourselves that there are true thoughts which we can't now think, but only when we can see that it is possible for us to acquire the concepts necessary to express those thoughts. I argued above that we have reason to believe that there are thoughts about our current situation which are expressible in Chinese, but which we can't now express, because we don't know Chinese. Our ability to conceive of thoughts which we can't *now* express is in this case dependent on our ordinary belief that we *would* be able to express new thoughts, if we learned Chinese. This reflects the fact that we can't separate our concept of a representation of the world from all of our beliefs about what the world is like. Our confidence that there exist thoughts which we can't now

---

[37] The views I attribute to Nagel in this paragraph are found in Chapters I, II, and V of Nagel 1986. He endorses the idea of the absolute conception of reality on page 15, footnote 1, in which he cites Bernard Williams's account (1978, pp. 64–65) of the idea.

express must be based on our understanding of how we *could* come to express those thoughts. Without any of our thoughts and beliefs to rely on, we have no idea what the representations are.[38]

We should therefore reject Nagel's skepticism about objectivity, and the related idea of an absolute conception of the world. Beginning with our meaningful ordinary use of language, we observed that our thoughts are partly determined by the things with which we are causally related. This means that our concept of a representation is inextricably connected with particular beliefs and thoughts whose contents we can (in principle) express. The story of the brain in a vat seems to show that we can conceive of a representation which is radically detached from our substantive beliefs. But this is an illusion, based in a misunderstanding of our ordinary concepts of meaning and thought.[39]

APPENDIX: AN APPARENT GAP IN PUTNAM'S ARGUMENT

Premise (ii) of Putnam's reasoning is ambiguous. It can be interpreted as making either an unrestricted or a restricted claim. The *unrestricted* claim is that if I were always a brain in a vat, I could not raise any question which has the same truth conditions as the question *Am I always a brain in a vat?* The *restricted* claim is that if I were always a brain in a vat, I could not ask *Am I always a brain in a vat?* by using the words "Am I always a brain in a vat?" Putnam's reasoning only *directly* establishes the restricted claim. This claim is sufficient to establish the conclusion, since the first premise is stated using the words 'brain' and 'vat'. But one might ask whether there is some *other* way of raising a very troubling skeptical worry about our current cognitive

---

[38] The argument in this paragraph is similar in spirit to Donald Davidson's argument (1974). Unlike Davidson, however, I believe that it is important to acknowledge that we can conceive of true thoughts which we can't now think (but only when we can see that our circumstances don't make it impossible for us to acquire the concepts necessary to express those thoughts). Thus I agree with Hilary Putnam's criticism (1987) of Davidson's argument against the possibility of alternative conceptual schemes. On the other hand, I believe that Putnam's and Davidson's positions are closer than they may first appear. On one crucial point they agree: the idea of a representation that portrays the world using concepts we don't possess and can't acquire does not make sense.

[39] The reasoning in this chapter shows that once Putnam's causal constraint in meaning is properly understood, it undermines the intelligibility of the absolute conception of the world, which is one form of what Putnam calls "metaphysical realism." This suggests that, contrary to the standard interpretation, the rejection of "metaphysical realism" is implicit in Putnam's early views on meaning and reference. In Ebbs 1992, I develop this aspect of my interpretation of Putnam's views of meaning and reference. According to my reconstruction of Putnam's views, our participation in ongoing inquiries subjects our statements to norms which it is the task of philosophy to describe and clarify. I argue that once this conception of the starting point and the task of philosophy of language is properly understood, we can see that "metaphysical realism" has no content.

situation. (If so, then Putnam's conclusion would not rule out the possibility of skepticism about the objectivity of our thoughts. The arguments in Sections 2.10–2.12 against Nagel's skeptical worries would not be undermined, however, because Nagel's worries were supposed to arise in part from the *assumption* that a brain which is always in a vat is unable to express the thought that it is a brain in a vat.) It helps to approach this question indirectly, by first asking whether a brain which is always in a vat can express a thought which has the same truth conditions as the thought that it is always in a vat. Putnam's argument establishes that a brain which is always in a vat can't use the sentence 'I am always a brain in a vat' to say something true. But perhaps the brain can express a thought which has the same truth conditions as the thought that it is always a brain in a vat *without using its words 'brain' and 'vat'*. And if a brain which is always in a vat can express such a troubling thought, why can't we? There may be a way that *we* can express a deeply troubling thought about our situation without using the words 'brain' and 'vat'. And if we can express such a troubling thought, we can ask whether it is true.

Consider the situation in which a certain brain y has always been and always will be in a vat. Suppose that a person x is able to interpret all of y's utterances, and that x knows that y is always a brain in a vat. In this situation, x bears a certain complex relation R to y. For instance, in order for x to be able to interpret all of y's utterances, x must bear certain causal relations to y, and to the things with which y is causally related.

These causal relations will be part of the complex relation R. In order for the example to work, we must assume that the causal relations which exist between x and y are not direct enough to enable y to have thoughts about the kinds of things which exist only outside the vat. So y can't ask whether it is a brain which is always in a vat by using the sentence "Am I always a brain in a vat?" Nevertheless, perhaps we can use relation R to construct a counter-example to the claim that a brain which is always in a vat can't express a thought which has (nearly) the same truth conditions as the thought that it is always a brain in a vat. And perhaps we can use R to construct a similarly troubling thought about our cognitive situation.

Suppose that

(a) A brain which is always in a vat can express thoughts involving R.

(a) is not obvious, since it is not clear what is required in order for a subject to be able to express thoughts involving R. But if (a) is true, then a brain which is always in a vat could raise the following question:

(b) Does someone bear R to me?

If the answer is "yes," then the brain is always in a vat. (The thought that someone bears R to *y* does not have the *same* truth conditions as the thought that *y* is always a brain in a vat, but it *implies* that *y* is always a brain in a vat, and so it is sufficiently troubling to raise a skeptical question about the brain's cognitive perspective.) But unlike those who stand outside the vat, the brain is unable to express the thought that if the answer is "yes," then it is always a brain in a vat. The brain has no reason to believe that the answer to (b) is "yes." But if (a) is true, then the brain can raise the question expressed by (b). This is an apparent counterexample to the claim that a brain which is always in a vat can't raise *radically* skeptical worries about the objectivity of its cognitive perspective.

If *y* can raise skeptical doubts about the objectivity of its cognitive perspective, why can't we? It seems that we can raise the question expressed by (b), applied to ourselves. We know that we are not always brains in vats, since this follows from the restricted reading of premise (ii) of Putnam's argument. But we don't know whether (b) is true, when it is applied to ourselves. If it is true, our cognitive perspective must be limited in something like the way the cognitive perspective of a brain in a vat is limited. But we are unable to state in an informative way what the consequences of (b)'s truth would be. We don't have any reason to believe that the answer to (b), as applied to ourselves, is "yes." But if (b) makes sense when applied to ourselves, then we can at least raise a question about the objectivity of our cognitive perspective.

Before we can accept these counterexamples, we must determine whether (b) really makes sense, applied by a brain which is always in a vat, or to ourselves. It is not easy to make progress on this question. Here is one difficulty: it seems that I can't conceive of the spatio-temporal location of a person who bears R to me. And if I can't conceive of the spatio-temporal location of a person who bears R to me, I can't make sense of the idea that someone might bear R to me. It seems that the brain which is always in a vat would be similarly unable to grasp the thought it attempts to express with (b). This reflects the fact, emphasized in Section 2.12, that our understanding of a thought depends on our ability to connect it in some way with our substantive beliefs about the world.

CHAPTER 3

Ebbs on skepticism, objectivity, and brains in vats

Anthony Brueckner

In Chapter 2, Gary Ebbs considers various issues surrounding the attempt to reconstruct an argument against Cartesian skepticism from the materials furnished by Putnam's discussion of the semantics of the utterances of brains in vats.[1] Ebbs goes on to investigate the bearing of Putnam's discussion on a different sort of skepticism: that which concerns *objectivity* conceived in the manner of Thomas Nagel. In this paper, I wish to raise some questions concerning his claims about both the reconstructive issues and objectivity-skepticism.

3.1 RECONSTRUCTING PUTNAM

The main issue in the first half of Ebbs's paper is how to reconstruct an argument from the Putnamian materials for the conclusion

(iii) I am not always a brain in a vat.

Ebbs favors the following Putnam-style argument for (iii) (which is to be interpreted as concerning brains in vats who exist in a world whose only contents are brains in vats and a computer which stimulates them):

(i) I can raise the question: *Am I always a brain in a vat?*
(ii) If I were always a brain in a vat, I could not raise this question. (p. 28)

Call this argument *A*. Ebbs contrasts this reconstruction of Putnam with one I gave in Chapter 1. On Ebbs's presentation of my reconstruction, the argument makes appeal to a disquotation principle

(T) My utterances of 'I am a brain in a vat' are true if and only if I am a brain in a vat.

---

[1] All page references in the text are to Chapter 2, this volume. Putnam's discussion is in Chapter 1 of Putnam 1981.

In discussing my reconstruction, Ebbs's practice is to "represent the content of the . . . [brain in a vat's] utterance of a sentence S with ⌜(S) in the image⌝" (p. 38). Here is Ebbs's version of my Putnamian argument (call it *B*):

(1) Either I am a brain in a vat (and I speak vat-English) or I am not a brain in a vat (and I speak English).

(2) Suppose I am a brain in a vat (and I speak vat-English).

(3) Then 'I am a brain in a vat' is true in my language (vat-English) if and only if (I am a brain in a vat) in the image. [(2), Theory of meaning]

(4) (I am not a brain in a vat) in the image. [Empirical fact (?)]

(5) So 'I am a brain in a vat' is not true in my language. [(3), (4)]

(6) Suppose I am not a brain in a vat (and I speak English).

(7) Then 'I am a brain in a vat' is true in my language (English) if and only if I am a brain in a vat. [(T), (6)]

(8) Hence 'I am a brain in a vat' is not true in my language (English). [(6), (7)]

(9) 'I am a brain in a vat' is not true in my language. [(1–8, Disjunction elimination]

(10) 'I am a brain in a vat' is true in my language if and only if I am a brain in a vat. [(T)]

(11) Therefore, I am not a brain in a vat. [(9), (10)][2]

Ebbs's first complaint about this argument is that my case for premise (4) "rests on a false verificationist account of the meaning of 'I am not a brain in a vat'" (p. 41). Following Putnam's fairly clear suggestion, I assumed that when Putnam speaks of *the image*, he means the stream of sense impressions given to the BIV. Thus, '(There are trees) in the image' is true if and only if the image contains sense impressions as of trees. '(I am a brain in a vat) in the image', then, is true if and only if I have sense impressions as of being a brain in a vat. In a world in which I am a brain in a vat, though, I do not have such sense impressions; instead, I have sense impressions as of being embodied in a normal environment.

Does this lead to a verificationist (or, better, phenomenalist) account of the meaning of 'I am a brain in a vat'? Well, only for a *brain in a vat's* utterances of the sentence. What is wrong with such an account, anyway, so long as it is recognized that the truth conditions of a normal speaker's utterances of the sentence are *not* verificationist? One reason (not given by Ebbs) is that sense impressions play the same causal role in the production of *both* a brain in a vat's utterances *and* those of a normal language-user. Putnam's views about reference should lead us to look for entities in the vat

---

[2] This presentation is on p. 15 of Chapter 2; it departs from mine in certain inessential respects.

world which play a causal role which is analogous to that played by trees, brains, and the like in the normal world. Putnam does in fact consider alternatives to the verificationist account (as I noted in the paper). Putnam, for example, considers the idea that 'There are trees' is true as uttered by the BIV if and only if computer state 666 obtains.[3]

Ebbs's own objection to the verificationist account of the truth conditions of 'I am a brain in a vat' as uttered by a brain in a vat is that it is possible for a brain in a vat's utterances of the sentence to be *true* even though he does not have the requisite sense impressions (ones which would somehow represent him as being envatted). In support of this claim, Ebbs gives the example of a brain in a vat who does not meet one of the conditions of Putnam's thought experiment: a brain in a vat who isn't *always* in a vat and whose utterances are accordingly able to have *disquotational* truth conditions (which are satisfied since it *is* a brain in a vat). However, my discussion in Chapter 1 (and just about all the other discussions in the relevant literature) was quite explicit in focusing only on *Putnamian* brains in vats, who are always envatted and who do not have causal contact with ordinary unenvatted experiencers. To see how far off the mark the objection is, it is sufficient to note that it would apply to *any* view of the semantics of an envatted brain's utterances of 'I am a brain in a vat' according to which these utterances do not have disquotational truth conditions. But if we are talking about brains in vats who meet the conditions of Putnam's thought experiment, and we take Putnam's semantic views seriously, then we will agree that a brain in a vat's utterances of 'I am a brain in a vat' do not have disquotational truth conditions. Thus, even if the verificationist truth conditions for envatted utterances are unsatisfactory, this is not for the reasons adduced by Ebbs.

Though Ebbs objects to my explanation of why (4) is true (since it depends on the objectionable assignment of truth conditions), he thinks that an alternative explanation is available to Putnam. Ebbs's representation of the content of a BIV's utterance of 'I am always a brain in a vat' is

($) (*I am always a brain in a vat*) *in the image.*

He says that he is not sure that he understands ($) (p. 42). If that is so, then it is at least prima facie unclear how he can argue, as he does, that

---

[3] How is the right computer state to be specified? One possibility is that it is the state which standardly causes the brain in a vat to assent to 'There are trees' via the production of various sense impressions. Applying this idea to 'I am a brain in a vat', we still get the result that the sentence is false as uttered by the brain in a vat in virtue of the ongoing non-obtaining of any computer state causing assent to 'I am a brain in a vat' via the state's production of various sense impressions.

the claim expressed by ($) (whatever it is) is *false of a brain in a vat*. His actual argument is hard to follow:

> For if the brain *were* always a brain in a vat in the image (whatever *that* means), then it would not be causally related with the images of brains and the images of vats, and so it could not claim that *(I am always a brain in a vat) in the image.* But we are assuming that it can claim that *(I am always a brain in a vat) in the image.* (p. 42)

If we do not know what it is to be a brain in a vat in the image, then how do we know whether or not such a thing would be causally related to images of brains and images of vats? And why would it be required that a brain in a vat in the image be causally related to images of brains in order to refer to brains in the image unless we assume some sort of objectionable verificationist account of the relevant truth conditions?

After providing the reconstruction B which Ebbs finds to be inferior to his A, I objected to B in various ways. Ebbs does not find my main objection to be even prima facie worrisome. He states it as follows: "even if . . . [B] is valid it is compatible with skepticism about what one means" (p. 43) This wasn't quite my objection. I worried that the Putnamian semantic views underlying B (which underlie Ebbs's A as well) *generate* skepticism about meaning within the pertinent dialectical context. The objection was, roughly, that if you accept Putnam's semantic views while remaining agnostic on the question of whether you are in a vat world or a normal world (as the anti-skeptic does in constructing his anti-skeptical argument B), then you cannot claim to know whether your utterances have the disquotational truth conditions embodied in (T) or instead strange, non-disquotational truth conditions. Thus you cannot fairly claim knowledge of the disquotational premise (10) of argument B.

This objection may well be flawed, but Ebbs's response to it is problematic. He holds that I can know that I am not speaking vat-English – thereby coming to know that my utterances do not have strange truth conditions – by appeal to a variant of argument A (call it *A'*):

(i')   I can express the thoughts (about vats, brains, etc.) necessary to define vat-English as the language spoken by a brain which is always in a vat.
(ii') If I were always a brain in a vat, then I could not express those thoughts.
(iii) I am not always a brain in a vat.[4]

Now we can turn to the question whether A really is superior to B (as Ebbs maintains). Ebbs has not considered the possibility that A and B might be

---

[4] See p. 44 of Chapter 2 for the relevant passage.

quite similar in a certain crucial respect. B appeals to disquotation in premise (10). My question about that argument was: Can I claim knowledge that my utterances have disquotational truth conditions, given B's underlying externalist semantic assumptions, and given agnosticism on the question whether I am in a vat world or a normal world? An exactly parallel question can be raised about premise (i′) of A′ and about the corresponding premise (i) of the original A: Can I claim knowledge that my sentence 'Vat-English is the language spoken by a brain which is always in a vat' expresses the thought that *vat-English is the language spoken by a brain which is always in a vat* (rather than some thought about *the image*), given A′'s underlying externalist semantic assumptions (which are B's as well), and given agnosticism on the question whether I am in a vat world or a normal world?[5] There may well be an acceptable affirmative answer to both these questions. That is, there may well be convincing reasons for thinking that the externalist semantic assumptions underlying A, A′, and B engender neither skepticism about knowledge of meaning and truth conditions nor skepticism about knowledge of the contents of one's thoughts.[6] However, Ebbs's response to the skeptical difficulty allegedly afflicting B rests upon the unargued assumption that since no parallel difficulty afflicts A′ (and A), A′ can thus be used to remove the difficulty allegedly afflicting B. But there is really no significant difference between A and A′, on the one hand, and B, on the other, when it comes to the sort of objection I made to B. Skepticism about knowledge of content is on a par with skepticism about knowledge of meaning and truth conditions.

Ebbs maintains that Putnam is clearly attracted to demonstrating, in the manner of B, that

(iv) Whether or not I am always a brain in a vat, my utterances of 'I am always a brain in a vat' are false.

But according to Ebbs, argument A established

(iii) I am not always a brain in a vat

without recourse to the (problematic, on Ebbs's view) metalinguistic claim (iv). So what is the explanation of Putnam's overall position? The

---

[5] The parallel question for A: Can I claim knowledge that my sentence 'I am always a brain in a vat' expresses the thought that *I am always a brain in a vat*, given A's underlying semantic assumptions, and given agnosticism on the question whether I am in a vat world or a normal world?

[6] See, e.g., Burge 1988a. See also Brueckner 1992a, for an extended discussion of the problem of reconciling semantic externalism with knowledge of meaning, truth conditions, and content. In that paper, I defend a reconstruction of Putnam which is similar to Ebbs's, and I try to provide an answer to skepticism about knowledge of the truth conditions of one's utterances.

explanation, says Ebbs, is that Putnam wishes to forestall a move by a skeptic concerned with Nagelian *objectivity*. This skeptic maintains that there is "an absolutely objective third-person perspective on our current situation" from which it may turn out that we are always brains in vats (p. 45). We may be brains in vats who argue, in the manner of Putnam, for a conclusion we express by saying 'We are not always brains in vats', which conclusion really means that *(We are not always brains in vats) in the image* (p. 45). Ebbs's view is that Putnam wishes to block this objectivity-skeptic's move by arguing from the metalinguistic (iv), as in argument B.

According to Ebbs, we should interpet Putnam as attempting to answer the objectivity-skeptic by putting forward

(v) Whether or not we are always brains in vats, we can conclude that we are not always brains in vats

and then inferring

(vi) We are not always brains in vats.

Thus there is no absolutely objective third-person perspective from which it can be seen that we are always brains in vats who only succeed in concluding that *(We are not always brains in vats) in the image*. If the metalinguistic (iv) is to play a role in this answer to the objectivity-skeptic, as Ebbs maintains, then it is presumably this: the pluralized version of (iv) is conjoined with disquotation to yield (v).

The odd thing about Ebbs's interpretation of Putnam here is that Putnam could have refuted the objectivity-skeptic by establishing (vi) *via* A, rather than via the B-style disjunctive, metalinguistic reasoning. So Ebbs hasn't in the end found any real role for the disjunctive, metalinguistic reasoning in Putnam's overall position, given the assumption that Putnam's core reasoning about brains in vats is given in A.

3.2 NAGELIAN OBJECTIVITY

Ebbs wants to show how Putnam's ideas about brains in vats bear on a more sophisticated skepticism about objectivity than that just considered. Thomas Nagel says,

If I accept … [Putnam's] argument, I must conclude that a brain in a vat can't think truly that it is a brain in a vat, even though others can think this about it. What follows? Only that I can't express my skepticism by saying "Perhaps I am a brain in a vat". Instead I must say, "Perhaps I can't even think the truth about what I am, because I lack the necessary concepts and my circumstances make it impossible for me to acquire them!" If this doesn't qualify as skepticism, I don't know what does.[7]

Ebbs maintains that Nagel is not entitled to a premise which is necessary to formulate his skepticism about objectivity:

(6) For all we know, there is some representation (or other) which is related to our representation as ours is related to the ... [brain in a vat's] representation. (p. 49)

(One's *representation* of the world is *all one's beliefs and thoughts about the world*.) Ebbs holds that if we accept the anti-individualist conception of meaning, reference, and content, which stems from Putnam's Twin-Earth thought experiments, then we see that we cannot conceive of the 'possibility' allegedly countenanced in (6).

Let us consider Ebbs's reasoning to show the incoherence of (6). He seems to proceed from the claim that anti-individualism yields

(*) There is no way to conceive of a thought or belief unless we have some idea of the social and physical environment on which its individuation depends. (p. 51)

From (*) he seems to infer

(**) We cannot conceive of a thought involving concepts which we cannot acquire.[8]

Now in conceiving of the alleged 'possibility' countenanced in (6), we would need to conceive of putative *alien concepts* which are not acquirable by us, in the same way that our concepts are not acquirable by a brain in a vat.[9] But (**) tells us that we cannot and hence do not possess a second-order concept of such alien concepts. So we cannot really conceive of the 'possibility' allegedly countenanced in (6).

The first thing to note about this reasoning is that it involves a type of formulation which is close to paradoxical when taken literally. For example, consider (**). If this claim is true, then the English phrase 'thought involving concepts which we cannot acquire' does not express any concept. If it

---

[7] Nagel 1986, p. 68.

[8] Ebbs says, "To understand the possibility that our conceptual resources are limited ... [in the way alleged in (6)], we must be able to conceive of a representation which portrays the world using concepts we don't possess and can't acquire" (p. 50). However, "the idea of a representation that portrays the world using concepts we don't possess and can't acquire does not make sense" (p. 52, fn. 38).

[9] I assume throughout that Ebbs has in mind some account of the conditions under which a concept is *acquirable* by a being. Ebbs would need to have, for example, some account of when the acquisition of a concept would somehow be precluded by the being's intellectual and sensory capacities.

did express a concept (a second-order concept of thoughts and their constituent concepts), then, contra (**), we *would* be able to conceive of a thought involving concepts which we cannot acquire. Given, then, that the phrase in question does not express any concept, it follows that the sentence 'We cannot conceive of a thought involving concepts which we cannot acquire' (this is (**)) is not meaningful. Ebbs's claims, however, obviously could be reformulated in the formal mode so as to take this difficulty into account. Still, it seems intuitively implausible to hold that the phrase in question fails to express any concept. Perhaps Ebbs could somewhat modify his claims. Consider what an anti-individualist would say about the English phrase 'natural kind concept whose individuation conditions do not at all depend upon the environment in which it is used'. The anti-individualist does not have to say that this phrase fails to express a concept. It is perfectly meaningful, he might say, and hence it expresses a genuine concept. However, this concept has an empty extension (in all possible worlds). No possible natural kind concept has such individuation conditions. Ebbs might take a similar line with regard to the phrase 'concept which we cannot acquire'. It expresses a concept with an empty extension, he might say. We can conceive of – and speak meaningfully about – such concepts. But there are none, and there could not be any. This, I think, would suffice for Ebbs's purposes.

Let us set aside these questions and consider Ebbs's case for (**). First consider (*), which appears to function as a premise in the reasoning. This thesis is too strong. To see this, first note that Ebbs allows that I can conceive of thoughts (and concepts) which I cannot now "express" (and cannot now think), say, due to my current ignorance of Chinese.[10] It seems that Ebbs should also allow that, contrary to (*), I can conceive of thoughts which (a) I cannot now think in virtue of the character of my current environment, and (b) whose environmental individuation conditions elude my present powers of conceptualization. Indeed, the Twin-Earth thought experiments which underlie anti-individualism (which itself is supposedly the basis for (*)) seem to presuppose that I can conceive of such thoughts. We have no idea of what XYZ is like. 'XYZ' is just a dummy name for some liquid of which we have no concept, since it is absent from our environment and composed of alien elements. Still, we are apparently able to conceive of the thoughts of our Twin-Earth counterparts, thoughts whose individuation depends on the character of some liquid of which we have no concept.

---

[10] This seems to be a rather unfortunate example to illustrate what appears to be Ebbs's point. Does Chinese really differ significantly from English in its expressive power?

If we cannot form any conception of our counterparts' thoughts, as (*) would have it, then (*) ultimately rests on incoherent thought experiments. Of course, we cannot determinately refer to some particular Twin-Earth thought just by saying 'thought which involves the concept of twater, which concept applies to the liquid XYZ'. This is because, as noted, 'XYZ' has no determinate reference. The point is rather that the thought experiments underlying anti-individualism seem to presuppose that the phrase 'thoughts whose individuation conditions depend upon environmental features for which we lack a concept' expresses a concept. This concept is employed in thinking about the relevant counterfactual situations in the anti-individualist thought experiments.

Let us try to modify (*) in order to get around this difficulty. Note first that if I were placed in the Twin-Earth enviroment, then I would eventually acquire the concept of twater in virtue of my interactions with XYZ. Further, if I were so placed, then I could come to form a concept of the physical environment on which the individuation of my concept *twater* depends. I could come to form the concept *the liquid XYZ*. Finally, it is *possible* for me to be placed in the Twin-Earth environment. Accordingly, let us consider the following modification of (*):

(*') There is no way to conceive of a thought or belief unless we *can acquire* some idea of the social and physical environment on which its individuation depends.

Now it can be said that we *can* conceive of our Twin-Earth counterparts' thoughts, insofar as it is possible for us to acquire a concept of the pertinent environmental individuating conditions.

(**) apparently follows from (*'). (*') tells us that if I can conceive of a concept C, then it is possible for me to conceive of the environment upon which the individuation of C depends. If it is possible for me to conceive of that environment, then it would seem to follow that it is possible for me to be in that environment in a way which would enable me to acquire C. So if I can conceive of C, then C is acquirable. This is what (**) says.

Does (*') follow from anti-individualism? It is not at all obvious that it does, and Ebbs gives no argument whatsoever for this connection. The anti-individualist views found in Putnam and Burge concern the way in which the individuation of *first-order*, empirical concepts (e.g., *tree*, *water*) depends upon physical and social environment. These views contain no claims concerning second-order, 'pure' concepts such as *concept* and *thought*. But surely, Ebbs might say, we can quite naturally *extend* the anti-individualist views to such concepts. But how exactly are we to extend the familiar views to the case of second-order concepts? According to these views, 'water', as used by a Twin-Earth counterpart of me, will express a different concept from mine if the enviromental factors causally relevant to his uses of the term are sufficiently different from mine. So, by extension, Ebbs might say, 'concept', as used by a counterpart of me in a radically alien environment, will express a different concept from mine if the causally relevant enviromental factors are sufficiently different from mine. This way of putting the claim, though, implies that my counterpart's uses of 'concept' would express a *concept*, and Ebbs, I take it, would deny this. Further, in what sense could a being in a radically alien environment from mine be a *counterpart* of me? Presumably we are not to imagine that, as in the Twin-Earth-thought experiments, my alien counterpart would be a phenomenological twin of me who speaks a language which is syntactically indistinguishable from mine.

Let us try to understand the envisaged extension of anti-individualism as follows. In (6), we are invited to conceive of a being who thinks thoughts which it is tempting for us to express as follows: "Those puny humans have concepts which are impoverished in comparison to our concepts, which their environmental circumstances prevent them from acquiring, just as the brains in vats are prevented from acquiring the puny humans' concepts." On the extension of anti-individualism currently under consideration, the being's word which we are inclined to translate as 'concept' cannot be so translated. The word, whatever it is, does not express the concept expressed by our word 'concept', given the difference between our environments. Indeed, such a being would not possess concepts at all, in virtue of the alien character of those parts of his environment that are appropriately related to that representation (if we can call it that) of his which we are inclined to mistranslate as meaning what our word 'concept' means.[11]

The trouble with this quick defense of Ebbs's anti-individualism about second-order concepts is that it is not obviously plausible to hold that the extension of the term 'concept' gets fixed by one's environment in a manner which is analogous to the fixing of the extension of 'water'. In the latter cases, the relevant reference-fixing circumstances are causal connections between speakers' uses of 'water' and samples of the liquid H_2O. In the former case, though, is it at all plausible to maintain that the relevant reference-fixing circumstances are causal interactions between speakers' uses of 'concept' and concepts?[12]

---

[11] This result does not require that our phrase 'concept which we cannot acquire' expresses no concept.

[12] Here is another way to defend Ebbs's extension of anti-individualism. Suppose we hold that the extension of our term 'concept' is determined by which concepts we in fact use the term to refer to (even if there is no illuminating *causal* story to be told about the relevant reference relation). None of

In criticizing Nagel's skepticism about objectivity, Ebbs has, in effect, put forward the interesting proposal that anti-individualism can be extended to second-order, 'pure' concepts such as *concept*. This proposal deserves further investigation. It seems to me that it is an open problem whether the proposal can be plausibly developed.

the concepts we in fact use are used in the sort of alien environment we are invited to imagine in (6). Thus, any alien 'representation' which we would be inclined to translate as meaning what our word 'concept' means cannot be so translated. In order to have that meaning, the 'representation' would need to be applied to our concepts, which are not employed in the alien environment. The trouble with this line of reasoning, though, is that it rests on two problematic assumptions. First, it is assumed that our concepts are absent from the envisaged alien environment (in the sense that they are not employed there). But it is not clear that this is Nagel's picture: the alien conceptual framework might well contain much of our framework as a proper part. Second, it is assumed that since our concepts are absent from the alien environment, all concepts are absent. A parallel claim would be that since our cars are absent from some alien possible world, all cars are absent. Why is the claim about concepts any more plausible than the claim about cars?

CHAPTER 4

The dialectical context of Putnam's argument that we are not brains in vats

Gary Ebbs

In Chapter 3 Brueckner raises a number of questions about my arguments in Chapter 2. He challenges central details of my proposed reconstruction of Hilary Putnam's argument that we are not brains in vats, and raises doubts about my attempt to show that Putnam's argument undermines skepticism about objectivity. I shall argue that Brueckner's challenges and doubts can be traced back to a misunderstanding of the dialectical context of Putnam's argument.

4.1 TWO RECONSTRUCTIONS OF PUTNAM'S ARGUMENT

In Chapter 2 I propose that we reconstruct Putnam's argument that we are not brains in vats as follows:

Argument A
  (i)   I can raise the question: *Am I always a brain in a vat?*
  (ii) If I were always a brain in a vat, I could not raise this question.
  (iii) So I am not always a brain in a vat.

Here I take "I am always a brain in vat" as short for "I am a permanently envatted brain whose neuro-receptors are stimulated, throughout its life, in exactly the same way that an ordinary embodied brain's neuro-receptors are stimulated." I claim that (i) is obviously true, despite doubts that have been raised about it, and that the key premise of the argument is (ii), which is a consequence of Putnam's discoveries about our ordinary concepts of meaning and reference.

I contrast this reconstruction of Putnam's argument with the reconstruction that Brueckner offers in Chapter 1. Brueckner's alternative reconstruction relies on the otherwise unimpeachable assumption that we are each in a position to accept

(T) My utterances of 'I am always a brain in vat' are true if and only if I am always a brain in a vat.

The leading idea behind Brueckner's reconstruction is that *whether or not we are always brains in a vat* – where we take each of these alternatives to be epistemically possible, and to *remain* epistemically possible, even *after* we have reached our conclusion – our utterances of "I am a brain in vat" are not true, and hence, by (T), we may conclude that we are not always brains in vats. Brueckner's reconstruction of Putnam's argument builds in this disjunctive style of reasoning:

Argument B
(1) Either I am always a brain in a vat (and I speak vat-English) or I am not always a brain in vat (and I speak English).
(2) Suppose I am always a brain vat (and I speak vat-English).
(3) Then 'I am always a brain in vat' is true in my language (vat-English) if and only if (I am always a brain in a vat) in the image. [(2), theory of meaning]
(4) (I am not always a brain in vat) in the image. [Empirical fact (?)]
(5) So 'I am always a brain in vat' is not true in my language. [(3), (4)]
(6) Suppose I am not always brain in a vat (and I speak English).
(7) Then 'I am always a brain in vat' is not true in my language (English). [(T), (6)]
(8) Hence 'I am always a brain in a vat' is not true in my language. [(6), (7)]
(9) 'I am a brain in a vat' is not true in my language. [(1)–(8), Disjunction elimination]
(10) 'I am always brain in vat' is true in my language if and only if I am always a brain in a vat. [(T)]
(11) Therefore, I am not always a brain in a vat.

In Chapter 2 I raise two problems for Brueckner's reconstruction. First, it assumes (at steps (2)–(4)) that the truth conditions for the utterances of a brain that is always in a vat can be defined in terms of how things appear to the brain in a vat – what sensory impressions it has – and this conflicts with Putnam's theory of meaning. Second, it invites a peculiar and paradoxical sort of skepticism about one's knowledge of what thoughts one expresses by using one's own sentences.

In Chapter 2 I also claim that my reconstruction, Argument A above, does not have either of these problems, and is therefore preferable to Brueckner's reconstruction, Argument B above. In response to the first problem, Brueckner defends his verificationist interpretation of the meanings of utterances of a brain that is always in a vat. And in response to the second problem, Brueckner argues that my own reconstruction, Argument A, is equally vulnerable to skepticism about one's knowledge of what thoughts one expresses by using one's own sentences. I shall examine both of Brueckner's responses, but in reverse order, starting with his response to the second problem, which is the deeper of the two. His response reveals that he understands the dialectical context of Putnam's argument very differently from the way I do. For reasons I shall explain, our different conceptions of this dialectical context underlie and explain our disputes about how to understand Putnam's argument and its consequences.

4.2 BRUECKNER ON "THE PERTINANT DIALECTICAL CONTEXT" FOR EVALUATING A AND B

Brueckner reports that in Chapter 1, he

worried that the Putnamian semantic views underlying B (which underlie Ebbs's A as well) *generate* skepticism about meaning within *the pertinent dialectical context*. The objection was, roughly, that if you accept Putnam's semantic views *while remaining agnostic on the question of whether you are in a vat world or a normal world (as the anti-skeptic does in constructing his anti-skeptical argument B)*, then you cannot claim to know whether your utterances have the disquotational truth conditions embodied in (T) or instead strange, non disquotational truth conditions. Thus you cannot fairly claim knowledge of the disquotational premise (1) of argument B. (Chapter 3, p. 58; my underlining)

This makes clear that Brueckner takes the "pertinent dialectical context" to be one in which we are "agnostic on the question of whether we are in a vat world or a normal world." Brueckner understands this to mean that we suppose throughout the argument that we may actually be brains that are always in vats. We also accept that our utterances of 'I am always a brain in a vat' express different thoughts in English and in vat-English. Since we are agnostic on the question of whether we are in a vat world or normal world, we have no choice but to conclude that we don't know what thought our utterances of 'I am always a brain in a vat' actually express.

In Chapter 2, I try to allay this doubt by pointing out that "Vat-English is *defined* as that language spoken by a brain which is always in a vat. It follows from Putnam's theory of meaning that if I were such a brain, I could not characterize the language it speaks as vat-English. For if I were such a brain, then I could not express the thoughts necessary to define vat-English" (p. 44). Brueckner reconstructs this argument as follows:

Argument A′
  (i′) I can express the thoughts (about vats, brains, etc.) necessary to define vat-English as the language spoken by a brain which is always in a vat.
 (ii′) If I were always a brain in a vat, then I could not express those thoughts.
(iii′) Therefore, I am not always a brain in a vat.

Brueckner argues that Argument A′ does not really allay the sort of doubt he raised for Argument B. He reasons as follows:

My question about that argument [B] was: Can I claim knowledge that my utterances have disquotational truth conditions, given B's underlying externalist semantic assumptions, and given agnosticism on the question whether I am in a vat world or a normal world? An exactly parallel question can be raised about premise (i′) of A′: Can I claim knowledge that my sentence 'Vat-English is the language spoken by a brain which is always in a vat' expresses the thought that *vat-English is the language spoken by a brain which is always in a vat* (rather than some thought about *the image*), given A′'s underlying externalist semantic assumptions (which are B's as well), and given agnosticism on the question whether I am in a vat world or in normal world? (Chapter 3, p. 59)

Brueckner concludes that "there is really no significant difference between A and A′, on the one hand, and B, on the other, when it comes to the sort of objection I made to B." (Chapter 3, p. 59) His argument for this conclusion depends on his understanding of what he calls the pertinent dialectical context, according to which we are agnostic on the question whether we are in a vat world or in normal world, and we remain agnostic about this question throughout the argument.

4.3 WHAT IS THE PERTINENT DIALECTICAL CONTEXT?

I grant that an anti-skeptical argument must begin with an attitude of agnosticism about whether we are in a vat world or normal world. But I do not accept Brueckner's understanding of the sense of agnosticism that is relevant to the dialectical context of Putnam's argument. For Brueckner's understanding of the agnosticism rules out an important kind of response to a skeptical argument, one that begins by entertaining the possibility that a given skeptical hypothesis is coherent, and may actually be true, and ends by concluding that the hypothesis, while meaningful, cannot actually be true.

Brueckner's argument B presupposes that the skeptical hypothesis that I am always a brain in a vat is not only meaningful, but may actually be true, regardless of Putnam's reflections about meaning. He builds this assumption into his premise (1), where it is assumed both that I may actually be a brain that is always in a vat, and that if I am a such a brain, then I speak vat-English. In my view, this misrepresents Putnam's argument. For Putnam aims to show that the assumption that we are brains in vats is self-refuting. His point is that while it may at first *seem* to be a coherent possibility, we discover after further semantic reflections that it is not coherent, and that we cannot make sense of actually being a brain that is always in a vat. By starting with premise (1), Brueckner prevents himself from representing this aspect of Putnam's reasoning. Brueckner in effect begs the question about whether any reflections about the supposition that we are always brains in vats could convince us that the supposition that we are always actually brains in vats cannot actually be true. Unlike argument B, my Argument A does not stipulate from the start, as Brueckner's does, that the supposition that we are actually always brains in vats is coherent, and possibly actually true. My argument allows that the supposition may be coherent, and also that we may discover that it is not. Hence Argument A does not beg the question against the possibility of a discovery that what at first seems to be a fully coherent possibility, one that for all we know is true, is in fact not coherent, and cannot actually be true. That is the main reason that I prefer my reconstruction to Brueckner's.

This does not get us very far unless we understand how an argument could come to undermine our initial assumption that a given statement may actually be true. Let us first consider a statement that we cannot suppose to be true at all. For example, consider the statement that $x \neq x$, where 'x' is taken to refer to some object. Clearly, I am not agnostic about whether $x \neq x$, for any such interpretation of 'x'. Hence I would not start any argument for the conclusion that $x = x$ by being agnostic about whether $x = x$ or $x \neq x$. This is true, of course, even though the sentence '$x \neq x$' is meaningful. In this case, and in many others, meaningfulness should not be understood in terms of the possibility of truth. The sentence '$x \neq x$' is meaningful, but inconsistent, hence not possibly true. Now let us consider the following statement:

(Δ) There is a barber who lives in Spencer, Indiana and who shaves all and only those persons who live in Spencer, Indiana but do not shave themselves.

This statement follows a familiar form that is known to be contradictory, and hence we know that the statement is not true. When one first encounters a statement of this form, however, one might very well suppose that it may actually be true. It takes a bit of reasoning to see that it is inconsistent, hence not true. Without yet knowing whether the statement is consistent, we may try to get clearer about the conditions under which it would be true, if it were consistent. The obvious first step is to suppose that there is such a barber, call him w. This is to suppose

(Δ$_w$) w lives in Spencer, Indiana and w shaves all and only those who live in Spencer, Indiana but do not shave themselves.

And now we may ask if w shaves himself. Either w shaves himself or he does not. If w shaves w, then it follows from (Δ$_w$) that w does not shave w. And if

w does not shave w, then it follows from (Δ_w) that w shaves w. Either way, there is a contradiction. We made no assumptions about w except (Δ_w). Our reasoning therefore shows that (Δ) is inconsistent. We may at first have supposed that (Δ) may actually be true, but on further reflection we find that it is inconsistent, and hence that we cannot make sense of its being true.

Now imagine the following objection to this argument: "The argument begs the question against our initial assumption that (Δ) may actually be true. We were at first *agnostic* about whether (Δ) is true. Now, by claiming that there can be no one who both does and does not shave himself, we are in effect begging the question against the epistemic possibility that (Δ) is true. If (Δ) is contradictory, then since it is epistemically possible that (Δ) is true, it is epistemically possible that this particular contradiction is true. We cannot rule that out without simply begging the question against our initial agnosticism about whether or not (Δ) is true."

This is of course a weak objection to our argument that (Δ) is not true. The natural and correct reply to the objection is that we were mistaken in believing (Δ) may actually be true, and we discovered our mistake by going through the above reasoning.

I suggest that Putnam's argument, as represented by A above, should be understood in an analogous way. We begin by supposing that we may actually always be brains in vats. We then reflect on what is required for us to express the statement and wonder whether it's true, and we realize that if it were true we could not actually express it and wonder whether it's true. In this respect, the statement undermines itself. We cannot entertain it, and wonder whether it is true, without concluding that it is not true. And this is exactly how argument A presents Putnam's reasoning. It does not begin, as Brueckner's argument B does, by supposing at the start that Putnam's reasoning does not undermine the supposition that we are actually brains in vats. The dialectical context is quite different. We begin by entertaining the thought. We then consider Putnam's semantical reflections about what is required to express such a thought. And we then realize that we could not express the thought if it were actually true. We do not *remain* agnostic about whether the thought is true after we have reflected on the conditions that are required for expressing it, as Brueckner's reconstruction of Putnam's argument assumes.

When I wrote Chapter 2, I believed that by presenting and defending Argument A, I thereby made the dialectical context clear enough so that readers would realize that skepticism about self-knowledge is not engendered by Putnam's reflections about meaning. After reading Brueckner's Chapter 3, I realized that Brueckner and others have *independent* reasons for thinking that skepticism about self-knowledge is coherent and that they presuppose these reasons when they reconstruct Putnam's argument. Contrary to what Brueckner and others have claimed, however, neither Putnam's views about meaning nor his argument that we are not always brains in vats engender this skepticism. It must be *added* to Putnam's reasoning, either as an explicit premise, such as premise (1) of Argument B, or as a background assumption about the pertinent dialectical context, as in Brueckner's assumption that we must be, and remain, agnostic about whether or not we are actually always brains in vats.

In Section 2.2 of Chapter 2, I tried to inoculate the reader against this aspect of Brueckner's reasoning by stressing that "If our ordinary concepts of meaning and thought have the consequence that we cannot have thoughts about brains in vats unless we are causally related with brains in vats, the charge that Putnam is begging the question is out of place" (p. 30). I did not make the point as clearly as I could have, however, since I thought that it was obvious that the dialectical setting of Putnam's reasoning is one in which we discover that a supposition leads to absurdity, not one in which we take that assumption to be fully coherent, and to remain coherent, despite our anti-skeptical argument. I approached the issue, instead, by imagining someone who complains that by taking for granted that we are causally related with brains and vats, we are begging the question against the supposedly genuine possibility that we are always brains in vats. This is a weak objection if the dialectical context is analogous to one in which we discover, perhaps to our surprise, that a statement that we thought could actually be true is self-refuting or incoherent. And this is how I saw, and still see, the dialectical context of Putnam's argument. Unlike Brueckner, I take Putnam to be showing that while it might at first have *seemed* that we may actually always be brains in vats, after thinking things through, and, in particular, after reflecting about the conditions under which our words 'brain' and 'vat' could refer, respectively, to brains and vats, we find that we cannot coherently suppose that we are always brains in vats. The simple point, to repeat, is that if we were always brains in vats, we could not entertain the thought that we are, and this contradicts the obvious fact that we can entertain that thought. Hence, like (Δ), the thought that we are always actually brains in vats leads to a contradiction, and hence cannot be true.

4.4 PUTNAM'S DISJUNCTION EXPLAINED

Brueckner's and my disagreement about the dialectical context of Putnam's argument carries over to a disagreement about how to understand some of

Putnam's disjunctive formulations of his brain in the vat argument. Consider, for instance, Putnam's claim that

(iv) Whether or not I am always a brain in a vat, my utterances of 'I am always a brain in a vat' are not true.

What could the point of this disjunctive claim be, if not to highlight our agnosticism about whether we are actually always brains in vats? The answer, I suggest, is that this disjunctive style of reasoning is simply a vivid way of exploring and making explicit the absurd consequences of supposing that we are always brains in vats. Putnam derives a contradiction from the supposition that we are always brains in vats by relying on the observation that if we were, then we could not express the thought that we are always brains in vats. Since we can express that thought, we can conclude that we are not always brains in vats. This adds nothing to Argument A, but just expresses it in a different way.

The reasoning skirts paradox by never suggesting or implying that we do not know what thoughts our utterances express. Putnam did not seriously consider the supposed possibility that we do not know what thoughts our utterances actually express, and when I wrote Chapter 2, I did not either. Brueckner's Chapter 3 prompted me to try to say why I believe it is incoherent to suppose that we can both raise possibilities for ourselves, and at the same time doubt that we know what thoughts are sentences express, and in later papers, starting with Chapter 6, "Can We Take Our Words at Face Value?," I tried to do so. I shall not try to summarize these attempts here, since they are contained and developed in detail in later chapters in this volume. In the rest of this chapter I shall focus on other consequences of Brueckner's and my disagreement about the dialectical context of Putnam's argument. My point here is just that Putnam's use of the disjunctive style of reasoning is not a sign that he accepts the sort of agnosticism about whether we are actually always brains in vats that is crucial to Brueckner's reconstruction of his argument. On my reading, then, the disjunctive representation of the brain in the vat argument that Putnam sometimes offers does no more than highlight our initial puzzlement about whether we may actually always be brains in vats, and helps to explain how Putnam thinks that we can come to see that this supposition is incoherent.

In a sense, therefore, I agree with Brueckner (see Chapter 3, p. 60) that I have not found any real role for the disjunctive, metalinguistic reasoning in Putnam's overall position, beyond simply reformulating his Argument A. This does not count against my interpretation, however, since Brueckner and I disagree about the dialectical context, and on my view of that context, the disjunctive reasoning has no special role to play, but just helps to highlight our initial puzzlement about whether it makes sense to suppose we are actually always brains in vats.

4.5 REJECTING VERIFICATIONISM

I turn now to the first problem I mentioned above – that Brueckner's reconstruction of Putnam's argument assumes (at steps (2)–(4)) that the truth conditions for the utterances of a brain that is always in a vat can be defined in terms of how things appear to the brain in a vat – what sensory impressions it has – and this conflicts with Putnam's causal theory of meaning.

Before we look at details, it is important to keep in mind that this issue only arises if one takes seriously the idea that a brain that is always in a vat has thoughts and uses a meaningful language. Brueckner is committed to taking this idea seriously by his understanding of the dialectical context of Putnam's argument (see Brueckner's explanation of why in Chapter 5, p. 102), whereas I am not. As I noted in Chapter 2 (p. 37) Argument A does not presuppose that the brain that is always in a vat has any thoughts or means anything at all by its utterances. I explored questions about how to interpret utterances of a brain that is always in a vat not because I found the question independently interesting, or integral to Putnam's reasoning, but to contrast Argument A with Argument B.

Brueckner interprets the truth conditions mentioned in steps (2)–(4) as follows:

a BIVs utterance of 'I am a BIV' would be true iff he were a BIV-in-the-image. As I understand it, those truth conditions are equivalent to these: the BIVs utterance would be true iff he had sense impressions as a being a BIV. But by Putnam's hypothesis, a BIV never has such a sense impressions. . . . Thus . . . a BIVs utterance of 'I am a BIV' would never [be] true . . . (Chapter 1, p. 12)

The problem, as I argued in Chapter 2, is that this reasoning rests on a verificationist account of the meaning of 'I am always a brain in a vat'. We can see this by reflecting on the meaning of the closely related English statement, 'I am a brain in a vat'. As I put it in Chapter 2,

a person's brain might have been removed and placed in a vat *without her knowledge*. This is a possibility which Putnam's argument can't rule out, since it is compatible with the causal constraint on interpretation. But in that possible situation, her utterance of 'I am a brain in a vat' would be *true*, even though she would not have sense impressions as of being in a vat. Thus there is no way to read off from one's *sense impressions* whether or not one is a brain in a vat. Parallel reasoning suggests that a brain which is always in a vat can't conclude that *(I am not a brain in a vat) in the image* from the fact that it never has the sense-impressions as of being a brain in the vat in the image. (Chapter 2, p. 41)

Brueckner replies to this reasoning as follows:

Ebbs gives the example of a brain in a vat who does not meet one of the conditions of Putnam's thought experiment: a brain in a vat who isn't *always* in a vat and whose utterances are accordingly able to have *disquotational* truth conditions (which are satisfied since it *is* a brain in a vat). However, my discussion in the paper in question (and just about all the other discussions in the relevant literature) was quite explicit in focusing only on *Putnamian* brains in vats, who are always envatted . . . (Chapter 3, p. 57)

This reply misses my point. My argument (quoted above) is compressed, however, so let me expand on it here. By hypothesis, the sense impressions of a brain that is *always* in a vat will be no different from the sense impressions of a brain that is only sometimes in a vat, and hence no different from the sense impressions of a brain that is never in a vat. So the anti-verificationist point goes through for the interpretation of *our* utterances of 'I am always a BIV'. No one disputes this, I assume. What about for the utterances of 'I am always a BIV' made by a brain that is always in a vat? I hinted at "parallel reasoning," but should have made it explicit. I assumed that Putnam's causal account of meaning requires that we interpret the utterances of a brain in a vat in a way that *mirrors* the structural relationships between sense impressions and truth conditions that hold for our language. We should therefore think of '( ) in the image' not as defined in terms of sensory impressions, or images, as Brueckner does, but as a structure-preserving function from sentences to truth conditions that is constrained by Putnam's causal theory of meaning. If we grant this assumption – and surely we have no better guide than this for interpreting the brain's utterances, given Putnam's causal theory of meaning – then just as we cannot read off from *our* sensory impressions whether or not we are brains in vats, so a brain that is always in a vat cannot read off from *its* sensory impressions whether or not it is always a brain in a vat in the image.

These clarifications are not likely to persuade Brueckner, however, for he believes the entire line of reasoning is wrong. He writes:

To see how far off the mark the objection is, it is sufficient to note that it would apply to any view of the semantics of an envatted brain's utterances of 'I am a brain in a vat' according to which these utterances do not have disquotational truth conditions. But if we are talking about brains in vats who meet the conditions of Putnam's thought experiment, and we take Putnam's semantic views seriously, then we will agree that a brain in a vat's utterances of 'I am a brain in a vat' do not have disquotational truth conditions. Thus, even if the verificationist truth conditions for envatted utterances are unsatisfactory, this is not for the reasons adduced by Ebbs. (Chapter 3, p. 57)

Contrary to Brueckner's claim, however, my objection does not "apply to *any* view of the semantics of an envatted brain's utterances of 'I am a brain in a vat' according to which these utterances do not have disquotational truth conditions." For if we think of '( ) in the image' as a structure-preserving function from sentences to truth conditions that is constrained by Putnam's causal theory of meaning, in the way I assumed in Chapter 2, then we will specify the truth conditions of a brain in vat's utterances non-disquotationally, by filling in the following schema:

(Φ) '_____' is true if and only if (_____) in the image.

where '( ) in the image' is not understood in a verificationist way. I have no objection to such a specification, even though it plays no essential role in Argument A.

 Here it is also important to see that it is odd and misleading to say of a given sentence that it has (or does not have) disquotational truth conditions. For every speaker is in a position to apply (T) directly to her own utterances. In particular, a brain that is always in a vat can accept the sentence "'I am a BIV' is true if and only if I am a BIV." Of course, we cannot express what that sentence states in disquotational terms if we do not speak vat-English. Similarly, Twin-Oscar accepts the sentence, "'Water is a liquid' is true iff water is a liquid." This sentence is true, as spoken by Twin-Oscar, but *we* (who do not live on Twin Earth and have never been there) must express what Twin-Oscar uses that sentence to say in a nondisquotational way, perhaps as follows: 'Water is a liquid' (as spoken by Twin-Oscar) is true if and only if twin-water is a liquid. Hence it is not quite right to say that his sentence has or does not have disquotational truth conditions. The question whether or not a given sentence has disquotational truth conditions can only be answered from a particular speaker's point of view. A speaker who can directly use sentences of a given language *L* can apply (T) directly to its sentences, and thereby specify disquotational truth conditions for its sentences. Speakers who cannot directly use sentences of *L* must specify the truth conditions for those sentences nondisquotationally, if they specify them at all. (These observations contain the seeds of an argument against the intelligibility of Brueckner's suggestion that for all I know my own sentences have "nondisquotational" truth conditions. I shall not explore this matter further here, however, since I do so in other chapters in this volume.)

 If I am right about how to understand the function '( ) in the image', then what reasons could Putnam give for premise (4) of Brueckner's reconstruction? Recall that this question does not even arise on my reconstruction, Argument A, which does not presuppose that the brain that is always in a vat means anything at all by its utterances. Nevertheless, Putnam seems in places to be committed to premise (4), with '( ) in the image' understood in a non-verificationist way. I explained this in Chapter 2 as follows:

if the brain *were* always a brain in a vat in the image (whatever *that* means), then it would not be causally related with the images of brains and the images of vats, and so it could not claim that *(I am always a brain in a vat) in the image*. But we are assuming that it can claim that *(I am always a brain in a vat) in the image*. Given this assumption, we can see that the claim itself must be false. (Chapter 2, p. 42)

I regret that my account of this reasoning was so compressed. Let me try to expand on it. The reasoning results from the assumption that the sentences of Argument A may be used by a brain that is always in a vat to construct an argument that it is not always a brain in a vat in the image. I assume, once again, that '( ) in the image' is a structure-preserving function from sentences to truth conditions that is constrained by Putnam's causal theory of meaning. I also assume that if a given sentence is true in English, then '( ) in the image' maps it to a sentence that is true in vat-English. Since (i)–(iii) is sound, its image under the mapping '( ) in the image' must then also be sound. The reasoning in the paragraph just quoted must therefore be sound, even if we don't know what it states, because we don't know how to provide an informative specification of the '( ) in the image' function.

In the above passage, I should have been more careful about the use of the term 'cause', since this term, too, may not mean what it does in English when it is used by a brain that is always in a vat. However, I assume that Putnam's causal account of meaning, including the word 'cause', should also be mapped by '( ) in the image' to true sentences of vat-English. Hence not only can we say that Putnam's causal account of meaning requires that the typical causes of tokenings of the brain's words 'brain' and 'vat' are, respectively, *(brains) in the image* and *(vats) in the image*, but, also, a *(brain) in the image* that is always in a *(vat) in the image* is not *(causally) in the image* related to *(brains) in the image* and *(vats) in the image*. The notion of *(cause) in the image* may be the same as the notion of cause. Whether or not it is the same, however, I suppose that the image of (i)–(iii) for vat-English is sound, and so (4) is true.

Brueckner asks

If we do not know what it is to be a brain in a vat in the image, then how do we know whether or not such a thing would be causally related to images of brains and images of vats? And why should it be required that a brain in a vat in the image be causally related to images of brains in order to refer to brains in the image unless we assume some sort of objectionable verificationist account of the relevant truth conditions? (Chapter 3, p. 58)

I admit that it is difficult to answer these questions simply on the basis of the compressed presentation of the reasoning that I offer in Chapter 2. I hope it is now clear, however, how to answer Brueckner's two questions. The answer to the first question – "If we do not know what it is to be a brain in a vat in the image, then how do we know whether or not such a thing would be causally related to images of brains and images of vats?" – is that we don't need to know what it is to be a brain in the vat in the image to stipulate that '(   ) in the image' is constructed in accordance with Putnam's causal constraints on meaning, and this implies that a person must be causally related, at least sometimes, to things to which his or her terms apply. Hence it is a constraint on our interpretation of the utterances of a brain that is always in a vat that if its terms 'brain' and 'vat' refer, respectively, to *(brains) in the image* and *(vats) in the image*, then it is causally related, at least sometimes, to *(brains) in the image* and *(vats) in the image*. The answer to the second question – "Why should it be required that a brain in a vat in the image be causally related to images of brains in order to refer to brains in the image unless we assume some sort of objectionable verificationist account of the relevant truth conditions?" – is that the notion of *image* in question here is not verificationist, and not necessarily even identified with sensory impressions, but just what is captured by the '(   ) in the image' function, as constrained by Putnam's causal account of meaning and reference.

None of this is actually important to understanding Argument A, since, as I emphasized above, Argument A does not presuppose that the brain that is always in a vat has any thoughts or means anything at all by its utterances. I have taken the time here to track down Brueckner's misunderstandings of my discussion of his premise (4) only to highlight some features of Putnam's reasoning that Brueckner's dialectical strategy prevents him from seeing.

4.6 CONCEIVING OF A THOUGHT

In my discussion of Nagel's skepticism about objectivity, I wrote that "the idea of a representation that portrays the world using concepts we don't possess and can't acquire does not make sense" (Chapter 2, fn. 38). I expressed this claim in terms that I took from Thomas Nagel's discussion of Putnam's argument that we are not always brains in vats. Brueckner understands me to have claimed that

(**) We cannot conceive of a thought involving concepts which we cannot acquire.

And he exploits an ambiguity in the phrase "conceive of" to raise trouble for my position:

If this [(**)] claim is true, then the English phrase 'thought involving concepts which we cannot acquire' does not express any concept. If it *did* express a concept ... then, contra (**), we *would* be able to conceive of a thought involving concepts which we cannot acquire. (Chapter 3, pp. 61–62)

What this shows is that if (**) is to represent my position, we cannot take the phrase 'thought involving concepts which we cannot acquire' to be without meaning. Instead, and in keeping with my understanding of the dialectical context, as explained above, we should interpret this phrase so that, like the open sentence '$x \neq x$', it is meaningful, but not true of anything. Brueckner realizes this, and provides the following analogy:

Consider what an anti-individualist would say about the English phrase 'natural kind concept whose individuation conditions do not at all depend upon the environment in which it is used'. The anti-individualist does not have to say that this phrase fails to express a concept. It is perfectly meaningful, he might say, and hence it expresses a genuine concept. However, this concept has an anti-extension (in all possible worlds). No possible natural kind concept has such individuation conditions. Ebbs might take a similar line with regard to the phrase 'concept which we cannot acquire'. It expresses a concept with an empty extension, he might say. We can conceive of – and speak meaningfully about – such concepts. But there are none, and there could not be any. (Chapter 3, p. 62)

Brueckner also notes that I take the following statement to support (**):

(*) There is no way to conceive of a thought or belief unless we have some idea of the social and physical environment on which its individuation depends. (Chapter 2, p. 51, cited in Chapter 3, p. 61)

Brueckner writes,

contrary to (*), I can conceive of thoughts which (a) I cannot now think in virtue of the character of my current environment, and (b) whose environmental individuation conditions elude my present powers of conceptualization. ... the Twin-Earth thought experiments which underlie anti-individualism (which itself is supposedly the basis for (*)) seem to presuppose that I can conceive of such thoughts. (Chapter 3, p. 62)

But it is precisely to accommodate such cases that I wrote in (*) that in order to conceive of a thought or belief "we must have some idea of the social and physical environment on which its individuation depends." We would not accept the Twin-Earth thought experiments unless we did have some idea of the social and physical environments in question. We know that twin-water is a liquid that is found in the lakes and streams on Twin Earth, for instance, we know that our twins on Twin Earth have ordinary perceptual interactions with Twin-water, and so on. My thought was that this is enough for us to have some idea of the social and physical environment on which the twin concepts' individuation depends. To have some idea of the social and physical environment on which the individuation of a given concept depends is not necessarily to be able to express that concept directly, but roughly to understand its relationship to an environment that is for the most part describable in our own current vocabulary.

Brueckner paraphrases (*) as follows:

(*′) There is no way to conceive of a thought or belief unless we *can acquire* some idea of the social and physical environment on which its individuation depends. (Chapter 3, p. 63)

But this paraphrase of (*) rests on a misunderstanding of what I meant by having "some idea" of the social and physical environment on which the individuation of a given concept depends. A better paraphrase of (*) would be

(*″) There is no way to conceive of a thought or belief unless we have some idea of how we could come to be able to express it ourselves.

And Brueckner raises an objection to (*′) that, if correct, would also apply to (*″). The objection is that in order to support (*′), one would have to develop an anti-individualistic account of second-order concepts such as *concept* and *thought*. But, Brueckner reminds us,

The anti-individualist views found in Putnam and Burge concern the way in which the individuation of *first-order*, empirical concepts (e.g., *tree*, *water*) depends upon physical or social environment. These views contain no claims concerning second-order, 'pure' concepts such as *concept* and *thought*. (Chapter 3, p. 63)

Here is it important to ask why Brueckner believes that to support either (*′) or (*″), we need an anti-individualist account of *concept* and *thought*. Putnam's and Burge's observations about particular first-order concepts established general truths about how the individuation of first-order empirical concepts depends on the social and physical environment of the person who expresses them. We may therefore generalize to say that we if we accept anti-individualism, we have no understanding of first-order empirical concepts, such as tree and water, apart from our background beliefs about how such concepts are individuated. This is not an application of anti-individualism to the concept of *concept*, it is a generalization about *first-order empirical concepts* that is supported by Putnam's and Burge's observations about particular first-order empirical concepts. It goes hand-in-hand with Putnam's causal constraint on meaning and reference.

By reflecting on Putnam's and Burge's observations about particular first-order concepts, we come to realize that some apparently gripping thoughts, such as Nagel's thought that there are concepts we cannot acquire, are self-undermining. This was the point that my claim (*) was meant to summarize. In his response to this claim, Brueckner once again understands the dialectical context differently from the way I do. He assumes that there are concepts and thoughts that we cannot acquire, and is therefore puzzled by my conclusion that there are not. And he seems to think that I could only come to that conclusion if I provide an anti-individualistic interpretation of the second-order notions of concepts and thought. This understanding of the dialectical situation is evident in the following passage:

> [Nagel invites us] to conceive of a being who thinks thoughts which it is tempting for us to express as follows: "Those puny humans have concepts which are impoverished in comparison to our concepts, which their environmental circumstances prevent them from acquiring, just as the brains in vats are prevented from acquiring the puny humans concepts." On the extension of anti-individualism currently under consideration, the being's word which we are inclined to translate as 'concept' cannot be so translated. The word, whatever it is, does not express the concept expressed by our word 'concept', given the difference between our environments. Indeed, such a being would not possess concepts at all, in virtue of the alien character of those parts of his environment that are appropriately related to that representation (if we can call it that) of his which we are inclined to mistranslate as meaning what our word 'concept' means. (Chapter 3, p. 64)

Brueckner focuses on the meaning of our word 'concept'. In my view, however, the problem with his imaginary being is much deeper. His supposition that there is such a being falls apart without any help from reflections about what this supposed being means by the word 'concept'. Without any idea of the social and physical environment in which such "words" would be "uttered," we cannot even pretend to express this imaginary being's "thoughts." Brueckner (speaking for Nagel) has offered us just a string of letters and spaces to which we can give no substantive meaning. We understand the phrase "representation that we cannot acquire," but we see no way in which there could be any such representation, if we generalize from Putnam's and Burge's examples, and accept Putnam's causal constraint on meaning.

Brueckner does not see this problem with his own example because he takes for granted that there might be beings whose representations of the world are so vastly superior to our own that we could never acquire them. This assumption plays the same role for Brueckner here as his assumption that for all we actually know we are always brains in vats plays in his reconstruction of Putnam's argument, Argument B above. In each case, we are supposed to start with the assumptions, and then show that they are incoherent, or problematic, by somehow interpreting, or reinterpreting, the words that we use to express them.

Brueckner's criticisms of my arguments in Chapter 2 shows that he understands their dialectical contexts very differently from the way I do. In each case, I suggest, our dialectical situation is like that of the demonstration that (Δ) is inconsistent, hence not true. We begin with agnosticisim about whether or not (Δ) may actually be true, and discover that (Δ) cannot be true. Similarly, I have argued, we begin with agnosticism about whether or not it may actually be true that we are always brains in vats, and, by Argument A, we come to see, just by reflecting on the meanings of our own words and the natures of our own thoughts, that it cannot actually be true that we are always brains in vats. Finally, we begin with agnosticism about whether or not there could be a representation that is related to ours in the way that ours is related to a brain in a vat's, and we come to see, just by reflecting on our own language and extensions of it that we can imagine, that we cannot understand how there could be a representation that is related to ours in the way that ours is related to a brain in a vat's. In each of these arguments, we start with our own best understanding of the statements, expressed in our own current language, not in some imaginary one, and, after reflecting on the statements, realize that we do not understand how they could be true.

CHAPTER 5

Trying to get outside your own skin

Anthony Brueckner

5.1 INTRODUCTORY

Trying to entertain skepticism about knowledge of the contents of your own thoughts is like trying to get outside your own skin.[1] Externalist semantic views, though, have the appearance of generating such skepticism, as well as a correlative skepticism about knowledge of your own sentences' meanings and truth conditions. Several writers have defended externalism against this charge, holding that there is really nothing to the appearance in question. They say that, even assuming externalism, it can be seen that the skeptical views in question are at best false and at worst incoherent. In this chapter, I would like to assess a number of such responses to skepticism about knowledge of content, meaning, and truth conditions. I will argue that the responses fail to resolve the prima facie epistemological problems which plague externalism.

5.2 GENERATING CONTENT SKEPTICISM

Skepticism about knowledge of content, meaning, and truth conditions (for brevity, I will call this *content skepticism*) seems to be engendered by externalist semantic analyses of two well-known scenarios: those involving Twin Earth and Putnamian brains in a vat.[2] In the Twin-Earth thought experiment, we imagine my doppelgänger inhabiting a world in which XYZ rather than H_2O fills out the seemingly watery parts of the external environment. My twin's term 'water' does not refer to water, since there is no water in his causally relevant surroundings. His term 'water' expresses a concept which, unlike my concept *water*, applies to all and only samples of XYZ. Let us call this concept *twater*. So my twin's term 'water' differs in meaning

---

[1] I think that Tyler Burge said this.
[2] See Putnam 1975 and Burge 1982 for seminal discussions of Twin Earth. See Putnam 1981 for the seminal discussion of what happens when externalism meets brains in a vat.

from mine and refers to twater, the liquid composed of XYZ. Accordingly, his utterances of the sentence 'Water is wet' are true iff twater is wet. When he thinks a thought which he would express via an utterance of that sentence, the thought has the content *that twater is wet*. This is a distinct content from that which is expressed by my utterance of 'Water is wet', i.e., the content *that water is wet*. Correlatively, my utterances of that sentence have different truth conditions from my twin's utterances of the sentence: 'My utterances are true iff water is wet.'

My twin and I are indistinguishable in respect of *individualistic properties*: qualitative phenomenological and experiential properties (nonintentionally characterized), behavioral properties, neurophysiological properties, and functional properties (again, nonintentionally characterized).[3] Despite our phenomenological and introspective indistinguishability, though, our thought-contents differ (along with the contents of other intentional states expressible by 'water'-sentences). Our utterances of 'water'-sentences also differ at the levels of meaning, reference, and truth conditions. These semantic differences derive from differences between our external causal environments.

In Putnam's fantasy involving brains in a vat, we are to imagine my envatted twin inhabiting a world containing only brains in a vat and a supercomputer systematically stimulating the brains. My brain-in-a-vat counterpart is phenomenologically and introspectively indistinguishable from me, and his treeish sense experience leads him to think a thought which he expresses by uttering (in thought) the sentence 'Trees are green'. The Putnamian semantic analysis of this situation is as follows. My twin's term 'tree' refers to the entities which play a causal role with respect to his tokenings of 'tree' which is analogous to that role played by trees with respect to my tokenings of 'tree'. In the vat world, computer states, or maybe electrical impulses which stimulate the brain, play the role in question.[4] Accordingly, my twin's sentence 'Trees are green' is true iff the appropriate computer state obtains. The thought that he thinks via thinking that sentence does not have the content *that trees are green*. Rather, it has some such content as *that computer state 666 obtains*. As in the Twin-Earth

---

[3] For simplicity of exposition, let us consider for now a younger version of me who has no beliefs about the chemical structure of water; otherwise my twin and I would be distinguishable in respect of our assents to (and dissents from) sentences about chemistry.

[4] Putnam also considers the possibility that my vat-twin's tokens of 'tree' refer to *trees in the image*, where *the image* is the sequence of experiences had by the twin. On this sort of interpretation of my twin's language, his sentence 'Trees are green' is true iff trees in the image are green in the image. See Putnam 1981, Chapter 1.

scenario, the semantic differences between me and my envatted counterpart derive from differences between our external causal environments.

Some terminology will be convenient at this point. Let us say that tokens of a sentence S, as uttered in an object language L, have *disquotational truth conditions relative to a metalanguage L'* iff there is a true sentence of L' which consists of S surrounded by quotation marks, followed by an L'-translation of the phrase 'is true in L iff', followed by S itself. Let us say that when tokens of a sentence, as uttered in a given object language, have disquotational truth conditions relative to *my* language, they have disquotational truth conditions simpliciter (leaving implicit the relativization to my language as metalanguage). Let us say further that when sentence-tokens have truth conditions but do not have disquotational truth conditions, they have *nondisquotational truth conditions*.

We can apply the notion of a truth condition to thoughts and other intentional states in the following way. If a sentence S correctly expresses the content of a thought (or some other intentional state) T, then T's truth conditions are just those of S. If S has disquotational truth conditions, then we may say that T has disquotational truth conditions. Accordingly, my envatted twin's thoughts have nondisquotational truth conditions.

We can construct an argument for skepticism about knowledge of content and truth conditions which parallels a standard Cartesian skeptical argument regarding knowledge of the external world.[5] The first premise rests upon the following Closure Principle:

If S knows that φ, and S knows that φ entails ψ, then S knows that ψ.

Let 'SK' stand for the proposition that my thoughts and sentences have nondisquotational truth conditions. I know that if my thoughts and sentences have disquotational truth conditions, then they do not have nondisquotational truth conditions. Thus, by Closure we have

(I) If I know that my thoughts and sentences have disquotational truth conditions, then I know that $\sim SK$.

The second premise of the argument is the one which will call for the most discussion:

(II) I do not know that $\sim SK$.

From (I) and (II) it follows that

---

[5] See Nozick 1981 and Stroud 1984 for recent influential discussions which portray Cartesian skepticism as in the text.

(III) I do not know that my thoughts and sentences have disquotational truth conditions.

The case for (II) is as follows. We first note that even though the discussions of the Twin-Earth and vat scenarios were couched in terms of possible worlds containing my *doppelgängers* ensconced in twater and vat environments, there are possible worlds in which *I* am ensconced in such environments. In such worlds, my thoughts and sentences have nondisquotational truth conditions. In twater worlds, my sentence 'Water is wet' expresses the thought-content *that twater is wet* (rather than *that water is wet*). In vat worlds, my sentence 'Trees are green' expresses the thought-content *that computer state 666 obtains* (rather than *that trees are green*). So it appears that *SK* is a genuine skeptical *counterpossibility* to the proposition that my thoughts and sentences have disquotational truth conditions, where ψ is a *counterpossibility* to φ just in case ψ is a logically possible proposition which is logically incompatible with φ. The crucial question regarding premise (II), then, is whether I can rule out *SK*. That is, do I know that the actual world is not a possible world in which *SK* is true? Do I know that ∼*SK*?

SK worlds are introspectively, phenomenologically, and experientially indistinguishable from normal worlds in which my thoughts and sentences have disquotational truth conditions. The differences in external causal environments which induce differences in content and differences in sentential meanings and truth conditions do not induce any corresponding experiential, introspective, or phenomenological differences. In vat worlds and twater worlds, things seem to me just as they seem in normal, water-filled, nonvat worlds. On the face of it, then, it appears that I cannot discriminate between normal worlds in which my thoughts and sentences have disquotational truth conditions and *SK* worlds in which my thoughts and sentences have nondisquotational truth conditions. Thus we have a prima facie case for premise (II)'s claim that I do not know that ∼*SK*.[6]

The principles behind this intuitive reasoning could be put as follows. The first principle is that knowledge that φ requires having justification for believing that φ. The second is this Underdetermination Principle:

(UP) Suppose that I am considering a hypothesis *H* and a competing incompatible skeptical hypothesis *SK*. If my evidence and reasons (and whatever other considerations are available) do not favor *H* over *SK*, then I do not have justification for rejecting *SK*; hence I do not know that ∼*SK*.[7]

---

[6] See Chapter 1 for a discussion of this reasoning.
[7] See Brueckner 1994a and Brueckner 1994b for discussion of (UP).

When applied to $\sim SK$, these principles appear to yield the conclusion that I lack knowledge that $\sim SK$ in virtue of lacking justification for believing that $\sim SK$. I lack such justification in virtue of my inability to discriminate the hypothesis that $\sim SK$ from the hypothesis that SK.

It is worth noting that exactly parallel reasoning will yield the Cartesian skeptical conclusion that I do not know that I am sitting. Indeed, the argument would appeal to my inability to discriminate those SK worlds in which I am envatted (call them SK' worlds) from $\sim SK'$ worlds (worlds in which I am not envatted). Since I know that the proposition that I am sitting entails that $\sim SK'$, and since [by (UP)] I do not know that $\sim SK'$, it follows by Closure that I do not know that I am sitting.

Suppose it is said that I at least know that I am not in a twater world, since I know that my world contains H_2O instead of XYZ. The content skeptic could respond by describing a "switching" scenario in which we conceive of Earth and Twin Earth as coexisting within a single possible world.[8] We accordingly imagine a situation in which I am unwittingly switched from Earth to Twin Earth and allowed to remain long enough to begin thinking *twater*-thoughts via my 'water'-sentences, only to be switched back to Earth. There I remain long enough for *water*-thoughts to displace *twater*-thoughts, only to be switched back to Twin Earth. . . . Granted, even in such a bizarre scenario, whether or not I am in an environment containing XYZ rather than H_2O is not inaccessible to ordinary empirical investigation in the way in which the question whether I am a brain in a vat *is* inaccessible. Still, in the normal case, one has not recently undertaken the required chemical inquiry and, by the foregoing skeptical considerations, one lacks knowledge that one is not involved in a switching scenario. Therefore, by Closure, in the normal case, one lacks knowledge that one's thoughts and sentences have disquotational truth conditions.

Some philosophers have responded to the Cartesian skeptical argument about external-world skepticism by denying the Closure Principle and thereby removing the rationale for the argument's Closure-based premise. The same response could be made to the argument for content skepticism. It might be maintained that it is possible for one to know that one's thoughts and sentences have disquotational truth conditions without knowing that they lack nondisquotational truth conditions. I will not pursue this strategy here, since it raises questions which concern the nature of knowledge in

---

[8] See Burge 1988a and Boghossian 1989 for discussion of switching scenarios.

general rather than the nature of knowledge of content, meaning, and truth conditions in particular.[9]

Some philosophers have responded to Cartesian skepticism by denying that 'I am a brain in a vat' expresses a logically possible proposition. Verificationists and idealists might be seen as adopting such a strategy. Similarly, one might maintain that there is no possible world in which my thoughts and sentences have nondisquotational truth conditions. If this were so, then I could claim to know that ~*SK* in virtue of knowing that *SK* is a necessarily false proposition. I will not pursue this strategy here. If one accepts semantic externalism, then it seems that one is committed to the claim that *SK* is a logically possible proposition. Externalism is the thesis that semantic facts depend upon external causal environment in ways that are illustrated by thought experiments involving possible worlds in which one's twin's thoughts and sentences have nondisquotational truth conditions. If there are such possible worlds, then there are possible worlds in which *I*, like my twin, think thoughts and utter sentences with nondisquotational truth conditions. For example, according to the externalist, in a possible world in which *I* am a brain in a vat, my sentence 'Trees are green', as uttered by me in that vat world, is true iff computer state 666 obtains. My utterance of that sentence expresses a thought with the content *that computer state 666 obtains*. The utterances of sentences I produce in such worlds, then, have nondisquotational truth conditions relative to the language I am currently speaking. In other words, the utterances have, in the terminology introduced earlier, nondisquotational truth conditions simpliciter.

5.3 *SK* AND THE CONCEPT OF TRUTH

Let us, then, grant that *SK* is a logically possible proposition. Still, it would be natural at this point to hold that I can rule out *SK* as being actually false *on straightforward a priori grounds*. One might plausibly say that the correctness of my own application of disquotation to my own sentences is guaranteed by the meaning of the truth predicate. The guarantee is simply built into the concept of truth. Disquotation, indeed, affords us our most fundamental grip on the concept of truth. On this view, I know that my sentences do *not* have nondisquotational truth conditions in much the same way that I know that bachelors are not female.

---

[9] See Dretske 1970 and Nozick 1981 for influential rejections of Closure. See also Brueckner 1985 for a discussion of various ways of rejecting and defending Closure.

It is not clear, however, that an externalist can avail himself of this quick, clean way of dismissing *SK*. Let us look more closely at the concepts of reference and of truth that the externalist employs. I think that the view that I am calling "semantic externalism" has a core that the externalist would claim to know in an a priori manner. The core is, roughly, the thesis that semantic facts (and facts about mental content) depend upon facts concerning one's causal environment in ways which are illustrated in the thought experiments we have considered. While I obviously cannot have a priori knowledge concerning the details of my actual causal environment and its relations to my thoughts and utterances, I *can* know a priori that, e.g., *if* an individualistic twin of me is a Putnamian brain in a vat, *then* his uses of 'tree' do not refer to absent trees. I know a priori, then, that such a creature's utterances of 'Trees are green' lack disquotational truth conditions. The externalist seems to be working with a concept of reference which has a built-in causal component: According to this concept, there are causal constraints on the reference relation.

This opens up the possibility that the concept of *truth* that the externalist employs will not provide an a priori (since, allegedly, conceptual) guarantee that disquotation can be correctly self-applied. To see this, first note that in virtue of the causal component in the externalist's concept of reference, I can know a priori that if x is in the extension of my term 'cat', then x satisfies the causal constraints on reference: Either x bears some appropriate causal relation to me or x is an instance of a kind some of whose members bear such a relation to me. Now suppose that the following disquotation thesis about reference is also knowable a priori (since, we suppose, it is guaranteed by the concept of reference): x is in the extension of my term 'cat' iff x is a cat. This thesis is assumed by our current opponent of *SK*, who maintains that it is knowable a priori (since guaranteed by the concept of truth) that my utterances of 'Cats fear water' are true iff cats fear water. It would then follow that it is knowable a priori that if x is a cat, then x (or one of its kind) bears some appropriate causal relation to me. But it is far from clear that I can know anything a priori about my causal relations to cats (or even that I can know that if they exist, then I am causally related to them in a certain way).

The upshot is that even if there is a concept of truth according to which I can know a priori (on straightforward conceptual grounds) that my sentences have disquotational truth conditions, the externalist apparently is not employing that concept. He is apparently employing concepts of reference and of truth which are such that disquotation is not obviously guaranteed simply in virtue of the content of the concepts. Therefore, the externalist is not in a position to rule out *SK* on conceptual grounds of the pure and simple sort just considered.

5.4 THE COVARIANCE OF FIRST-ORDER AND
SECOND-ORDER CONTENT

I would like to consider a response to the argument for content skepticism in which premise (II) is denied. The strategy starts from Davidson's remark that "what determines the contents of thoughts also determines what the thinker thinks the contents are."[10] The point is put nicely by Sydney Shoemaker in application to Twin Earth: "[W]hatever fixes the content of the first-order belief I express by saying 'There is water in the glass' also fixes in the same way the embedded content in the second-order belief I express by saying 'I believe there is water in the glass'."[11]

What exactly is the relevance to content skepticism of this point about the covariance of first-order and second-order content? Let us begin by supposing that I sincerely utter the sentence 'Cats fear water'. My sincere utterance of that sentence expresses a first-order belief having a first-order content concerning cats.[12] It would be natural to report this content by using disquotation: The content of my belief is *that cats fear water*. Now consider a belief sentence to which I sincerely assent, in which the foregoing sentence is embedded in a 'that'-clause: 'I believe that cats fear water'. My sincere utterance of that sentence expresses a second-order belief having a second-order content, presumably the content *that I believe that cats fear water*. One way of restating the Davidsonian point in application to the present example is as follows.[13] What determines the first-order content of the belief expressed by my utterance of 'Cats fear water' also determines the second-order content of the belief expressed by my utterance of 'I believe that cats fear water'. The second-order content is *that I believe a certain first-order content*. The second-order content *contains* an embedded first-order content. The Davidsonian point, then, appears to have the consequence that the "contained" first-order content *is the same as* the first-order content of the first-order belief expressed by my utterance of the unembedded 'Cats fear water'. Now let us ask: How could it come about that my second-order sentence

---

[10] Davidson 1988, p. 664.   [11] Shoemaker 1994; the quotation is from note 7.
[12] Throughout this chapter, I often specify intentional states (e.g., thoughts and beliefs) in terms of the sentences that speakers use to express them. This practice is not symptomatic of an allegiance to some "language-of-thought" hypothesis according to which thinking necessarily involves sentence-like mental representations. Instead, the reason why I so often discuss intentional states in conjunction with the sentences that can be used to express them is as follows. Since I am discussing content skepticism, I often need to be able to refer to intentional states in a manner that is neutral as to their content. For example: 'the belief – whatever its content is – that is expressed by my utterance of "I am thinking that water is wet" ', as opposed to 'my belief that I am thinking that water is wet'.
[13] See Shoemaker 1994, p. 260 and Boghossian 1992 for presentations of the Davidsonian point which are similar to that in the text.

'I believe that cats fear water' is *false*, thereby expressing a mistaken second-order belief about what I believe? For this to occur, there would have to be a divergence between (*a*) the first-order content of the first-order belief expressed by my sincere utterance of 'Cats fear water' (i.e., the first-order content that I believe) and (*b*) the first-order content that is contained in the second-order content of the second-order belief expressed by my second-order sentence (i.e., the first-order content that I believe that I believe). However, as we have just seen, the Davidsonian point precludes such a divergence. Hence, the second-order sentence is true, not false.[14] This is to say that my second-order sentence, insofar as it is true, does not express a mistaken second-order belief on my part concerning what I believe.[15]

One drawback of the approach just sketched is its assumption that belief contents are of such a nature that a second-order content can *contain* a first-order content.[16] It is not clear, however, how we are to understand this notion of containment. Do contents have parts? In general, it would be nice if the Davidsonian strategist could avoid commitment to any specific view of the nature of belief contents. Similarly, it would be nice if he could also avoid commitment to any specific view of the semantics of belief sentences. Unfortunately, the Davidsonian strategy as just reconstructed here will be rejected by a classical Fregean.

According to such a theorist, the sentence 'Cats fear water' does not express a uniform sense across unembedded and embedded sentential contexts. The sentence expresses its customary sense – a proposition – when standing alone in an unembedded context, but in a singly embedded context, the sentence expresses its singly indirect sense – a distinct proposition. On such a theory, then, it will be problematic to hold that the sentence expresses a single content that can stand "unembedded" and that is "embedded" in some straightforward way in the second-order content expressed by the second-order sentence.

However, on such a theory, the sense of the second-order sentence's 'that'-clause will determine a first-order content (i.e., a customary sense which in this case is a proposition) *as its referent*. Which first-order content? This content will be the sense of my unembedded sentence 'Cats fear water'.

---

[14] Here is a different way of putting the point. The second-order sentence will express a correct belief if the second-order content of that belief is a *true* content. According to that second-order content, I believe a certain first-order content. Given the Davidsonian point, the first-order content that the second-order content represents me as believing is the same as the content of the first-order belief of mine that is expressed by my sincere utterance of 'Cats fear water'. So what the second-order content represents to be the case *is* the case. So the second-order content is true. So my belief of it is correct.

[15] Davidson (1984b) also argues for a connection between first-person authority and the constraints governing radical interpretation. I discuss his view below in Section 5.8.

[16] See Burge 1988a for a discussion of self-knowledge in which the notion of content containment plays a role.

This sense is a proposition; call it *P*. My sincere utterance of that unembedded sentence expresses a belief, indeed a belief of *P* (the proposition which constitutes the unembedded sentence's customary sense). Now the Fregean can say that the second-order sentence 'I believe that cats fear water' is going to be true. This is because that belief sentence is true iff I believe the proposition to which its 'that'-clause refers (the proposition which is determined as referent by the singly indirect sense expressed by the 'that'-clause). But this proposition, as we noted, is just *P*, and we noted that I do believe *P* (in virtue of my sincere utterance of 'Cats fear water').

In general, what the Davidsonian strategist needs to show is that so long as the same facts fix both first-order and second-order content, the content of a first-order belief and the content of the corresponding second-order belief will be so related (by containment or in the foregoing Fregean way) that the second-order sentence expressing the second-order belief *is true*. Let us assume that the Davidsonian can provide an account which has this consequence.

Suppose that I utter 'Cats fear water' on New Year's Eve 1984 and that the content of the belief thereby expressed is *that cats fear water*. Suppose that on New Year's Eve 1994, I utter the sentence 'I believe that cats fear water' at the end of my first decade as an unwitting resident of Twin Earth. Then the appropriate relation (containment, Fregean determination, or whatever) will not obtain between the content of the first-order belief expressed by the 1984 utterance and the content of the second-order belief expressed by the 1994 utterance. Still, the appropriate relation *will* obtain between that 1994 second-order content and the first-order content of the belief expressible by my New Year's Eve *1994* utterance of 'Cats fear water'. That is enough to make the 1994 second-order sentence true.

John Heil presents a version of the Davidsonian strategy which differs in some respects from the reconstruction just presented.[17] He argues that the environmental states of affairs that, according to the externalist, help fix first-order and second-order content do not need to be *known* by the thinker in order to play their content-determining role. I would like to note two things in connection with Heil's point. First, it is not clear that the reconstruction of the Davidsonian strategy I provided depends upon the assumption that externalism is correct, as does Heil's version. Even if individualistic facts alone are sufficient to determine the contents of one's intentional states, first- and second-order content will still covary in the manner described above. On this conception of the Davidsonian strategy, the aim is to answer the content skeptic by pointing to features of self-knowledge which are in

---

[17] See Heil 1988. See also Brueckner 1990 for a critical discussion of Heil.

place no matter whether or not externalism is correct. If this strategy succeeds, then it shows that externalism does not generate content skepticism without focusing upon any special properties of externalism.

The second point I would like to note about Heil's version of the Davidsonian strategy is that it does not make use of the following consequence of the covariance of first- and second-order content: My second-order sentence 'I believe that cats fear water' is *true* and hence does not express a mistaken belief about what I believe. Granted, if externalism is correct, that second-order belief has its content regardless of whether I know about content-determining circumstances. But nothing follows regarding the question whether that second-order belief is *correct* and therefore is at least a candidate for constituting a piece of *knowledge* about what I believe.

Tyler Burge makes some claims about self-knowledge which fall in the general vicinity of the Davidsonian strategy I have reconstructed.[18] According to Burge, the thought which I express by the sentence 'I am thinking that water is clear' is guaranteed to be a *true* thought. Suppose that the thought in question is a second-order thought with the content *that I am thinking that water is clear*. In order to think a thought with that second-order content at t, I must at t think a thought with the content *that water is clear*. This is Davidsonian content-containment at work. The containing second-order content, then, is made true by my act of thinking it: The containing content represents me as thinking the contained first-order content that I think in thinking the containing content.

According to Paul Boghossian, this mechanism of self-verification does not operate in cases in which I think a thought expressible by the sentence 'I believe that water is clear'.[19] The pertinent second-order content is *not* guaranteed to be true by my act of thinking it. Suppose that the content in question is *that I believe that water is clear*. I can think a thought with that content even if I do not believe that water is clear. In such a case, the second-order thought would be a thought with a false content.[20] However, if I use

---

[18] See Burge 1988a.   [19] See Boghossian 1989, p. 21.

[20] Boghossian also maintains that Burge's mechanism of self-verification does not extend to thoughts about one's desires and fears, since, like belief, these are "standing" mental states. The reasoning in the text suggests that the mechanism does not extend to *any* propositional attitudes other than thinking. Burge 1988a makes no claim to the contrary. He puts forward the mechanism as directly applying only to thoughts about one's thoughts. I will note two further points about self-verification. First, insofar as Burge is concerned with *self-knowledge*, he must consider not just the *thought* expressible by 'I am thinking that water is clear'. (He speaks of "thinking knowledgeably" that one is thinking that p; see Burge 1988a, p. 654.) Burge must also consider the *belief* expressible by 'I am thinking that water is clear'. This is because a piece of *knowledge* expressible by that sentence will involve a *believing* of a second-order content and not just a *thinking* or an *entertaining* of the content. Second, before discussing the mechanism of self-verification, Burge gives the following two paradigms of "authoritative self-knowledge": 'I think (with this very thought) that writing requires

the sentence 'I believe that water is clear' *to express a belief about what I believe*, then it appears that that belief's correctness is guaranteed by the covariance of first-order and second-order content. Thus, even if Burge's mechanism of self-verification does not extend to thoughts about what one believes, the related Davidsonian mechanism we have been discussing guarantees the correctness of one's beliefs about one's beliefs.[21]

5.5 COVARIANCE AND CONTENT SKEPTICISM

The Davidsonian strategy under discussion does not provide a successful answer to skepticism about knowledge of the contents of one's thoughts and other intentional states. The covariance of first-order and second-order content guarantees at most that when I sincerely utter a belief-sentence like 'I believe that cats fear water', thereby expressing a belief with a second-order content, the sentence is true. So the second-order belief thereby expressed is a true, i.e., correct, not mistaken, belief about what I believe. However, a true belief about what I believe need not amount to *knowledge* about what I believe. So it is far from clear that the Davidsonian strategy has the materials to show that one's correct second-order beliefs constitute self-*knowledge*.[22]

concentration', and 'I judge (or doubt) that water is more common than mercury' (1988a, p. 649). Unlike in the first of the paradigms, in the second it is possible to entertain or think the *false* content *that one judges (or doubts) that p*. This is why Burge did not attempt to explicate authoritative self-knowledge about one's doubtings and judgings in terms of the mechanism of self-verification. I would like to thank Burge for clarifying in conversation this part of his view.

[21] Boghossian (1989) makes the following additional objection to Burge's views about self-verification. On Burge's view, a self-verifying thought *T* about what I am thinking only affords me knowledge about what I am thinking *at the time of T's occurrence*. Burge's mechanism does not yield knowledge about what I was formerly thinking. Suppose that I know now (at t_1) that I am thinking that water is clear, by means of the mechanism. Years pass. Now (at t_2) I cannot use the mechanism in order to come to know what I was thinking at t_1. Indeed, I might have been switched from Earth to Twin Earth at t_1 plus one second, so that I now think only *twater*-thoughts. This situation leads Boghossian to put forward the following "platitude":

if *S* knows that *p* at t_1 and if at (some later time) t_2, *S* remembers everything *S* knew at t_1 then *S* knows that *p* at t_2. (1989, p. 23)

In light of this "platitude," there are two possible explanations for why I fail to know at t_2 what I was thinking at t_1: Either I have forgotten or I never knew in the first place, via the mechanism, what I was thinking at t_1. The first explanation is not successful, since there will be hypothetical cases with the structure under consideration in which "we ought to be able to exclude memory failure by stipulation" (1989, p. 23). We simply imagine someone with as good a memory as any human has ever possessed. Thus Boghossian concludes that the mechanism of self-verification never provided me with knowledge at t_1.

The "platitude" that this objection rests upon is dubious. I know now (at t_1) that I am here now, but this knowledge is context-bound. I lose it irretrievably when I move into a different spatiotemporal context. In the different context, I can know at t_2 that I was at <x, y, z> at t_1. But that is a different piece of knowledge from my t_1-bound knowledge. Maybe knowledge gained by Burge's mechanism is similarly context-bound and constitutes another counterexample to the "platitude."

[22] For more on this point, see 1992a, Section 2.

Worse than that, the Davidsonian strategy only guarantees that whatever second-order belief it is that is expressed by my sincere utterance of 'I believe that cats fear water', that belief is true (i.e., correct, not mistaken). But which second-order belief is expressed by that utterance? Is it a belief with the second-order content *that I believe that cats fear water*? Or is it a belief with the second-order content *that I believe that cats fear twater*? The Davidsonian strategy does not yield an answer to that question. It only tells us that *if* the first-order content of the belief expressed by my utterance of 'Cats fear water' is the content *that cats fear water*, *then* the second-order content of the belief expressed by my utterance of 'I believe that cats fear water' is the true content *that I believe that cats fear water*. On the other hand, if the first-order content in question is *that cats fear twater*, then the second-order content in question is *that I believe that cats fear twater*. Either way, the second-order belief, whatever is its content, is true.

The proponent of the Davidsonian strategy might well point out that just as first-order and second-order content covary, second-order and third-order content also covary. This has the consequence that when I sincerely utter the sentence 'I believe that I believe that cats fear water', I thereby express a true third-order belief. So the question of *which* true second-order content is expressed by my utterance of 'I believe that cats fear water' can be correctly answered by my uttering 'I believe that I believe that cats fear water'. That sentence expresses a true third-order belief about my second-order beliefs.

Now consider the following diagram:

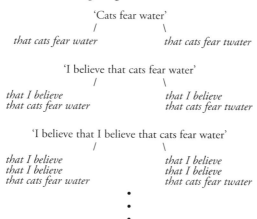

The pairs of italicized sentences in the diagram formulate truth conditions for the quoted sentences under which they appear. These alternative candidates for truth conditions for the quoted sentences are at the same time alternative candidates for formulating the content of the beliefs expressed by sincere utterances of the quoted sentences. The basic problem facing the Davidsonian strategy is as follows. The strategy at most establishes that each belief-sentence in the hierarchy expresses (when sincerely uttered by me) a true belief about what I believe. But the strategy leaves open the question of whether the left-hand members of the pairs in the diagram correctly formulate my sentences' truth conditions and my beliefs' contents or, instead, the right-hand members do. The skeptic about knowledge of content and truth conditions at this point will complain that the Davidsonian strategy does not afford me knowledge of which side of the diagram correctly describes the facts about my beliefs' contents and my sentences' truth conditions.

5.6 IS CONTENT SKEPTICISM REALLY SKEPTICISM AT ALL?

It might be held that the view I have been calling "content skepticism" is not really a form of skepticism at all. Here is one version of this charge, due to Kevin Falvey and Joseph Owens.[23] Suppose that a skeptic argues that I do not know that $\sim SK^*$, where SK^* is a skeptical counterpossibility to some proposition P which I claim to know on the basis of perception (let SK^* be the proposition that I am the victim of some form of sensory deception). His reasoning, we will suppose, is based upon the consideration that if the counterpossibility SK^* were true, then I would nevertheless mistakenly believe that $\sim SK^*$ This is because, if SK^* were true, things would seem just as they actually seem. Given the way things actually seem, I actually believe that $\sim SK^*$. So if SK^* were true, then I would still believe that $\sim SK^*$. Thus I would be mistaken if I were in a situation in which the counterpossibility obtained. Since I am prone to error in this way regarding the question whether SK^* is true, I do not know that $\sim SK^*$. Falvey and Owens sum this up by saying that "the Cartesian skeptic undermines the reliability of perceptual beliefs by describing a counterfactual situation in which perceptual experiences identical to my actual ones would lead me to form a false belief with the same content as my actual belief."[24]

---

[23] See Falvey and Owens 1994.
[24] Falvey and Owens 1994, p. 122. Falvey and Owens' analysis of the Cartesian skeptic's reasoning is similar to Robert Nozick's analysis (1981, Chapter 3). There Nozick interprets the skeptic as arguing that I fail to know that $\sim SK$ in virtue of my violation, with respect to $\sim SK$, of the following condition for knowledge:

If S knows that φ, then if φ were false, S would not mistakenly believe that φ.

Things are different, though, when it comes to content skepticism. I claim to know that I believe that water is clear. The content skeptic puts forward the counterpossibility that I believe that twater is clear, and he maintains that I do not know that that is not the case. In reply, I claim that I *do* know that I do not believe that twater is clear. Does this belief amount to knowledge? Suppose that I were in a world in which I believed that twater is clear (a world in which the skeptical counterpossibility under discussion is true). Given the covariance of first-order and second-order content, in such a world my sentence 'I believe that water is clear' would express a true belief with the second-order content *that I believe that twater is clear*. In other words, I would correctly believe that I believe that twater is clear. So if I were in a possible world in which the content skeptic's possibility obtains, then I would *not* mistakenly believe that I am *not* in such a world. So we see, according to Falvey and Owens, that the skeptic "cannot appeal to Twin-Earth thought experiments in support of the claim that beliefs formed on the basis of introspection are unreliable."[25] Thus the content skeptic cannot argue that my belief that I do not believe that twater is clear fails to amount to knowledge. At least, he cannot argue for this conclusion in a manner which parallels the Cartesian skeptic's reasoning, as analyzed above, to show that I do not know that $\sim SK^*$. In that case, consideration of a relevant counterfactual situation revealed that my perceptual beliefs are unreliable, in the sense that I am prone to error about perceptual matters in such situations.

So there is a relevant difference between Cartesian external-world skepticism and content skepticism: Given the covariance between the various levels of content represented in the above diagram, I am not prone to error on the question of what I believe. Not only *would* I lack mistaken beliefs about what I believe in various pertinent counterfactual situations, but, further, I do not *in fact* have mistaken beliefs about what I in fact believe. However, it seems that this is not enough to block content skepticism, because I still cannot rule out the hypothesis that the right-hand side of the diagram correctly describes my thought contents. The Davidsonian strategists have so far put forward no considerations which favor the common-sense hypothesis over that skeptical hypothesis. At this point the content skeptic could appeal to (UP). From this Underdetermination Principle, it would apparently follow that I am not justified in rejecting the skeptical hypothesis. Given that justification is required for knowledge, it would then

---

[25] Falvey and Owens 1994, p. 122.

follow that I do not know that I am not "on the right-hand side" of the diagram.[26]

The skeptic's position is this: I fail to know that I do not believe that twater is clear, even though the belief that I express by my utterances of 'I believe that water is clear' is true. This second-order belief, whatever it is, is true, but it may be the belief that I believe that twater is clear, rather than the belief that I believe that water is clear.

As David Christensen in effect notes in a slightly different context, the content skeptic I am presently considering would have me describe my current situation as follows: My utterances of 'I believe that water is clear' are true even though it may be that I do not believe that water is clear.[27] Christensen objects that "it is not entirely clear . . . that the term 'skepticism' is wholly appropriate here."[28] He says that the skeptic's hypothesis

> ends up calling true the very sentences [in our example, 'I believe that water is clear'] whose negations it is using [i.e., it uses, as opposed to mentions, 'I do not believe that water is clear'] to contradict the beliefs it seeks to cast doubt on [i.e., the belief that I believe that water is clear].[29]

This characterization has it that the content skeptic is assuming that I believe that I believe that water is clear and is wishing to cast doubt on that belief by suggesting that maybe I do *not* believe that water is clear. The "skeptic" compounds the confusion by adding that 'I believe that water is clear' is true as uttered by me.

However, this is not the content skeptic's strategy. He does not assume that I have the belief that I believe that water is clear, a belief that might be mistaken and therefore fails to amount to knowledge. Instead, he suggests that the right-hand side of the diagram might well correctly describe my belief contents, in which case I do not believe that I believe that water is clear. As for the "calling true" part of Christensen's criticism, this is simply a description of the point we have been emphasizing: The content skeptic acknowledges that the belief-sentences appearing in quotes in the diagram are all true, none expressing a mistaken belief about what I believe.[30]

---

[26] See my Brueckner 1994a, Section 1, for a related discussion.   [27] See Christensen 1993.

[28] Christensen 1993, p. 308. Christensen is discussing skepticism about knowledge of whether one's sentences have disquotational truth conditions. I am extending his remarks to skepticism about knowledge of content. The objection that follows in the text applies equally to Christensen's claims about the "disquotation skeptic."

[29] Christensen 1993, p. 308.

[30] For discussion of the relation between content skepticism and the hierarchy depicted in the diagram, see Genova 1991 and Brueckner 1992b.

5.7 STIPULATIVE EXCLUSION OF THE CONTENT
SKEPTIC'S COUNTERPOSSIBILITY

Let us now consider a strategy for ruling out the content skeptic's counter-possibility which focuses upon the role of stipulative definition in the generation of the skeptical problem. Let us consider a version of content skepticism which arises from reflection upon the Putnamian brain-in-a-vat scenario. Let us call the language spoken by a brain in a vat 'vat-English'. When the content skeptic maintains that I do not know whether my sentences and thought contents have disquotational truth conditions or, instead, nondisquotational truth conditions, he can be represented as maintaining that I do not know whether I am speaking English or vat-English.[31] But according to Thomas Tymoczko, "Vat-English is always something other than the language we are speaking."[32] The idea seems to be that 'English' by definition refers to whatever language I am speaking, and the term 'vat-English' is then stipulatively defined so that it refers to a language which is distinct from English. So I know that I am not speaking vat-English in virtue of (1) knowing the stipulative definition of 'Vat-English' used in constructing the brain-in-a-vat thought experiment, and (2) knowing that I am speaking the language I am speaking. Since I know in this way that I am not speaking vat-English, I know that I am not speaking a language whose sentences, as I utter them, have nondisquotational truth conditions.

However, my practice in the previous paragraph gives the lie to this stipulative strategy. At the beginning of the paragraph, I introduced the term 'vat-English' simply by saying that it is to refer to the language spoken by a brain in a vat. If it is insisted that 'English' refers to whatever language I am speaking, then I suppose that the content skeptic would have to be represented as suggesting that English might well be identical to Vat-English. This will be consistent so long as 'vat-English' is defined in the manner of the current paragraph.

These maneuvers seem to skirt the real issue raised by the content skeptic. Call my language whatever you want: *Brucknerese, Brenglish, English*. . . . Does my language consist of sentences with strange semantic properties or with the normal ones I take them to have? Do my utterances of the sentences of my language have disquotational or nondisquotational truth conditions?

If these remarks succeed against the stipulative strategy as applied to the brain-in-a-vat scenario, then it seems that they ought to succeed against the strategy's application to the Twin-Earth scenario. However, there is a

---

[31] See Chapter 1, Section 1.5.   [32] Tymoczko 1989; the quotation appears on 284–5.

version of the stipulative strategy that appears to work in the case of Twin Earth. In sketching that thought experiment, we are supposed to imagine a world replete with a liquid which is superficially indistinguishable from H_2O but chemically different. We are not told which elements constitute the liquid in question. However, we are told that the term 'XYZ' is to refer to the liquid in question. But *which* liquid? Clearly, we have not been provided with resources sufficient to determine some particular liquid as referent for 'XYZ'. We are told that the term 'twater' is to be understood as expressing the concept expressed by Twin-Earth speakers' uses of 'water' in referring to samples of XYZ. Since 'XYZ' has not been given a determinate referent, no concept has been uniquely specified in the foregoing way. We are told that Twin-Earth thinkers do not think thoughts with the content *that water is clear* but instead think thoughts with the content *that twater is clear*. But no determinate content for the Twin-Earth thoughts has been successfully specified by the foregoing remark. This is in accordance with externalist theory. A speaker who has only been in contact with H_2O and has never encountered a twin liquid cannot think a thought with the same content as that expressed by a doppelgänger's utterance of 'Water is clear', where the doppelgänger has only encountered some liquid or other which is a twin of H_2O. When we say, 'My twin has contact only with XYZ and thus thinks that twater is clear', this is best seen as shorthand for 'My twin has contact only with some or other liquid which is distinct from H_2O and thus thinks a thought with some or other content which is distinct from the content *that water is clear*'. Further, whatever content is borne by the thought expressed by my twin's utterance of 'Water is clear', this is a content which I cannot now entertain, in virtue of my current external circumstances.

These remarks indicate how the stipulative strategy can be deployed with respect to the question whether, when I think a thought expressible by the sentence 'Water is clear', I am now thinking a thought with the content *that water is clear*, or, instead, a thought with the content *that twater is clear*. My use of 'thought with the content *that twater is clear*' does not refer to a determinate content which is now thinkable by me. At best, the term refers to some range of thoughts which are not currently thinkable by me; the term is on a par with 'thought involving concepts which I lack'. Since I know that my sentence 'Water is clear' expresses a thought which *is* now thinkable by me, I know that I am not now thinking a thought with the content *that twater is clear*.

However, this strategy runs into problems when the possibility of switching enters the picture. Let us assume that the unwitting victim of shuttling between Earth and Twin Earth loses his concept *water* and gains some substitute concept after he has resided on Twin Earth for a sufficiently long period. He utters the sentence 'Water is clear' at some time *t* during his odyssey. Either (*a*) he expresses a *water*-thought at *t* and is at *t* incapable of entertaining the pertinent twin thought or (*b*) he expresses some twin thought at *t* which is not a *water*-thought (call it a *twater*-thought, if you like) and is at *t* incapable of entertaining a *water*-thought. What if *I* am involved in such a switching scenario? Can I rule out this apparent possibility by the stipulative strategy?

To answer this question, let us consider whether the following description of my situation is coherent. Either (*i*) the clear liquid stuff around me is water or (*ii*) it is some twin liquid which is not water. Without undertaking a chemical investigation, I cannot say whether (*i*) or (*ii*) is the case. If (*i*) is the case, then I am now thinking *water*-thoughts, and I cannot now entertain any twin thought which I would think if (*ii*) were the case. If (*ii*) is instead the case, then I am now thinking a thought which is not a *water*-thought. Indeed I cannot think *water*-thoughts if (*ii*) is the case.

While the foregoing description of my situation might seem coherent, it is not. To suppose that (*ii*) is the case is to suppose that I am in a waterless world containing a liquid which is a twin of water. According to the foregoing description, if our supposition is correct, then I cannot now think *water*-thoughts. But entertaining the supposition requires thinking *water*-thoughts, since the supposition is that I am in a waterless world. It is incoherent to suppose that I am in a waterless world and yet lack the ability to think thoughts involving the concept of *water*.

The situation is puzzling, since the following universally quantified conditional seems true:

(*) For all *x*, if *x* is in a waterless world (at the appropriate time in a switching scenario), then *x* cannot think *water*-thoughts.

But when I attempt to instantiate (*) to my own case, I pass into the incoherence just noted.

In a somewhat different context, Paul Boghossian discusses the conception of switching scenarios we have been using. He remarks that

on *this* way of telling the switching story, S [a switching victim] cannot even frame the hypothesis he is called upon to exclude. Someone may not have the concept of counterfeit money, but if there is a lot of counterfeit money in his vicinity, then he must be able to exclude the hypothesis that the coin in his hand is counterfeit before he can be said to know that it is a dime. The fact that he cannot so much as frame the relevant hypothesis does not absolve him of this requirement.[33]

---

[33] Boghossian 1989, p. 25 n. 12.

The point seems to be that in order for me to know that I am thinking that water is clear, I must possess the ability to exclude a certain relevant skeptical hypothesis *which, according to externalism, I cannot frame*. As against this, we may note that since I cannot frame, or conceive, of the skeptical hypothesis, I cannot justifiably believe that it does not obtain: I cannot exclude it. I do not have the conceptual resources to even *try* to exclude the hypothesis. It seems that Boghossian has not placed a reasonable requirement on knowledge here. It would follow from the requirement that an Earthling fails to know that he is drinking from a glass containing water in virtue of his inability to exclude the hypothesis that he is drinking from a glass containing a twaterspout. He cannot exclude that hypothesis since he cannot even frame it, but that hardly seems to reflect badly on his epistemic situation.

So it appears that a version of the stipulative strategy can be deployed when the content skeptic seeks to use the Twin-Earth scenario to generate his skepticism. The problem, as we have seen, arises because on the conception of switching we have adopted, one cannot think both *water*-thoughts and their twins while one remains a resident of a single planetary environment. When the content skeptic appeals to the Putnamian brain-in-a-vat scenario in order to generate his skepticism, this difficulty does not arise. This is because one can, from within a single causal environment, entertain both of the competing candidate thoughts upon which the content skeptic focuses. For example, if one is in a normal, non-vat world, then one can think both *tree*-thoughts and *computer-state*-thoughts. The content skeptic, then, could rely exclusively upon the brain-in-a-vat scenario in generating his skepticism, due to the foregoing difficulties he encounters in connection with the Twin-Earth scenario.

Another option for the content skeptic is to deny the assumption that in the switching scenario, the unwitting traveler can at no point think both *water*-thoughts and *twater*-thoughts. For example, Boghossian maintains that on a reasonable externalist view the traveler will be able to entertain both Earth and Twin-Earth thoughts at a single time.[34] He imagines a switching scenario in which *S* meets Luciano Pavarotti while swimming in Lake Taupo in New Zealand on Earth. Years later, *S* encounters Twin Luciano on Twin Earth. When *S* then says, 'Here comes Luciano Pavarotti', the singular term refers to Twin Luciano. When *S* says later that day, 'I still remember when, to my great amazement, Luciano Pavarotti emerged from Lake Taupo', *S*'s singular term then refers to the Earthly Luciano. According to Boghossian,

---

[34] See Boghossian 1992.

it is plausible to say this because the thought which S thereby expresses is a member of a class of thoughts that

are caused and sustained by *previous* perceptions long gone. In the normal case, they owe little, if anything, to current perceptions and cognitive transactions with one's environment. They would be expected, therefore, to retain their earthly interpretations even when tokened on twin earth.[35]

Maybe a similar situation could arise for S's uses of 'water'. While first on Earth, S only encounters water in and near Lake Taupo. Upon moving to Twin Earth, his family moves to Twin New Jersey, and his experience of twater is confined to that region. When S says in Twin New Jersey, 'The water in Lake Taupo is beautiful', it could be maintained that he thereby expresses a *water*-thought. This would be a situation in which S has the ability to think both *water*-thoughts and *twater*-thoughts. Maybe I am in such a situation. Maybe I started out with only the ability to think *water*-thoughts but now possess the ability to think *twater*-thoughts as well. So when I now think the sentence 'Water is clear', am I thinking a *water*-thought or a *twater*-thought?

5.8 IT IS *MY* LANGUAGE

In discussions of the brain-in-a-vat brand of content skepticism, Christopher S. Hill and David Christensen both object to the idea that I cannot straight-forwardly apply disquotation to my own sentences.[36] They say that there is no problem in ruling out the content skeptic's hypothesis that my sentences (and thought contents) have nondisquotational truth conditions. Hill and Christensen both suggest that the content skeptic fails to properly distinguish between (*a*) cases involving normal self-applied disquotation and (*b*) cases involving the application of disquotation to another speaker's sentences or involving self-applied disquotation to sentences that I do not fully understand.

Suppose that I am asked to consider in thought some speaker X who utters the sentence 'Trees are green'. If I am not told whether X is in a vat world or a normal world, then I cannot say whether or not his utterances of the sentence are true iff trees are green. It would seem to follow that if I do not know whether I am in a vat world or a normal world, then I cannot say whether or not *my* utterances of the sentence in question are true iff trees are green.[37] Christensen responds as follows:

---

[35] Boghossian 1992, pp. 19–20. [36] See Hill 1990 and Christensen 1993. [37] See Chapter 1, p. 25.

There is something initially troubling about this objection. On closer analysis, however, it seems to me to trade on a failure to account for an important asymmetry in the conditions for applying disquotation. Of course one may not apply disquotation to *another* speaker's words without first knowing that his words are being used univocally with one's own words. We can even easily imagine situations – being in a mixed language crowd – where one would really need additional information of this type before one could apply disquotation with any confidence. However, it is not at all obvious why one should think that this problem can infect *self-applied* disquotation. On the contrary, it would seem that in one's own case, no such additional information could possibly be useful. One can preclude the problematic possibility of equivocation *a priori*.[38]

I will return to Christensen's point below.

I do not understand the set-theoretical sentence 'Omega is a regular cardinal'. I am therefore not in a position to claim to know that 'Omega is a regular cardinal' is true iff omega is a regular cardinal. At best, I can claim to know that the sentence "'Omega is a regular cardinal' is true iff omega is a regular cardinal" is true. My situation with respect to my sentences 'Trees are green' and 'I am not a brain in a vat' is parallel, according to the content skeptic. If I do not know whether I am in a vat world or a normal world, then I am not in a position to apply disquotation to those sentences. Hill responds as follows:

> Brueckner wants to say that he does not know the meaning of either 'Omega is a regular cardinal' or 'Brueckner is not a brain in a vat'. But the sense in which this is true of the former sentence is quite different from the sense in which it is true of the latter. He does not know the meaning of the former in the sense that he does "not understand the technical terminology in the sentence"[39] – that is, in the sense that the sentence lacks a fully determinate meaning in his idiolect. This cannot be said of the latter sentence. . . . In general, in order to know that '*S*' is true if and only if *S*, I need only know the meaning of the word 'true' and have reason to believe that the embedded sentence has some determinate meaning or other in my idiolect.[40]

As against this, it is not at all clear that I can apply disquotation to my utterances of 'I am not a brain in a vat' on the ground that I have reason to believe that the sentence *has some determinate meaning or other in my idiolect*. Presumably, I need to know *which* determinate meaning the sentence has in my idiolect in order to apply disquotation. If all I know is that the sentence *either* has a determinate meaning which determines disquotational truth conditions *or* a different determinate meaning which determines nondisquotational truth conditions, then clearly I cannot on this basis apply disquotation to the sentence.

---

[38] Christensen 1993, p. 305.　　　[39] Here Hill is quoting page 25 of Chapter 1　　　[40] Hill 1990, p. 110 n. 4.

Do I know what my utterances of 'I am not a brain in a vat' and 'Trees are green' mean simply in virtue of knowing that it is *my* language, and not someone else's, that I am now speaking? If so, then, as Christensen suggests, there is no difficulty in straightforwardly applying disquotation to my own utterances. This move, though, does not seem very effective in the present dialectical context. The content skeptic is suggesting that if externalism is correct, then it yields the unfortunate consequence that there is a sense in which I do not understand my own language: I do not know whether my own sentences have disquotational or, instead, nondisquotational truth conditions. The Hill–Christensen response (as I am understanding it) involves the claim that since it is *my* language, of course I understand it: I understand the meanings of my own utterances and thus can legitimately self-apply disquotation. But this is too close to being a flat denial of the content skeptic's conclusion to constitute an effective reply to his skeptical argument.

Davidson's remarks on first-person authority can be seen as a variation on the theme: It is my language. Let us first note a fairly recent statement by Davidson:

Knowledge of the contents of our own minds must, in most cases, be trivial. The reason is that, apart from special cases, the problem of interpretation cannot arise. When I am asked about the propositional contents of my mind, I must use my own sentences. The answer is usually absurdly obvious: my sentence 'Snow is white', like my thought that snow is white, is true if and only if snow is white.[41]

This seems to be no more than an expression of the point we have just been discussing: Insofar as I use my own language to characterize the contents of my thoughts, I am at liberty to self-apply disquotation. Therefore, "the problem of interpretation cannot arise." I cannot wonder about how to interpret *my own words*.

However, in a famous earlier discussion of the same issues, Davidson says,

there must be a presumption that speakers, but not their interpreters, are not wrong about what their words mean. The presumption is essential to the nature of interpretation – the process by which we understand the utterances of a speaker. This process cannot be the same for the utterer and for his hearers. . . . [T]here can be no general guarantee that a hearer is correctly interpreting a speaker; however easily, automatically, unreflectively and successfully a hearer understands a speaker, he is liable to general and serious error. In this special sense, he may always be regarded as interpreting a speaker. The speaker cannot, in the same way, interpret his own words.[42]

[41] Davidson 1991, pp. 163–164.   [42] Davidson 1984b, p. 110.

There seem to be two intertwined strands of argument in this passage, one new and one old. First, Davidson seems to be saying that interpretation cannot succeed unless interpreters are right about what their own words mean. There is not space to discuss why this point would follow from Davidson's views of interpretation. For our present purposes, though, it is enough to note that the content skeptic can reply by accepting Davidson's point and then by denying that successful interpretation (say, of another by me) is possible. The second strand in the passage seems familiar. Since it is my language, the idea that I might try to *interpret* it is absurd. Interpreting a language is coming to know what its sentences mean. But it cannot be supposed that I do not know what my own sentences mean.

5.9 WHEN METALANGUAGE CONTAINS OBJECT LANGUAGE

I have just criticized a defense of disquotation which rests entirely on the bald assertion that since it is *my* language that I am speaking, I therefore understand the meanings of my utterances. Let us now consider an alternative defense of disquotation that focuses in a different way upon the apparent triviality that it is my language that I am speaking.

Consider the sentence

(1) X's utterances of 'Trees are green' are true iff trees are green.

An utterance of (1) is guaranteed to express a truth so long as the metalanguage in which the utterance is made contains the object language to which the mentioned sentence belongs. This is so in virtue of the meanings of quotation marks and the truth predicate. If we cannot say whether or not the metalanguage in which an utterance of (1) is couched is X's language, then we cannot say whether the utterance of (1) is true. If the metalanguage is some language semantically different from the language X speaks, then it does not contain the relevant object language – X's language – and all bets are off.[43] If I utter (1), then the question whether I thereby say something true thus depends on whether my language (the metalanguage) diverges from X's language (the object language).

Let us apply these considerations to my utterances of the sentence

(2) My utterances of 'Trees are green' are true iff trees are green.

---

[43] Even if metalanguage and object language diverge, (1) would express a truth when uttered in the metalanguage if that language's semantics happened to overlap the object language at the sentence 'Trees are green'.

In my uses of (2), the object language is my language, and the metalanguage is also my language. This is so for two reasons. When I utter (2), I refer to *my* utterances of the mentioned sentence, thereby determining *my* language as the relevant object language. And when I utter (2), I use *my* language as the metalanguage. Thus, given the form of (2), my utterances of (2) are guaranteed to be true. When I utter (2), divergence between metalanguage and object language is not possible, and such divergence is required for the falsity of an utterance of (2). Thus, we seem to have a defense of disquotation which differs from that which we considered in the previous section.[44] The current defense rests upon the rather trivial fact that in stating disquotational truth conditions for my own utterances, my own language is both metalanguage and object language.[45]

When a brain in a vat utters

(2) My utterances of 'Trees are green' are true iff trees are green,

he says something true. This is because for such an utterance, the metalanguage is the brain-in-a-vat's language, and so is the object language.[46] Though some writers have found this to be a source of support for self-applied disquotation, consideration of the brain-in-a-vat's utterance of (2) will set us on the road to a rejection of this defense of disquotation.[47] When a brain in a vat utters (2), the pertinent metalanguage contains the pertinent object language and thus the utterance expresses a truth. But I cannot on that basis conclude

(3) A brain-in-a-vat's utterances of 'Trees are green' are true iff trees are green.

Instead, I can at best conclude

(4) The sentence "My utterances of 'Trees are green' are true iff trees are green" is true as uttered by a brain in a vat.

Let us apply this line of thought to my own case. The defense of disquotation under consideration has rested entirely on the fact that when I utter (2), the pertinent metalanguage contains the pertinent object language. But

---

[44] The proposition expressed by my utterances of (2) is contingent, since it does not correctly formulate the truth conditions of the utterances of 'Trees are green' that I produce in, e.g., a vat world. According to the current defense of disquotation, the proposition in question can be known by me in an a priori manner. I can see that the proposition's truth is guaranteed by the form of (2) together with the meanings of the truth predicate and quotation marks. So if this defense of disquotation is successful, we would have an example of a contingent a priori truth.

[45] See Brueckner 1992a for such a defense of disquotation in the context of content skepticism.

[46] See Chapter 1, Section 1.3.

[47] For example, Christensen says, "disquotation is . . . a valid step *within* either English *or* vat-English" (Christensen 1993, p. 305).

now it appears that I cannot on that basis conclude *that my utterances of 'Trees are green' are true iff trees are green*. Instead, it appears that I can at best draw the meta-metalinguistic conclusion

(5) The sentence "My utterances of 'Trees are green' are true iff trees are green" is true as uttered by me.

In fact, this point was already implicit in my exposition of the current defense of disquotation. I said that when the pertinent metalanguage contains the pertinent object language, an utterance of

(1) *X*'s utterances of 'Trees are green' are true iff trees are green

is guaranteed *to express a truth. Which* truth is left open, unless in addition to knowing that metalanguage contains object language, I know the correct way to state *X*'s sentences' truth conditions in my language. Similarly, my utterances of (2) are guaranteed to express a truth given the relation of containment between metalanguage and object language. That leaves it open as to which truth is thereby expressed, unless in addition to knowing that metalanguage contains object language, I know the correct way to state my sentences' truth conditions in my language. Is the truth in question *that my utterances of 'Trees are green' are true iff trees are green*? Or is it *that my utterances of 'Trees are green' are true iff computer state 666 obtains*? The fact that the pertinent metalanguage contains the pertinent object language does not by itself answer that question.[48]

5.10 THERE IS NO TRANSCENDENTAL STANDPOINT

There is a response to content skepticism according to which such skepticism is incoherent because it presupposes the existence of a standpoint which is merely illusory. A version of this response can be reconstructed from Peter Hylton's discussion of Quine's thesis of the indeterminacy of translation.[49] Suppose that Quine is right in maintaining that there is no fact of the matter as to whether 'Gavagai' correctly translates into English as 'Here is a rabbit' or, instead, as 'Here is an undetached rabbit part'. Hylton considers the claim that it would follow that there is no fact of the matter as to what *my* sentence 'Here is a rabbit' means and what its parts refer to, since there exist competing stimulus-synonymous translations of my sentence

[48] I thank Earl Conee for repeatedly urging that the "metalanguage contains object language" defense of disquotation is unsuccessful (contrary to what I had claimed in Brueckner 1992a). His objections on this score were an impetus to writing this paper.
[49] See Hylton 1991–92. The locus classicus of the indeterminacy thesis is Chapter 2 of Quine 1960.

into Gavagese. And if there is no fact of the matter as to what my sentence means, then I do not *know* what it means. There is nothing there to be known beyond the facts about the sentence's stimulus meaning. Hylton is anxious to rebut this line of reasoning, which is put forward by John Searle as constituting a reductio of the Quinean indeterminacy thesis.[50]

Hylton offers an interesting interpretation of Quine in which he attempts to explain why the indeterminacy thesis is compatible with a sane, non-skeptical view of self-knowledge. The details of this interpretation go beyond our present purview, but I would like to discuss Hylton's account of what happens when we try to entertain skepticism about knowledge of our own language:

What has gone wrong here, from Quine's point of view, is that we are attempting to speak of objects and of reference transcendentally, i.e. in abstraction from any language or theory, as if we could somehow occupy a God's-eye point of view. But for Quine reference, like truth and reality, is immanent: speaking of reference only makes sense from within some language and theory of the world. To say what some word refers to is, inevitably, to be speaking some language.[51]

Saul Kripke's discussion of Wittgenstein-inspired skepticism about meaning displays an awareness of the sort of worry expressed by Hylton.[52] Kripke presents a skeptical argument whose first stage is aimed at showing that there is no fact of the matter as to whether *in the past* I used 'plus' to denote the plus function or, instead, the *quus* function (a function which diverges from the plus function in the values it assigns to arguments greater than those I have as yet considered). In this first stage of the Wittgensteinian skeptical argument, Kripke avoids raising the question of what I *now* mean by 'plus'

so as to avoid confusing questions about whether the discussion is taking place 'both inside and outside language' [in Rogers Albritton's phrase] in some illegitimate sense. If we are querying the meaning of the word 'plus', how can we use it (and variants like 'quus') at the same time?[53]

However, Kripke does not in the end think that there is a difficulty here that precludes the success of the second stage of the skeptical argument, in which he concludes that since there is no fact of the matter about which function I meant in the past, "neither can there be any such thing in the present either."[54]

What are we to make of Hylton's claim (on behalf of Quine) that the content skeptic is attempting to speak transcendentally, that he is attempting to occupy a God's-eye point of view? Hylton says that that is the attempt

---

[50] See Searle 1987.   [51] Hylton 1991–2, p. 280.   [52] See Kripke 1982.   [53] Kripke 1982, p. 12.
[54] Kripke 1982, p. 21.

to speak "in abstraction from any language or theory." This is echoed by the Albrittonian idea of a discussion which takes place outside of language (as well as inside language!). But the content skeptic would be a fool to deny Sweeney's point: "I gotta use words when I talk to you."[55] If Hylton's Quinean objection is to have any force against the content skeptic, it must involve more than the reminder that the content skeptic must use language (his own, presumably) in stating his skepticism. The content skeptic surely does not need to be reminded of *that*. Whatever further content the objection might have must concern the *consequences* of Sweeney's truism.

Hylton maintains that once one recognizes that to raise skeptical questions about language is "to be speaking some language," it follows that one must "take it for granted" that what appear to be referring terms of that language really are referring terms and that they "obey the disquotational rules which are characteristic of reference."[56] However, as we have seen in the previous section, it is quite unclear how the mere fact that one is speaking one's own language licenses self-application of disquotation. Hylton's Quinean approach seems to add nothing new in this connection.

Gary Ebbs discusses the question whether Putnam's views on the semantics of the brain-in-a-vat's utterances raise problems for our knowledge of the truth conditions of our own utterances.[57] He holds that to question whether our own utterances have disquotational truth conditions is to try to detach ourselves from our own language in an illegitimate way. He says, "We can't detach ourselves from the very facts on which the meaningful use of language depends."[58] He continues, "the idea that we can somehow detach ourselves from the very facts which give our words their meaning, and wonder which of two very different languages we are actually speaking, is very odd."[59] The facts to which Ebbs alludes are the external facts which, according to semantic externalism, help fix meanings, truth conditions, and content. The content skeptic, however, does not attempt to detach himself from these facts. His claim is that since he does not know the nature of the pertinent external facts to which he is attached, he does not know the semantic facts which the external facts help determine. The content skeptic, then, does not attempt to detach himself from the facts on which the meaningfulness of his language depends. He would like to get closer to them, so as to know them better.

Ebbs cites a remark from Tyler Burge which he takes to illustrate his own point about trying to detach oneself from the meaning-determining facts:

---

[55] See Eliot 1963. I thank Paul Benacerraf for locating Sweeney's line.   [56] Hylton 1991–2, p. 280.
[57] Chapter 2; see especially Section 2.8.   [58] Chapter 2, p. 44.   [59] Chapter 2, p. 44, fn. 30.

The idea that we can attempt to determine what our thoughts are from a vantage point that is neutral as to which of various alternative thoughts we are thinking seems to me to be not only deeply implausible but incoherent.[60]

Contrary to Ebbs's interpretation, Burge says nothing explicit here about attempting detachment from meaning-determining (or content-determining) facts. The point of the remark is not obvious, though. Of course, one cannot *occupy* a vantage point that is in fact neutral as to which of various alternative thoughts one is thinking, if doing so would require that, e.g., one is in fact neither thinking that water is clear nor that twater is clear. No matter what one's vantage point is, one is determinately thinking some thought or other via the sentence 'Water is clear'. But it is another matter to say that one cannot occupy a vantage point that is *epistemically neutral* as to which of various alternative thoughts one is thinking. From such a vantage point, one claims to lack knowledge as to which of various alternative thoughts one is thinking (and this negative claim is correct, according to the skeptic).

Kripke suggests that the fact that one must use one's own language in order to formulate skeptical problems regarding that language might show that such skepticism cannot be formulated (though Kripke apparently does not accept this suggestion). On the face of it, though, we *have* formulated content skepticism in the foregoing discussion. We are currently looking for more than metaphorical guidance in understanding why such prima facie coherent formulations involve some sort of underlying incoherence. Let us now turn to the question whether content skepticism is incoherent because it is somehow self-defeating.

5.11 IS CONTENT SKEPTICISM SELF-DEFEATING?

As a preliminary, consider an objection Searle made to the Quinean inde-terminacy thesis. Suppose that, as Quine argues, there is no fact of the matter as to whether the Gavagese speaker refers to rabbits or to rabbit stages when he utters 'Gavagai'. With regard to the Gavagese speaker, then, there is no difference between referring to rabbits and referring to rabbit stages. As noted above, Searle wishes to construct a reductio of Quine's argument for inde-terminacy, and he brings to bear Quine's teaching that *indeterminacy begins at home*. We accordingly consider a Gavagese speaker seeking to translate my sentence 'Here is a rabbit'. Searle says, "If the argument [for the indetermi-nacy of translation of 'Gavagai'] is valid, then it must have the result that there

---

[60] Burge 1988b, p. 93.

isn't any difference *for me* between *meaning* rabbit or rabbit stage, and that has the further result that there isn't any difference for me between *referring to* a rabbit and referring to a rabbit stage, and there isn't any difference for me between something's *being* a rabbit and its *being* a rabbit stage."[61] However, once I say that there is no difference between something's being a rabbit and its being a rabbit stage, I should then "recall that the whole argument about 'Gavagai' was understood by me (or you) only because we know the difference for our own case between meaning rabbit, rabbit stage, rabbit part, etc."[62] The point seems to be that the Quinean indeterminacy argument undermines itself in the following way: Its premises imply that no one understands the argument. So if Quine claims to understand his own indeterminacy argument, then he must reject at least one of its premises.

Let us see whether the same situation arises for the arguments for content skepticism. We may first note the following difference between the Quinean skeptic and the content skeptic: Unlike the Quinean, the content skeptic does *not* hold that there is no fact of the matter as to whether, e.g., I am thinking that water is clear or, instead, thinking that twater is clear. Like Cartesian skepticism about knowledge of the external world, content skepticism is epistemological in nature. There is a fact of the matter as to what I am thinking, according to the content skeptic. His claim is that I do not know *which* fact obtains. Similarly, the Cartesian skeptic holds that there are determinate facts about the way the external world is; I do not know, however, what the facts are.

Even so, insofar as the content skeptic says that I do not know whether or not my sentences have disquotational truth conditions, he is saying that I fail, to that degree, to understand my own language (as we have noted above). But if I do not understand my own language, then I do not understand the sentences which express a skeptical argument for the conclusion that I do not understand my own language.

This objection, however, is a bit too simplistic to have any real force against content skepticism. Consider the following content-skeptical argument.

(X) If I know that my sentence 'Grass is green' expresses the thought that grass is green, then I know that I am not a brain in a vat thinking thoughts with nondisquotational truth conditions.

(Y) I do not know that I am not a brain in a vat thinking thoughts with non-disquotational truth conditions.

[61] Searle 1987, p. 130.   [62] Searle 1987, p. 131.

So (Z) I do not know that my sentence 'Grass is green' expresses the thought that
        grass is green.

It is not as if the content skeptic holds that in the light of his skeptical
conclusion (Z), the sentences (X)–(Z) must be regarded by him as gibberish
which he cannot understand. He does hold that there is a certain limitation
on his understanding of those sentences. He holds that he does not know
whether the sentence 'Grass is green', as it is used in (X)–(Z), is true iff grass
is green or, instead, has nondisquotational truth conditions concerning, say,
the image. That is, if the skeptic is in fact a brain in a vat, then his sentence
'Grass is green' is true iff grass in the image is green in the image. Since the
skeptic claims that he does not know whether or not he is a brain in a vat, he
maintains that his sentence 'Grass is green' may well be true iff grass in the
image is green in the image. Similar remarks apply to the sentence 'I am not
a brain in a vat' as it is used in sentences (X) and (Y).

    Some remarks by Andrè Gallois suggest that this limitation on the skeptic's
understanding of his own argument will generate a problem for him in the
following way.[63] Even though sentences (X)–(Z) might well express propositions forming a sound argument if the sentences are interpreted as being in
English, this is not so if the sentences are interpreted as being in vat-English.
In particular, if, as the skeptic suggests, he is a brain in a vat speaking vat-
English, then his sentence

(*) I do not know that I am not a brain in a vat

expresses a false proposition, according to Gallois. If that is so, then the
argument expressed by (X)–(Z) under the vat-English interpretation has a
false premise. So if the skeptic holds that he does not know whether he is
speaking English (in which case his thoughts and sentences have disquotational truth conditions) or vat-English (in which case they do not), then he
cannot claim to know that he has a sound argument for that conclusion.

    Let us examine the basis for Gallois's criticism. Why, according to
Gallois, does sentence (*) express a false proposition when uttered by a
brain in a vat speaking vat-English? Gallois appeals to two facts to make his
case. The *first fact* is that if a brain in a vat, Ralph, speaking vat-English
utters the sentence

(**) I am not a brain in a vat,

---

[63] See Gallois 1992. His remarks concern a Putnamian argument against Cartesian skepticism, but they
apply equally to the content-skeptical argument in the text.

then Ralph thereby expresses the proposition that Ralph is not a brain in a vat in the image (rather than the proposition that Ralph is not a brain in a vat). The *second fact* is that the sentence

(***) I know that I am not a brain in a vat in the image

expresses a true proposition no matter whether the sentence is uttered by a brain in a vat such as Ralph or by someone who is not envatted. From these two facts, Gallois attempts to infer that the sentence

(****) I know that I am not a brain in a vat

expresses a true proposition as uttered by Ralph. If that did follow from the two facts, then Gallois would have shown that (*) expresses a false proposition as uttered by Ralph.

Gallois' reasoning is unsuccessful. Obviously, Ralph cannot argue as follows: "I know that I am not a brain in a vat in the image (since my experience does not represent me as being in a vat). So I know that I am not a brain in a vat." This is because Ralph is perfectly well aware that the following sentence expresses a truth as uttered by him:

(A) The experience of a brain in a vat does not represent him as being envatted; so he is not a brain in a vat in the image.

So from the fact that I am not a brain in a vat in the image, I cannot infer that I am not a brain in a vat. Ralph cannot make the corresponding inference either.

Suppose that Ralph instead argues as follows: "I know that the proposition that I am not a brain in a vat in the image is true (by the second fact above). I know that my sentence 'I am not a brain in a vat' expresses the proposition that I am not a brain in a vat in the image (by the first fact above). Thus I know that my sentence 'I am not a brain in a vat' expresses a true proposition." The glaring problem with this reasoning is that even though *we* know that Ralph's sentence 'I am not a brain in a vat' expresses the proposition that Ralph is not a brain in a vat in the image (since we are in the middle of a thought experiment in which we stipulate that Ralph is a brain in a vat), *Ralph* does not know that he is a brain in a vat whose sentences express propositions concerning the image.

Further, the most recent reasoning stops short of the desired conclusion. Even if the reasoning had successfully reached its metalinguistic conclusion, Ralph would have needed to continue as follows: "I know, by the foregoing reasoning, that my sentence 'I am not a brain in a vat' expresses a true proposition. *Which* proposition? It expresses the proposition that I am not a brain in a vat. Thus I know that the proposition that I am not a brain in a vat is true. In other words, I know that I am not a brain in a vat." But now Ralph's overall position is incoherent. In the first half of his reasoning, he endorses the sentence

(B) My sentence 'I am not a brain in a vat' expresses the proposition that I am not a brain in a vat in the image.

But in the second half, he endorses

(C) My sentence 'I am not a brain in a vat' expresses the proposition that I am not a brain in a vat.

Ralph cannot have it both ways.

I have examined one failed attempt to show that an argument for content skepticism is self-defeating in virtue of the limitation its conclusion places on one's understanding of the argument's premises. But of course there remains the worry that there might be other ways of making good the charge that content skepticism is in this way self-defeating.

5.12 CONCLUSION

Semantic externalism appears to generate content skepticism. Content skepticism has not been answered in any of the ways considered here. The externalist has more work to do.[64]

---

[64] I would like to thank Earl Conee, Kevin Falvey, Nathan Salmon, and the members of a seminar at the University of California, Santa Barbara in the winter of 1995 for helpful discussions of these issues. I also thank Christopher S. Hill for valuable criticisms of an earlier version of this chapter.

CHAPTER 6

Can we take our words at face value?

Gary Ebbs

My central aims in this chapter are to sketch my view of the starting point and methodology behind anti-individualism, and to use this sketch to clarify the relationship between our ordinary practices of attributing thoughts to a person, on the one hand, and self-knowledge – the familiar fact that in a wide range of ordinary cases a person knows the contents of his thoughts without special empirical investigation, on the other. My immediate purpose is to expose two misunderstandings of this relationship. The most fundamental and widespread misunderstanding is to think that we can make sense of attributing thoughts to a person even if he can't know the contents of his thoughts without special empirical investigation. A related misunderstanding is to think that a person can "know the contents" of his thoughts even if he suspends all his empirical beliefs. To expose these misunderstandings I'll explore the relationship between anti-individualism and some puzzling skeptical "possibilities" that apparently undermine self-knowledge.

In discussing these issues there is a danger of getting swamped by unusually heavy seas of language. I take for granted, for instance, that to say we have self-knowledge is to say we "know the contents" of our own thoughts without special "empirical" investigation. But these words are

For comments on earlier drafts I am grateful to Gary Hatfield, Charles Kahn, Mark Kaplan, Scott Kimbrough, Wolfgang Mann, Tom Meyer, Alan Richardson, Tom Ricketts, Jamie Tappenden, Jay Wallace, Joan Weiner, and Scott Weinstein. I am especially grateful to Mark Kaplan and Joan Weiner for their excellent advice about how to revise an earlier draft. A shortened earlier version of this paper was read at the Central Division Meetings of the APA in May 1994; the commentator was Jamie Tappenden. Jamie's questions and suggestions helped me to separate essential points from distracting details. Still earlier versions of the paper were read at CUNY, Columbia University, and the University of Pennsylvania; I am grateful for the questions and criticisms I received on those occasions. The comments and advice of two anonymous referees for *Philosophy and Phenomenological Research* led to further improvements. My work on the paper was supported in part by a summer research grant from the University of Pennsylvania Research Foundation.

commonly associated with ideas that prevent us from understanding the relationship between self-knowledge and anti-individualism. The word 'empirical' typically brings to mind the idea of a sharp distinction between "conceptual" and "empirical" consequences of our beliefs and thoughts – an idea that anti-individualism undermines, for reasons I'll explain below. We'll see that talk of "contents" and of "knowing the contents" of one's own thoughts is also misleading. If we don't keep our eye on such problematic expressions, entrenched ways of understanding them are sure to distort our picture of the phenomena they are supposed to describe. To signal my doubts about standard ways of thinking about self-knowledge and related issues, I'll sometimes put double quotation marks around words and phrases I find especially problematic.[1]

In the rest of this opening section, I'll sketch my view of anti-individualism, raise a skeptical problem for self-knowledge, and describe my strategy for dissolving it.

In my view, the anti-individualist starts by taking at face value our ordinary judgments about what individuals believe, what they are talking about, and when they agree or disagree with one another. For example, we ordinarily take for granted that if a competent English speaker who has at least a minimal mastery of the term 'water' sincerely utters the sentence 'There's water in the basement' in appropriate circumstances, he thereby expresses his belief that there's water in the basement, even if he doesn't know that water is H_2O. The anti-individualist's thought experiments clarify our understanding of such ordinary belief attributions. By means of these thought experiments we come to see that in a wide range of cases the procedures for properly evaluating an individual's beliefs and thoughts are partly settled by social and physical factors he knows very little about. I'll suppose that the contents of an individual's beliefs and thoughts are given by a description of how they should be evaluated. In this sense the anti-individualist's thought experiments show that the contents of an individual's beliefs and thoughts may be settled by social and physical factors he knows very little about.

At first it seems obvious that if the contents of our beliefs are settled in part by social and physical factors, then we don't know the contents of our beliefs unless we know those social and physical factors. It seems obvious,

---

[1] When this chapter was first published I used double quotation marks to highlight *all* occurrences of the problematic terms. I now find the frequent use of quotation marks in the original publication to be cumbersome and distracting, and so I removed most of them for this publication. At some critical points, however, I still use quotation marks to signal my doubts about how the quoted terms are standardly used.

for example, that if the procedure for properly evaluating a person's belief that there is water in the basement is settled in part by the fact that water is H_2O, then if that person doesn't know that water is H_2O, he doesn't know all that is involved in properly evaluating his belief that there is water in the basement, and so he doesn't know the content of that belief.[2]

But we should not be so quick to conclude that anti-individualism is incompatible with self-knowledge. Anti-individualists question the assumption that if the contents of our thoughts are settled in part by social and physical factors, we don't know the contents of our thoughts unless we know those social and physical factors.[3] More importantly, in my view, anti-individualists should say that just as there is an ordinary sense in which a competent speaker who does not know that water is H_2O may believe there is water in the basement, so there is an ordinary sense in which a competent speaker who believes there is water in the basement knows the content of that belief, even if he does not know that water is H_2O. On the picture of self-knowledge that I'll propose, to know the contents of our own beliefs is just to be able to use our sentences in discourse – to make and evaluate assertions, to ask questions, to describe possibilities, and so forth. To evaluate this proposal we must move beyond the facile first impression that anti-individualism is incompatible with self-knowledge.

Deeper doubts about the compatibility of anti-individualism and self-knowledge arise when we formulate skeptical possibilities that seem to call into question even our most basic presuppositions about the meanings of our words and the contents of our thoughts. Ordinarily I take for granted that when I sincerely utter the sentence 'There's water in the basement', I thereby express the thought that there's water in the basement. After a little reflection I realize that in a world in which my word 'water' doesn't refer to water, my sincere utterances of the sentence 'There's water in the basement' don't express the thought that there is water in the basement. But if I accept anti-individualism it seems I can raise the skeptical possibility that I am actually *in* a world in which my word 'water' does not refer to water. If

---

[2] Akeel Bilgrami (1992) expresses this first impression that there is a conflict between self-knowledge and anti-individualism (which he calls "externalism") as follows:

> if the contents of our thoughts are not constituted only by things internal to us in some suitably Cartesian sense, then it may seem at least *prima facie* natural to think that we will often not know what our thoughts are, since we may often not know crucial things about items external to us. (p. 235)

[3] For example, Tyler Burge (1988a) compares self-knowledge to perceptual knowledge, and argues that when skepticism is not at issue,

> Knowing one's own thoughts no more requires separate investigation of the conditions that make the judgment possible than knowing what one perceives. (p. 657)

I *am* in such a world, then when I utter the sentence 'There's water in the basement' I don't thereby express the thought that there's water in the basement. Moreover, I can describe any number of possible situations in which my word 'water' does not refer to water. How then can I know the contents of the thoughts I express with my sincere utterances of sentences containing the word 'water'?

If I know that my word 'water' refers to water, then of course I know that I am not in a world in which my word 'water' does not refer to water. But it seems that to know what I mean by 'water' and what thoughts I express when I sincerely utter sentences containing the word 'water', I must *first* discover which of many different possible worlds I am in. It also seems that I can't discover this without empirical investigation. So it appears that if we accept anti-individualism, we can make sense of skeptical possibilities that are incompatible with our most basic assumptions about the meanings of our words and the contents of our thoughts. Such skeptical possibilities apparently undermine our ordinary conviction that we needn't engage in a special empirical inquiry to "know the contents" of our thoughts.[4]

This skeptical reasoning is more challenging than our first facile impression that anti-individualism is incompatible with self-knowledge. Nevertheless, as I'll try to show, the reasoning sketched in the last two paragraphs also rests on a mistake. The skeptic invites us to suppose that *we may actually be in a world in which our word 'water' does not refer to water*. I'll argue that this supposition is incoherent, since if it were true we would not be able to express or understand it. The skeptic may reply that the incoherence of his supposition amounts to a *reductio ad absurdum* of anti-individualism. But I'll argue that the fault lies with the skeptic's supposition, which reflects a fundamental misunderstanding of anti-individualism.

The misunderstanding is to think that it makes sense to attribute a wide range of ordinary beliefs and thoughts to an individual who doesn't know the content of those beliefs and thoughts. In my view, to understand the

---

[4] Anthony Brueckner goes further, and argues that if anti-individualism is true, we can't know the contents of our beliefs *whether or not we appeal to empirical evidence*. In Brueckner 1990, he argues for this radical skeptical conclusion as follows:

I claim to know that I am thinking that some water is dripping. If I know that I am thinking that some water is dripping, then I know that I am not thinking, instead, that some twater is dripping. But I do not know that I am not thinking that some twater is dripping, since, according to externalism [anti-individualism], if I were on twin earth thinking that some twater is dripping, things would seem exactly as they now seem (and have seemed). So I do not know that I am thinking that some water is dripping. (p. 448)

Brueckner's reasoning is in essentials just like the reasoning I presented in the text, although his conclusion is a stronger (and correspondingly less plausible).

relationship between belief and self-knowledge we must investigate our actual practices of attributing beliefs to a person, and of judging whether or not he knows what he is talking about. As I have already suggested, careful descriptions of ordinary situations in which philosophers are inclined to say that a speaker knows the contents of his own beliefs and thoughts show that to know the contents of the thoughts we express with our sentences is just to be able to use our sentences in discourse – to make and evaluate assertions, to ask questions, to describe possibilities, and so forth. The same linguistic activities that lead us to attribute beliefs and thoughts to an individual also show that he knows the contents of those beliefs and thoughts.[5] It is therefore a misunderstanding to suppose that someone could express a wide range of beliefs and thoughts in the usual way, yet not know the contents of those beliefs and thoughts.[6]

A related misunderstanding is to think that an individual can know the contents of his thoughts even if he suspends all his "empirical" beliefs. As I see it, our understanding of belief and self-knowledge is inextricably linked to our assessments of whether or not an individual is competent in the use of language. A speaker is not competent in the use of language, nor does he know the contents of his beliefs, unless he takes for granted some background (or other) of empirical beliefs. To say that we know the contents of our beliefs without empirical investigation is to say that at any given time, relative to a background of revisable empirical beliefs, we need not engage in any special empirical investigation to be able to use our words to make and evaluate assertions, ask questions, and so on. Self-knowledge is neither purely formal, nor is it in need of special empirical justification.

---

[5] This view of self-knowledge conflicts with some standard philosophical models of what might be called the logical form of self-knowledge. For example, Tyler Burge (1988a) writes that

> Knowledge of one's own mental events . . . consists in a reflexive judgment which involves thinking a first-order thought that the judgment itself is about. The reflexive judgment simply inherits the content of the first-order thought. (p. 656)

In this sense Burge thinks that self-knowledge is second-order. In contrast, I think that our ordinary attributions of self-knowledge are *inextricable* from our ordinary attributions of first-order thoughts and beliefs. To assign different logical forms to them is to suggest that self-knowledge of first-order thoughts and beliefs must be somehow *constituted* by mental states *over and above* the first-order thoughts and beliefs themselves. This picture of self-knowledge is partly responsible, I think, for the widespread failure to see that it makes no sense to attribute first-order thoughts and beliefs to an individual who does not know the contents of his beliefs and thoughts without special empirical inquiry.

[6] Of course I don't deny that the phrase 'know the contents' could be interpreted in such a way that to know the contents of one's own beliefs and thoughts it is *not* enough to be able to use one's words in discourse.

Despite appearances, I'll argue, this view of self-knowledge does not beg the question against skepticism, since to characterize a possibility as skeptical we must have some idea of what that possibility is. Since we must take many of our beliefs for granted just to *understand* and *describe* possibilities that are in conflict with some of our beliefs, there are many supposedly skeptical possibilities whose descriptions show they are not actual. Properly viewed, anti-individualism deepens our understanding of belief and self-knowledge, and undermines certain entrenched intuitions about what is possible.

6.2 HOW THE TWIN-EARTH THOUGHT EXPERIMENTS WORK

In my view, anti-individualism is an inevitable consequence of taking at face value our ordinary judgments about what individuals believe, what they are talking about, and when they agree or disagree with one another. The Twin-Earth thought experiments do not *establish* anti-individualism, they *highlight our implicit commitment to it*. The thought experiments should be viewed as tools for investigating and clarifying our ordinary practices of attributing beliefs and thoughts to a person.

Let us look at a typical anti-individualistic thought experiment.[7] In the first step we consider Oscar, who lives on Earth, and is a competent English speaker. Let's assume that Oscar's use of the word 'water' *passes muster*[8] in his linguistic community, despite his ignorance of the molecular structure of water. Oscar's use of the word 'water' is judged competent: his sincere utterances of sentences containing the word 'water' are taken at face value and evaluated accordingly in the English-speaking community. Two aspects of Oscar's ordinary competence in the use of the word 'water' are especially important. First, Oscar typically applies the word 'water' to samples of *water*, even though he sometimes makes mistakes. And second, Oscar is disposed to submit the judgments he makes using his word 'water' to criticism and correction by more knowledgeable members of his linguistic community. Thus Oscar implicitly acknowledges that his own rough and ready criteria for applying 'water' do not determine the truth or falsity of the beliefs he expresses using that word.

Suppose that after several days of heavy rain, Oscar examines his basement, and sincerely utters the sentence 'There is water in the basement'.

---

[7] The thought experiment I present here is modeled on Putnam's classic thought experiments in Putnam 1975, and Burge's influential extensions and refinements of these thought experiments in Burge 1979.
[8] This is Putnam's phrase, taken from Putnam 1975, p. 247.

Since in Oscar's (and our) language this sentence means that *there is water in the basement*, and his use of the word 'water' passes muster in the sense just described, we see that by uttering the sentence 'There is water in the basement' in those circumstances, Oscar expresses his belief that there is water in the basement.

Note that we have not yet said anything about Twin Earth or Twin Oscar. Our judgment that Oscar believes that there is water in the basement is just a consequence of taking at face value our ordinary practices of attributing beliefs to competent English speakers. Our understanding of the concept of belief is expressed in such ordinary judgments. By accepting these judgments we are already implicitly committed to anti-individualism.

The second step of the thought experiment, in which we *contrast* Oscar's situation with that of his twin on Twin Earth, is designed to *illuminate* central aspects of the relationship between Oscar's beliefs and his normal environment. In the second step we consider Twin-Oscar, who has virtually the same physical structure and dispositions to behavior as Oscar.[9] Twin-Oscar lives on Twin Earth, which is exactly like Earth, except that where there is water on Earth, there is twin-water, a liquid with a different molecular structure, on Twin Earth. Twin-Oscar is a competent speaker of Twin-English, the language they use on Twin Earth, and his use of his word 'water' passes muster on Twin Earth, despite his ignorance of the molecular structure of twin-water, the liquid denoted by the word 'water' in his linguistic community. Moreover, like Oscar, Twin-Oscar is disposed to submit the judgments he makes using his word 'water' to criticism and correction by more knowledgeable members of his linguistic community.

Suppose that after several days of heavy twin-rain, Twin-Oscar examines his basement, and sincerely utters the sentence 'There is water in the basement'. Since in Twin-Oscar's language this sentence means (when translated into English) that *there is twin-water in the basement*, and he is a competent user of the Twin-English word 'water', we see that by uttering the sentence 'There is water in the basement' Twin-Oscar expresses his belief that there is twin-water in the basement.[10] Just as Oscar's sincere utterances of sentences of English are taken at face value and evaluated

---

[9] Since on Twin Earth there is no water, Twin-Oscar can't be molecule-for-molecule like Oscar; that is why I say he has "virtually the same physical structure" as Oscar. This is just a distracting detail of Putnam's original thought experiment, and the difficulties it raises need not affect the point of the thought experiment, or the conclusions we draw from it.

[10] Note that twin-water is an *imaginary* liquid, or a liquid that we imagine to be real on Twin Earth, an imaginary planet. Hence it is only a fiction that we can translate the imagined content of Twin-Oscar's beliefs into English. This is in contrast to descriptions of possible worlds in which counter-parts of ours express such real contents as that *water is in a liquid state at room temperature*.

accordingly within the English-speaking community, so Twin-Oscar's sincere utterances of sentences of Twin-English are taken at face value and evaluated accordingly within the Twin-English-speaking community. This shows that Oscar and Twin-Oscar express different beliefs with their sincere utterances of 'There is water in the basement'. Since Oscar and Twin-Oscar have the same physical structure and dispositions to behavior, the differences in their beliefs reflect differences in their social and physical environments.[11]

6.3 SELF-KNOWLEDGE IN CONTEXT

Before we consider skeptical possibilities that are supposed to undermine self-knowledge, let us first identify some common misunderstandings of it, and remind ourselves of the ordinary contexts in which it is rooted. For these preliminary observations I'll presuppose that skepticism is not in question.

Ideas we typically associate with the words "know" and "content" prevent us from properly describing the familiar fact that we can know the contents of our beliefs and thoughts without special empirical investigation. One obstacle is our tendency to take certain ordinary uses of the word "know" as our paradigm for understanding what it means to say a speaker "knows the contents" of his own thoughts without empirical inquiry. Ordinarily someone says "I know that the basement is flooded," for example, only if (first) there is some question about whether the basement is flooded, (second) the person is able to give a reason for his claim, and (third) there is an investigation that, if carried out, would settle the question.[12] If we take this ordinary use of "know" as our paradigm, we will be puzzled as to how a person could be said to know the contents of his own beliefs and thoughts without empirical investigation. For the question of whether someone knows the contents of his own beliefs and thoughts does not ordinarily arise, and there is no established practice of making, challenging, and defending claims to have self-knowledge.

---

[11] One might wonder why I say that *social* factors are partly responsible for the differences in Oscar's and Twin-Oscar's beliefs. The reason is that it is the use of the word 'water' among the experts in their respective communities which partly determines that 'water' is a natural kind term, and not a term whose correct application is only a matter of satisfying certain qualitative criteria, such as feeling wet, looking clear, having no taste, etc. Thus even the meanings of natural kind terms are partly settled by social factors. This point is often missed in standard expositions of anti-individualism.

[12] These three features common to many ordinary uses of the word "know" are identified by Norman Malcolm in Malcolm 1949; see page 203 for Malcolm's list of the three features.

Another obstacle to our understanding of self-knowledge is the word 'content'. The claim that a speaker "knows the contents" of his own beliefs typically brings to mind the idea of a relation between the speaker and something *x* that is the content of his belief. Sparked by this idea, some philosophers try to construct metaphysical theories of the special cognitive relationship a speaker bears to the contents of his own thoughts. In contrast, I assume that our understanding of "content" is exhausted by our actual practices of attributing and evaluating beliefs and thoughts. We may use the sentence 'Oscar believes that there is water in the basement' to express the content of one of Oscar's beliefs, and to say how this belief is to be evaluated. We need not suppose that contents are *objects* to attribute and evaluate beliefs in this way. In my view, to say that Oscar can tell without empirical inquiry that he believes there is water in the basement is not to presuppose that there is a mysterious cognitive relationship between Oscar and something *x* that is the "content" of his belief.[13]

To avoid such misunderstandings, I propose that we clarify the phenomenon of self-knowledge by looking at those aspects of our linguistic practices that lead us to say (misleadingly) that we "know the contents" of our own beliefs and thoughts without special "empirical" investigation. As I see it, self-knowledge is an ordinary aspect of competence in the use of language. The key point is that to know the contents of the thoughts we express with our sentences is just to be able to use our sentences in discourse – to make and evaluate assertions, ask questions, describe possibilities, clear up confusions, and so on. Thus the same linguistic activities that lead us to attribute beliefs and thoughts to an individual also show that he knows the contents of those beliefs and thoughts. Oscar's use of the word 'water' to make and evaluate assertions shows that when he sincerely utters the sentence 'There's water in the basement', he knows the content of his belief that there's water in the basement without special empirical inquiry.[14]

In this sense a speaker can know the contents of his beliefs without empirical investigation, even if such investigation would be required to

---

[13] Donald Davidson (1987) notes that the sense of mystery that surrounds the topic of self-knowledge stems in part from our tendency to picture the contents of our beliefs and thoughts as "objects before the mind."

[14] This sense of self-knowledge is of a piece with a familiar sense in which speakers know the meaning of their words, described and endorsed by Putnam in the following passage:

To know the meaning of a word may mean (a) to know how to translate it, or (b) to know what it refers to, in the sense of having the ability to state explicitly what the denotation is (other than by using the word itself), or (c) to have tacit knowledge of its meaning, in the sense of being able to use the word in discourse. The only sense in which the average speaker of the language "knows the meaning" of most words is (c). (1988, p. 32)

determine whether one of his beliefs has the same content as another. Kevin Falvey and Joseph Owens highlight this aspect of our ordinary practice with the following story:

Suppose that Rudolf is acquainted with cilantro. He knows it to be an herb that figures prominently in Mexican cuisine, and he is familiar with its distinctive aroma. He says ... "cilantro should be used sparingly," thereby expressing the thought that cilantro should be used sparingly. In addition, Rudolf frequently employs dried coriander in his cooking; indeed he is as familiar with coriander as he is with cilantro. Coriander, too, he thinks, should be used sparingly, and he says so ... "coriander should be used sparingly."[15]

Falvey and Owens assume that Rudolf is competent in the use of the terms 'cilantro' and 'coriander', and so he knows without empirical investigation what beliefs he expresses when he utters the sentences "cilantro should be used sparingly" and "coriander should be used sparingly." Falvey and Owens suggest that since coriander is cilantro, Rudolf's belief that cilantro should be used sparingly and his belief that coriander should be used sparingly have the same content.[16] Rudolf does not know that cilantro is coriander, and so he does not know whether these two beliefs have the same content. But this does not undermine our ordinary judgment that Rudolf is competent in the use of the terms 'cilantro' and 'coriander', and that without special empirical inquiry he knows the contents of his beliefs that cilantro should be used sparingly and that coriander should be used sparingly.

---

[15] Falvey and Owens 1994, p. 110.

[16] Falvey and Owens (1994) speak of one thought (or belief) being the "same" as or "different" from another, as in the following passage:

Is Rudolf's thought that cilantro should be used sparingly the same as or different from his thought that coriander should be used sparingly? ... Whether Rudolf's thoughts are the same or different is determined in part by relevant features of his environment, among which is the fact that cilantro is coriander. (p. 110)

In footnote 3 they suggest that two thoughts are the "same" if they have the "same content." They summarize the point of their cilantro example as follows:

facts about the world and the language he employs are relevant in determining sameness and difference in the contents of Rudolf's propositional attitudes, facts that he can come to know only by investigation of his environment. (p. 111, footnote 3)

I accept this way of speaking only if it is qualified by a strong dose of skepticism about the clarity of the word "content." The question of whether a belief expressed using a sentence S and a belief expressed using a different sentence S' "have the same content" is not well posed until we settle on some account of what content is. In my view, a deflationary anti-individualist has almost nothing general and informative to say about what content is. One might say that S and S' "have the same content" if they are properly evaluated in the same way, but this of course depends on what is meant by "proper evaluation." To elucidate this phrase, I recommend that we describe how we evaluate *particular* assertions and beliefs.

This and similar examples have led some philosophers to think that self-knowledge is independent of *all* "empirical" beliefs.[17] But in making and evaluating assertions, raising questions, clearing up confusions, and so on, we always take for granted some background or other of empirical beliefs.[18]

So when we say that we know the contents of our own thoughts *without* empirical investigation, we do not mean that our "self-knowledge" is independent of all our empirical beliefs. We mean that we are in a position to use our words in discourse without first engaging in a special empirical investigation of the "contents" of our thoughts.

6.4 SELF-KNOWLEDGE AND METALINGUISTIC BELIEFS

Our ordinary attributions of self-knowledge do not presuppose that the attributee has any metalinguistic beliefs. Yet we are each in a position to talk about our own words, even if we have never previously done so. I can say, for example, that *when I sincerely assert the sentence 'There is water in the basement' I thereby express the thought that there is water in the basement*, and that *my word 'water' refers to water*. And once I have made these statements I may wonder whether they are true.

I can see that if these statements were not true, then my sincere utterances of the sentence 'There is water in the basement' would not express the thought that there is water in the basement. I realize that if my sincere utterances of the sentence 'There is water in the basement' don't express the thought that there is water in the basement, then I don't know the content of my thought that there is water in the basement.[19] Since I take for granted,

---

[17] Falvey and Owens claim we know the contents of our own thoughts even if we doubt all our empirical beliefs. Against this I'll argue (in Section 6.9) that if we suspend all our "empirical beliefs," we have no idea what we are talking about.

[18] Putnam (1975) emphasizes the importance of empirical beliefs to a speaker's minimal competence in the use of a term. For instance, here is a passage from Putnam's discussion of linguistic stereotypes:

Suppose our hypothetical speaker points to a snowball and asks, 'is that a tiger?'. Clearly there isn't much point in talking tigers with *him. Significant communication requires that people know something of what they are talking about.* (p. 248, my emphasis)

Given the anti-individualist's starting point, this observation is not limited to communication, but has immediate consequences for our understanding of the content of a speaker's beliefs, and his own knowledge of what he is talking about. To take a person to be a competent speaker just is to take his utterances at face value, and to take for granted that he knows what he is talking about. There is no simple rule for determining whether or not a speaker is competent in the use of a language, no informative set of necessary and sufficient conditions for competence. The best we can do is investigate and elucidate various actual and counterfactual situations in which we judge that speakers are competent in the use of a term or a language.

[19] I am deliberately playing into the hands of the skeptical challenge developed in Section 6.5, by treating the supposition that *my sincere utterances of the sentence 'There is water in the basement' don't express the*

without special empirical inquiry, that I know the content of my thought that there is water in the basement, I naturally conclude, without special empirical inquiry, that my sincere utterances of the sentence 'There is water in the basement' express the thought that there is water in the basement, and that my word 'water' refers to water.

We are each in a position to see that if we have self-knowledge, then our disquotational metalinguistic statements of the forms 'my sincere utterances of the sentence '_____' express my thought that _____' and 'my word '_____' refers to _____' are true. Once we express such metalinguistic statements about our own words, we can see that if those statements aren't true, then we don't know the contents of our beliefs and thoughts. We take for granted that we know the contents of our beliefs and thoughts without special empirical inquiry, and so we naturally conclude that the disquotational metalinguistic statements of the forms 'my sincere utterances of the sentence '_____' express my thought that _____' and 'my word '_____' refers to _____' are true.[20]

6.5 HOW TO RAISE THE SKEPTICAL CHALLENGE

The skeptic about self-knowledge claims that our confidence in this conclusion should be undermined by skeptical possibilities that follow directly from the anti-individualist's thought experiments. In these thought experiments we hold constant a person's physical structure and behavior, described non-intentionally and without reference to his environment, while we stipulate that his environment is different in certain respects. When we generalize the anti-individualist's method of constructing thought experiments, we see that for each of us, one could describe countless *subjectively equivalent worlds* in which our sensory surfaces are affected in the same way, but our environments are radically different. In each of these worlds we express our beliefs and thoughts using sentence-tokens with

---

thought that there is water in the basement as the antecedent of a conditional. This *suggests* (but doesn't require) that the supposition *may actually be true*. In Section 6.6–6.7 I shall argue that we can't really make sense of the skeptic's supposition that for all I know on the basis of my first-person experiences, I may actually be in a world in which *my sincere utterances of the sentence 'There is water in the basement' don't express the thought that there is water in the basement*.

[20] I assume that each individual is in a position to use a disquotational truth predicate to generalize for himself the reasoning of the previous paragraph, and that he can *use* and *affirm* his own sentences of the forms 'my sincere utterances of the sentence '____' express my thought that ___' and 'my word '____' refers to ___'. Those who find it distracting to use a disquotational truth predicate here should just replace the schemata with particular metalinguistic statements, such as *my sincere utterances of the sentence 'Water boils at 212 degrees Fahrenheit' express the thought that water boils at 212 degrees Fahrenheit, my word 'water' refers to water, my sincere utterances of the sentence 'Gold is a metal' express the thought that gold is a metal, my word 'gold' refers to gold*, and so on.

the same syntactic shapes. Moreover, it *appears* that in each of these worlds our "first-person experiences" would be the same.[21] It is therefore tempting to conclude that from the first-person point of view, although we know which sentences we are using, this does not tell us which of our subjectively equivalent worlds we are actually in.

But if we can't tell solely on the basis of our first-person experiences which of our subjectively equivalent worlds we are actually in, then we can't tell solely on the basis of our first-person experiences that, for example, our sincere utterances of the sentence 'There is water in the basement' express the thought that there is water in the basement. And if we can't tell solely on the basis of our first-person experiences that our sincere utterances of the sentence 'There is water in the basement' express the thought that there is water in the basement, then it seems that without special empirical inquiry we can't know the contents of the beliefs and thoughts we express with that sentence. More generally, if we can't tell solely on the basis of our first-person experiences which of our subjectively equivalent worlds we are actually in, then it seems we can't know the contents of our own beliefs and thoughts without special empirical inquiry.

The skeptic's reasoning is most gripping when it is illustrated by descriptions of particular subjectively equivalent worlds in which the contents of our beliefs and thoughts are different from what we actually take them to be. For example, consider the subjectively equivalent world in which I am born, raised, and now live on Twin Earth, where the word 'water' refers to twin-water, not water. In that world my sincere utterances of 'There is water in the basement' express the thought that there is twin-water in the basement. This is a different thought from the one I actually take myself to express with my sincere utterances of 'There is water in the basement'. Using this subjectively equivalent world to illustrate his point, the skeptic about self-knowledge reasons as follows: "If I focus on my subjective experience of using my sentence 'There is water in the basement', I am unable to tell whether or not I was born, raised, and now live on Twin Earth, and so it seems that I can't know without empirical investigation whether I am expressing the thought that there is water in the basement, or the thought that there is twin-water in the basement."

---

[21] In my view this appearance is illusory. But to present the skeptic's reasoning in the most gripping way, I shall not directly question the illusion that our first-person experiences are the same in all our subjectively equivalent worlds. My use of the phrase subjectively equivalent world does not commit me either way.

We can describe another troubling possibility that is slightly closer to home. Among my subjectively equivalent worlds is one in which I am transported without my knowledge from Earth to Twin Earth. It seems that by our ordinary standards of belief attribution, we would say that after a time (let's say five years[22]), I count as a competent member of the twin-English-speaking community. Then my sincere utterances of 'There is water in the basement' express the thought that there is twin-water in the basement. Prior to the move, my sincere utterances of this sentence expressed the thought that there is water in the basement. Yet in that subjectively equivalent world I am unaware of the move. Using this subjectively equivalent world to illustrate his point, the skeptic about self-knowledge reasons as follows: "If I focus on my subjective experience of using my sentence 'There is water in the basement', I am unable to tell whether or not I was transported five years ago to Twin Earth, and so it seems that I can't know without empirical investigation whether I am expressing the thought that there is water in the basement, or the thought that there is twin-water in the basement."

To understand this skeptical reasoning, it is crucial to see that skepticism about self-knowledge does not follow just from the observation that in some of our subjectively equivalent worlds the contents of our beliefs and thoughts are different from what we take the contents of our beliefs and thoughts to be in the actual world. It is a mistake to move directly from (a) there are subjectively equivalent worlds in which our beliefs and thoughts are different from what we take them to be in the actual world, to (b) without special empirical investigation we can't tell whether or not we are in one of these strange subjectively equivalent worlds. To move from (a) directly to (b) is in effect to slide from "my beliefs and thoughts *might have been* different from what I actually take them to be," to "my beliefs and thoughts *may be* different from what I actually take them to be." Taken by itself, this move is unjustified. And anyone who thinks that anti-individualism is compatible with self-knowledge accepts (a) but

---

[22] Paul Boghossian (1989) takes for granted that the meanings of our terms and the contents of our thoughts could change in one day. This leads to the strange consequence that we may not know what thought our sincere utterances of 'There is water in the basement' expressed *yesterday*. Boghossian rightly questions whether the possibility of such a rapid change is compatible with the assumption that we had self-knowledge yesterday, or, for that matter, that we have self-knowledge today. In my view, however, our practices of attributing meanings and thoughts show that changes in the meaning of a sentence cannot occur in just one day. It is not clear exactly how *much* time is required for such changes to occur, but we need not settle this question to evaluate the skeptical reasoning I present in this section.

not (b). To challenge this position the skeptic needs to justify his move from (a) to (b).[23]

To get from (a) to (b), one might think it is enough to assert that all knowledge of contingent truths requires special empirical investigation. We saw in Section 6.4 that if we know the contents of our beliefs and thoughts without special empirical investigation, then we may also conclude without special empirical investigation that, for example, our sincere utterances of the sentence 'There is water in the basement' express the thought that there is water in the basement, and our word 'water' refers to water. One might accept this conditional, but insist that our acceptance of such contingent truths requires empirical justification of a kind we can't provide, and infer by *modus tollens* that we *don't* know the contents of our beliefs and thoughts without special empirical investigation.[24]

This argument may *appear* promising, but in fact it just begs the question against a principled anti-individualist, who has good reason to resist the widely accepted view that our acceptance of contingent truths requires special empirical justification. The key point is that from the anti-individualist's perspective, our ordinary understanding of self-knowledge is inextricable from our actual practices of attributing beliefs and thoughts, and hence also from our ordinary discriminations between competent and incompetent uses of language. In Section 6.3 I noted that our attributions of belief and self-knowledge to an individual always presuppose that he takes for granted some background (or other) of empirical beliefs. To say that an individual knows the contents of his own thoughts without special empirical inquiry is to say he is in a position to use his words in discourse without first engaging in a special empirical investigation of the contents of his thoughts. And in Section 6.4 I argued that if an individual knows the contents of his beliefs and thoughts without special empirical investigation, then if he can construct disquotational metalinguistic sentences of the forms

---

[23] The slide from "my beliefs and thoughts *might have been* different from what I actually take them to be," to "my beliefs and thoughts *may be* different from what I actually take them to be" is an example of the kind of modal fallacy that G. E. Moore identified in his classic papers Moore 1959a and Moore 1959b. Moore observed that anyone who claims to know that p, for some contingent proposition p, will accept that p might have been false; but to say "p may actually be false" is in effect to say "I do not know that p." Hence a skeptic who argues from "p might have been false" to "p may actually be false" begs the question of whether I know that p. Even if we accept that p might have been false, that by itself gives us no reason to conclude that p may actually be false.

[24] I'll argue in Sections 6.6–6.7 that it is a confusion to think we may *not* actually have self-knowledge – that we are merely *supposing* that we do have it. At this stage in the dialectic, however, I am presenting the skeptic's reasoning *as though* it makes sense to treat the presupposition that we have self-knowledge as the antecedent of a conditional that could be used, by modus tollens, to support the conclusion that we do *not* have self-knowledge.

'my sincere utterances of the sentence '_____' express the thought that _____' and 'my word '_____' refers to _____', he can accept without special empirical investigation that those metalinguistic sentences are true.[25] Thus, for instance, without special empirical investigation he can accept that his sincere utterances of the sentence 'There is water in the basement' express the thought that there is water in the basement, and that his word 'water' refers to water. In this sense he accepts some contingent truths without special empirical investigation.[26] To raise a serious skeptical challenge to this view of self-knowledge the skeptic must show us how to move from (a) to (b) without just taking for granted that to accept a contingent truth we must have special empirical justification.

How then does the skeptic justify the move from (a) to (b)? As I understand it, the skeptic's road from (a) to (b) is paved by the natural and tempting assumptions that (i) in all of our subjectively equivalent worlds our first-person experiences would be the same, and (ii) our self-knowledge must be justified by our first-person experiences. Neither (i) nor (ii) directly begs the question against the anti-individualistic view of self-knowledge sketched in the previous paragraph. Yet (i) and (ii), together with (a), lead the skeptic to conclude that our evidence for our self-knowledge claims does not discriminate between any of our subjectively equivalent worlds.

Given (i) and (ii), the *realism* implicit in anti-individualism – the recognition that our beliefs are not guaranteed to be true, and that our physical and social environments exist independently of us – supports the skeptic's claim that *for all we know on the basis of our first-person experiences we may actually be in any one of our subjectively equivalent worlds*. If we accept this claim we are apparently forced to accept (b) – that without special empirical investigation we don't know whether or not we are in one of these strange subjectively equivalent worlds. But if we can't tell without empirical investigation which of our subjectively equivalent worlds we are in, then we can't tell without empirical investigation what beliefs and thoughts we express with sincere utterances of our sentences. In this way we feel driven to conclude that anti-individualism is incompatible with self-knowledge.

---

[25] I take for granted that each individual is in a position to use a disquotational truth predicate to generalize for himself the reasoning of the second paragraph of Section 6.4, and that he can *use* and *affirm* his own sentences of the forms 'my sincere utterances of the sentence '____' express the thought that ____' and 'my word '____' refers to ____'. See note 20.

[26] One might wonder how these sentences *could* express contingent truths, if it is reasonable to accept them without special empirical justification. In Section 6.9 I address a sophisticated version of this concern.

6.6 WHY SKEPTICISM ABOUT SELF-KNOWLEDGE IS INCOHERENT

In our attempt to answer the skeptic's challenge, we are seduced into thinking that if we can *picture* ourselves existing in any one of our subjectively equivalent worlds, then we may *actually be* in any one of our subjectively equivalent worlds. And to say that we may *actually be* in any one of our subjectively equivalent worlds is to concede that we don't know the meanings of our words or the contents of our thoughts. Yet I shall argue that if we accept anti-individualism, then to show that we may actually be in any one of our subjectively equivalent worlds, it is not enough to *picture* ourselves existing in any of our subjectively equivalent worlds. The gripping idea that we may actually be in any one of our subjectively equivalent worlds is illusory.

There are two central components to the illusion. On the one hand there is the first-person subjective view of our use of sentences, and on the other, a radically external third-person objective view of the physical and social factors that determine the meanings of our sentences and thereby also determine the contents of our beliefs and thoughts. The subjective view of our use of sentences is based in the idea that we can somehow subtract any empirical assumptions we make about our social and physical environment from our first-person experience of using our sentences. This subtraction seems natural if we take for granted that our first-person experiences are the same in all of our subjectively equivalent worlds.[27] We assume that we can describe, from a fully "objective" point of view, an array of possible situations we may be in, and note that our subjective experience would be the same in each of them. This seems to lead inevitably to the conclusion that our knowledge of our beliefs and thoughts is limited to what little we can glean from our subjective experiences of using sentences of various syntactic types.

But this subjective view of our own sentence-use makes sense only if it is contrasted with a corresponding objective view of the external factors that determine the meanings of our sentences and the contents of the beliefs and thoughts. Those who accept the skeptical reasoning sketched in the previous section think that we *can* make sense of this contrast between the subjective and the objective view of our sentences. Why do they accept this?

The idea of an objective view of our subjective situation stems from a natural but fundamental misunderstanding of the anti-individualist's

---

[27] Note again that I don't myself accept this assumption.

thought experiments. The anti-individualist thought experiments are usually presented from the third-person point of view, with the subjects of the thought experiments viewed from the outside. From this third-person point of view, we assume that *we* know what features of the subjects' social and physical environments partly determine the contents of their beliefs and thoughts. We think *we* know the contents of the subjects' beliefs and thoughts, even if *the subjects themselves* can't tell without special empirical inquiry which subjectively equivalent world they are in. This sets up the contrast between the two perspectives: the subjective point of view of the subject of the thought experiment, and the objective point of view of the person conducting the thought experiment. To apply the conclusion of the thought experiments to ourselves, *we simply imagine ourselves in the position of the subject.* We assume that the contrast between the subjective first-person point of view and the objective third-person point of view can be easily applied to our own case. So we think of our own sentence-use from the subjective point of view, and imagine that from the objective third-person point of view our sincere utterances express thoughts whose contents we can't know without empirical investigation.

The trouble is that this radical contrast between the subjective and the objective points of view does not make sense. The incoherence of the contrast is brought home when we try to reason about our own thoughts from both perspectives. Consider the following elaboration on our earlier attempt to reach a skeptical conclusion:

Among my subjectively equivalent worlds is one in which five years ago I was transported without my knowledge from Earth to Twin Earth, and I am now a competent member of the Twin-English-speaking community. In that situation my sincere utterances of 'There is water in the basement' do not express the thought that there is *water* in the basement, they express the thought that there is *twin-water* in the basement. I can't tell without empirical investigation whether or not I am in this subjectively equivalent world. So I can't tell without empirical investigation whether my sincere utterances of 'There is water in the basement' express the thought that there is *water* in the basement or the thought that there is *twin-water* in the basement.

This reasoning slips back and forth between taking a "subjective" view of my use of sentences, and using them to describe "objective" possibilities. On the one hand, I am saying that I do not know what "objective" situation I am in, and so I don't know whether my sincere utterances of 'There is water in the basement' express the thought that there is *water* in the basement or the thought that there is *twin-water* in the basement. On the other hand, if I am to *use* my sentence 'There is water in the basement' to *describe* the possible world in which my sincere utterances of 'There is water in the basement' express the thought that there is water in the basement, I must take for granted that, viewed "objectively," my sincere utterances of 'There is water in the basement' express the thought that there is water in the basement. But the attempt to shift back and forth between the "subjective" and "objective" points of view on my use of sentences is deeply confused. For if I can use my sentences to describe possibilities at all, then in effect I undermine the general conclusion that all I know of the "contents" of my thoughts must be based in my "subjective" experience of using my sentences.

The skeptic apparently fails to see that to know the contents of the thoughts we express with our sentences is just to be able to use our sentences to make and evaluate assertions, to ask questions, and to describe possibilities. We can agree with the skeptic that doubts about disquotational metalinguistic statements should undermine our confidence that we know what we are talking about. But if such doubts undermine our confidence that we know what we are talking about, the same doubts also undermine our confidence that we can use our sentences to make and evaluate assertions, to ask questions, and to describe "objective" possibilities. When we use our words to express the skeptic's reasoning we in effect undermine the general conclusion that we don't know the contents of our thoughts unless we first find out which of our subjectively equivalent worlds we are in. To use our words to express the various objective possibilities that the skeptic raises is to *show* that we know the contents of our thoughts without special empirical investigation. Hence the skeptic's attempt to shift back and forth between the subjective and objective points of view on our use of language is incoherent.

One might think that this incoherence is the result of our being trapped within our subjective first-person point of view. Someone who accepts this account of the problem will still find the objective perspective intelligible, even if he can't express it from his first-person subjective point of view. Such a person may imagine a completely objective perspective on his own situation, expressed in some idealized philosophical metalanguage the meanings of whose sentences are independent of the environment he is in. When he is reasoning about his own situation from the objective point of view, he will then imagine that he is using the sentences of this idealized metalanguage, and this will shield his reasoning from the consequences of anti-individualism.

The trouble with this response is that if we accept anti-individualism we have no idea how we *could* express the thoughts we imagine ourselves to express using the idealized metalanguage. We can't express these thoughts in language, for the whole point of the idealized metalanguage is to take up a detached objective point of view on *all* of our linguistic behavior. But since we can't actually *express* the thoughts we imagine ourselves to express using the idealized metalanguage, our *imagining* these thoughts can't save the skeptical reasoning from incoherence.

Philosophers who feel they understand the skeptical reasoning may not find this reply immediately convincing. Such philosophers may insist that our theorizing about language and content must start with a metaphysical picture of the objective external world. Within this more encompassing metaphysical framework we can then ask whether and how it is possible for our words to refer to the independently conceived entities that we suppose to exist in the external world.

If we think of anti-individualism in this way, the problem summarized four paragraphs ago looks merely pragmatic: every time we *try* to express our skeptical concern that we are in some strange world in which our words do not mean what we think they mean, we end up expressing a different thought from the one (we imagined that) we were trying to express. Confident that we can make sense of this puzzling situation, we reason as follows:

When I think that perhaps I was transported to Twin Earth, and so my utterances of 'There is water in the basement' express the thought that there is twin-water in the basement, I find that I have not properly expressed my skeptical insight. I was trying to view my use of language from a perspective independent of both situations, and to observe that if I am in the world in which I was transported to Twin Earth, my sentences would not mean what I think they mean. The trouble is that if I accept anti-individualism, I must accept that the contents of my descriptions of these possibilities are themselves settled by the world I am actually in. So every time I try to express my metaphysical doubts from a perspective independent of my actual situation, my actual physical and social environments settle which thoughts I am expressing with my sentences, and my aim is frustrated. *I know what I am trying to say, but I can't express my meaning in language.*

Our initial confidence should falter when we realize that we can't express the "objective" skeptical possibilities that we imagine. Once we see that we can't express the "objective" skeptical possibilities that we imagine, we can see that the imagined metaphysical perspective is illusory, and thus the skeptical problem of the previous section dissolves.

The incoherence of the skeptic's reasoning is like the incoherence of an Escher drawing whose seemingly sensible parts don't fit together into a sensible whole. To raise a skeptical problem about self-knowledge, it is not enough to *picture* ourselves in place of one of our twins in a subjectively equivalent world, since a picture is not a thought, and the "possibility" our skeptic has "pictured" does not amount to a coherent possibility at all.

6.7 THE MISUNDERSTANDING BEHIND SKEPTICISM ABOUT SELF-KNOWLEDGE

Someone in the grip of the skeptical reasoning might regard the argument I just presented as a *reductio ad absurdum* of anti-individualism. This attitude presupposes that the skeptical reasoning is an inevitable consequence of anti-individualism. But the skeptic's illusion that we may actually be in any one of our subjectively equivalent worlds reflects a fundamental misunderstanding of anti-individualism. Anti-individualism starts by taking at face value our ordinary judgments about what individuals believe, what they are talking about, and when they agree or disagree with one another. From this perspective we see that when a competent speaker of English sincerely utters the sentence 'There is water in the basement', she thereby expresses her belief that there is water in the basement, and when a competent speaker of Twin-English sincerely utters the sentence 'There is water in the basement', she thereby expresses her belief that there is twin-water in the basement. I have already pointed out that there is an unproblematic sense in which competent speakers in both communities "know the contents" of their beliefs and thoughts without special "empirical" inquiry: they are able to use their words in discourse. The mistake behind the skeptical reasoning is to think that we can accept the anti-individualistic belief-attributions, even if we conclude that the attributees can't use their words in discourse, and hence don't know the contents of their beliefs and thoughts without special empirical inquiry.

I have already stressed that knowing the contents of one's beliefs without special empirical inquiry is an ordinary aspect of competence in the use of language. Since Oscar typically applies the word 'water' to samples of *water*, and he is disposed to submit the judgments he makes using his word 'water' to criticism and correction by more knowledgeable members of his linguistic community, we see that he is competent in the use of the English word 'water', and that without special empirical inquiry he knows the contents of the beliefs his sincere utterances of sentences that contain the English word 'water' express. Similarly, without special empirical inquiry Twin-Oscar knows the contents of the beliefs his sincere utterances of sentences that contain the Twin-English word 'water' express. This is not to speculate about psychological processes that occur inside Oscar's and Twin-Oscar's heads, but to describe our actual practices of attributing beliefs and self-knowledge.

The skeptic about self-knowledge may reply that to attribute the belief that there is water in the basement to a competent English speaker who sincerely utters the sentence 'There is water in the basement', we need not suppose that she knows the content of this belief without special empirical investigation, but only that she *believes* that she knows the content of her belief without special empirical investigation.

This reply presupposes that a competent English speaker can *believe* that she knows the contents of her beliefs without special empirical investigation, even if in fact she does not know the contents of her beliefs without special empirical investigation. But this presupposition does not make sense either. We saw in the previous section that I know the contents of my thoughts without special empirical inquiry if I can describe the objective possibility that my sincere utterances of the sentence 'There is water in the basement' express the thought that *there is water in the basement*, and not the thought that *there is twin-water in the basement*. We saw that I can't *simultaneously* accept that I am considering these possibilities, and that I may not be considering them after all. The same kind of reasoning shows that no one *else* can consider the possibility that her sincere utterances of 'There is water in the basement' express the thought that there is water in the basement unless *she* knows the contents of the thought expressed by her sentence 'There is water in the basement'.

At this point the skeptic about self-knowledge may simply insist that the anti-individualist's attributions do *not* express the contents of a competent speaker's beliefs and thoughts. But this is not to *discover* a problematic consequence of accepting anti-individualism. Instead it amounts to a rejection of anti-individualism. In most ordinary cases we can't make sense of the anti-individualist's attributions of a belief to an individual unless we see that she knows the content of that belief without special empirical inquiry. And if we can't make sense of anti-individualism, we can't accept it either.[28]

I conclude that if we are convinced that the anti-individualist's attributions make sense, we can't *also* insist that the attributees don't know the contents of their beliefs and thoughts without special empirical inquiry.

---

[28] If we were convinced by the skeptic's reasoning, we would try to find "beliefs" and "thoughts" that capture what is common to the subject's first-person point of view in all of her subjectively equivalent worlds. We may try to characterize these "beliefs" and "thoughts" in terms of what Brian Loar (1988) calls their "realization conditions." For an interesting critical discussion of Loar's notion of "realization conditions" see Stalnaker 1990.

One needn't think anti-individualism is incompatible with self-knowledge to be interested in a distinction between "wide" and "narrow" content. One might find a use for "narrow" content in cognitive psychological explanations, for example, even if one thinks that anti-individualism is compatible with self-knowledge.

This insistence would lead us back to the incoherent contrast, sketched in Section 6.6, between our "subjective" use of sentences, and the "objective" factors that determine the contents of our beliefs and thoughts. The illusion of such a contrast is fostered by a misunderstanding of the anti-individualist's thought experiments. We can make sense of the anti-individualist's attributions of particular beliefs and thoughts to a person only if we see that she knows the contents of those beliefs and thoughts without special empirical inquiry. Thus we cannot both accept the anti-individualist's attributions of beliefs and thoughts to a subject, and deny that she knows the contents of those beliefs and thoughts without special empirical inquiry.

6.8 THE PROBLEMATIC POSSIBILITIES ARE NOT ACTUAL

We are now in a position to see that the problematic possibilities described in Section 6.5 are not actual. We can see this by reflecting on our *description* of those possibilities. Consider the following argument:

(A1) I am now using this sentence to express the thought that there is water in the basement.
(A2) If I were in the world in which I was born, raised, and now live on Twin Earth, I could not use sentence (A1) to express the thought that there is water in the basement.
(A3) Therefore, I am not in the world in which I was born, raised, and now live on Twin Earth.

As a competent speaker, without special empirical investigation I know the content of the thought I express with sincere utterances of (A1). (A2) is a consequence of our observation that when a competent speaker on Twin Earth sincerely utters the sentence 'There is water in the basement' he thereby expresses the thought that *there is twin-water in the basement*. This is not the thought that there is water in the basement, since *water is not twin-water*. Thus I can see that I am not in a world in which I was born, raised, and now live on Twin Earth.

The same kind of reasoning shows that I am not in the world in which I was transported to Twin Earth five years ago:

(B1) I am now using this sentence to express the thought that there is water in the basement.
(B2) If I were in the world in which I was transported to Twin Earth five years ago, I could not use sentence (B1) to express the thought that there is water in the basement.
(B3) Therefore I am not in the world in which I was transported to Twin Earth five years ago.

As a competent speaker, without special empirical investigation I know the content of the thought I express with sincere utterances of (B1). (B2) is a consequence of our observation that when a competent speaker on Twin Earth sincerely utters the sentence 'There is water in the basement' he thereby expresses the thought that *there is twin-water in the basement*. This is different from the thought that there is water in the basement, since *water is not twin-water*. Thus I can see that I am not in a world in which I was transported to Twin Earth five years ago.[29]

From (A1)–(A3) and (B1)–(B3) we see that there are subjectively equivalent worlds whose descriptions show they are not actual.[30] This undermines the skeptic's conclusion that for all we know without special empirical inquiry we may actually be in any one of our subjectively equivalent worlds.

---

[29] I arrived at the form for arguments (A1)–(A3) and (B1)–(B3) by reflecting on the argument Putnam uses in Chapter 1 of Putnam 1981 to show that we are not always brains in vats. In Chapter 2, I defend and explore the consequences of the following version of Putnam's argument (due in essentials to Tymoczko 1989):

(1) I can raise the question: *Am I always a brain in a vat?*

(2) If I were always a brain in a vat, I could not raise this question.

(3) Hence I am not always a brain in a vat.

This reconstruction goes beyond Putnam's own presentation in Chapter 1 of Putnam 1981, but captures the spirit of it. I now think it is better to formulate the argument as follows:

(C1) I am now using this sentence to express the thought that I am not always a brain in a vat.

(C2) If I were always a brain in a vat, I could not use (C1) to express the thought that I am not always a brain in a vat.

(C3) Hence I am not always a brain in a vat.

If we use (C1)–(C3) instead of (1)–(3), we can avoid the loophole I worry about in the Appendix to Chapter 2. I don't have the space here to defend (C1)–(C3).

[30] There is no argument analogous to (B1)–(B3) that shows that I am not in the subjectively equivalent world in which I lived on Twin Earth from birth until five years ago, when I was transported without my knowledge to Earth, where I now count as a competent speaker of English. It is instructive to see that this strange possibility does not undermine self-knowledge, and it is consistent with anti-individualism. Let us consider a few of the details. After the change, what I used to call 'Twin Earth' is Earth, and what I used to call 'Earth' is Twin Earth. By supposition, before the change I was a competent speaker of Twin-English, the language they speak on Twin Earth, and so my utterances five years ago of 'There is water in the basement' expressed the thought that there is twin-water in the basement. Now that I have settled on Earth, however, my sincere utterances of 'There is water in the basement' express the thought that there is water in the basement. Without special empirical inquiry I accept that my sincere utterances of 'There is water in the basement' express the thought that there is water in the basement even though I don't know without special empirical inquiry whether or not five years ago my utterances of 'There is water in the basement' expressed the same thought. As we saw in Section 6.3, a speaker can know the contents of his beliefs without special "empirical" inquiry, even if special investigation *would* be required for him to find out whether one of his beliefs has the same content as another. The supposition that five years ago I lived on Twin Earth does not lead to incoherence, yet I am confident that it isn't true, since I am confident that there is no Twin Earth, and that even if there were, I could not have been transported from there to Earth without my knowledge.

6.9 SELF-KNOWLEDGE, BACKGROUND EMPIRICAL BELIEFS, AND SKEPTICISM

Viewed out of context, arguments (A1)–(A3) and (B1)–(B3) can look like tawdry attempts to pull a rabbit – knowledge of empirical facts – out of an empty hat – self-knowledge. To clarify the context and dispel the air of hocus-pocus surrounding arguments (A1)–(A3) and (B1)–(B3), in this section I'll sketch and criticize a position that combines a minimal disquotational picture of self-knowledge with a rejection of arguments like (A1)–(A3) and (B1)–(B3).

One might think that self-knowledge is restricted to knowledge of disquotational metalinguistic truths, and so it does not tell us, for example, whether or not water is twin-water. Since premises (A2) and (B2) both depend on the assumption that water is not twin-water, these premises depend on substantive empirical presuppositions that go beyond self-knowledge.[31] If we accept this

---

[31] One might be tempted to think that we can simply *stipulate* that water is not twin-water. If it is *true by stipulation alone* that water is not twin-water, then it is also true by stipulation that if we were in either of the two situations described in Section 6.5, our word 'water' would not refer to water. Such a stipulation would *seem* to be independent of our ordinary background of "empirical" beliefs.

The trouble is that if we accept anti-individualism, we can't make sense of the idea that it is true by stipulation, completely independent of any empirical facts, that water is not twin-water. For even if we now take for granted that water is not twin-water, this belief is not independent of our ordinary background of empirical beliefs.

To see this, it is enough to tell a far-fetched story about how we might someday discover that water is twin-water. To tell this story we must suspend some of our deeply entrenched empirical beliefs. We take for granted for example that Twin Earth is a fictional planet, a figment of Putnam's imagination. But suppose that (here we lapse into fiction)

Long ago, before Putnam wrote "The Meaning of 'Meaning'," he discovered a planet that looks exactly like Earth. He dubbed this planet 'Twin Earth', and conjectured that wherever there is water on Earth, there is a different liquid, which he called 'twin-water', on Twin Earth. His discovery got him thinking about the relationship between linguistic meaning and our social and physical environments, and this led him to develop the Twin-Earth thought experiments he presents in "The Meaning of 'Meaning'." He never told anyone (except some of his closest friends, who have kept it secret) that Twin Earth exists, since he was not sure that there is no water on Twin Earth, and this supposition is important to his thought experiments. He decided to keep his discovery of Twin Earth secret, and to ask readers to *suppose* that Twin Earth exists, and that on Twin Earth there is no water, only twin-water.

To understand this story we must suspend some of our ordinary empirical beliefs. What makes the story unbelievable is precisely that it conflicts with some of our most deeply entrenched background empirical beliefs. Yet if we are willing to suspend many of these empirical beliefs, we can "understand" the remote possibility that someday we will discover that water is twin-water. Thus suppose for example that (here we again lapse into fiction)

Sometime early in the next century Putnam makes his discovery of Twin Earth public. Astronomers study planet Twin Earth, and tentatively confirm Putnam's initial conjecture that the lakes, streams, and oceans of Twin Earth are filled with twin-water, and there is no water at all on Twin Earth. Philosophers are surprised to find that the planet they called Twin Earth really exists, but they soon adjust to this situation, and continue their exploration of our ordinary practices of belief ascription

restricted disquotational picture of self-knowledge, then it will seem that, contrary to my claim at the end of the previous section, there are no subjectively equivalent worlds whose descriptions alone show us that they are not actual. To establish that a particular subjectively equivalent world is not actual, empirical investigation is always required.[32]

In my view, this objection to arguments (A1)–(A3) and (B1)–(B3) reflects a confusion about the relationship between self-knowledge and background empirical beliefs. If we accept anti-individualism, it is a confusion to think that we can suspend all our empirical beliefs, and still know what we are talking about well enough to understand why the problematic possibilities sketched in Section 6.5, and disarmed by arguments (A1)–(A3) and (B1)–(B3), are supposed to be skeptical. It should go without saying that *to characterize a possibility as skeptical we must have some idea of what that possibility is*. Nevertheless, I shall argue, the restricted disquotational picture of self-knowledge reflects a failure to see the consequences of this truism.

According to the restricted disquotational picture of self-knowledge (i) I know without special empirical inquiry that such disquotational sentences as 'My sincere utterances of the sentence 'There is water in the basement' express the thought that there is water in the basement' and 'My word 'water' refers to water' are true, but (ii) my knowledge that these disquotational metalinguistic sentences are true can't *by itself* yield

---

using variations on Putnam's original Twin Earth thought experiments. They accept that their word 'twin-water' refers to a real liquid, the stuff that fills the lakes, streams, and oceans of Twin Earth. Finally, after several centuries astronauts from Earth make a trip to Twin Earth and discover that twin-water is really water after all, undermining our initial "stipulation," made several centuries earlier, that water is *not* twin-water.

This story shows that it is not true *by stipulation alone* that water is not twin-water. When we assume that water is not twin-water, we are tacitly supposing that Twin Earth is a figment of Putnam's imagination, and so the story I just told is pure fiction. The story is so far-fetched that in ordinary contexts our stipulation that water is not twin-water seems independent of any empirical assumptions. Nevertheless, the story shows that we do not know *by stipulation alone*, independent of all empirical assumptions, that twin-water is not water. A similar story can be constructed to show that we do not know by stipulation alone, independent of all empirical assumptions, that Twin Earth is not Earth. These stories should be taken in the same spirit as Putnam's fantasy (1962) of discovering that our term "bachelor" is a "law-cluster" term, even though we are sure it's a "one-criterion" term.

[32] The position I shall sketch is similar to the position defended by Falvey and Owens 1994. They present what amounts to a version of what I call the restricted disquotational picture of self-knowledge, claim that this picture of self-knowledge is compatible with anti-individualism, and argue that when we are evaluating skeptical arguments, we can't take any of our empirical beliefs for granted. Here is a characteristic passage:

I know the propositions expressed by all the T-sentences of a homophonic truth theory for English. It is partly in virtue of the fact that I possess this knowledge that it is correct to characterize me as a speaker of English. But what I may not know, and what I may for the purposes of the [skeptical] argument under discussion assume that I do not know, are the propositions expressed by the T-sentences of any *non*homophonic truth theory for English. (p. 127)

knowledge of any empirical or contingent facts. Someone in the grip of this picture of self-knowledge will reason as follows:

Since I know without empirical inquiry that these metalinguistic sentences are true, by the simple disquotational property of the predicate 'is true', I can infer that I know without empirical inquiry that *my sincere utterances of the sentence 'There is water in the basement' express the thought that there is water in the basement*, and that *my word 'water' refers to water*. Since this knowledge is available *without* any empirical inquiry, it can't amount to knowledge of empirical or contingent facts.

We can sum up this reasoning as follows: *self-knowledge is restricted to knowledge of disquotational metalinguistic truths, and so by itself it can't yield knowledge of empirical facts.*

Someone who accepts this restricted disquotational picture of self-knowledge can grant that in ordinary contexts where skeptical hypotheses are not in question, it is harmless to rely on commonsense empirical beliefs. He can even agree that relative to our commonsense background of empirical beliefs, our knowledge of disquotational metalinguistic truths *seems* to yield knowledge of substantive empirical facts. But he will insist that this is an illusion created by a failure to distinguish self-knowledge, which is empirically empty, from our commonsense "empirical" beliefs.

If we accept this picture of the relationship between self-knowledge and knowledge of empirical facts, we will think that (A1)–(A3) and (B1)–(B3) beg the question against the skeptical possibilities that they allegedly undermine. We will think that at best our self-knowledge yields empirically empty versions of (A1) and (B1), and so we will see no reason to accept premises (A2) and (B2), which both depend on the assumption that water is not twin-water. We will reason as follows:

Whether or not we are actually in either of the situations described, we have the purely disquotational, empirically empty knowledge that our word 'water' refers to water. But this does not tell us what water is. In particular, it does not tell us whether or not water is twin-water. If we take for granted that water is not twin-water, then we in effect simply beg the question of whether our word 'water' refers to twin-water. In the context of the skeptical hypotheses raised in Section 6.5, we are not entitled to assume that water is not twin-water.

We can sum up this skeptical reasoning as follows. *Self-knowledge is knowledge of purely disquotational metalinguistic truths, and so it does not tell us whether or not water is twin-water. This shows that premises (A2) and (B2) depend on substantive empirical presuppositions that go beyond self-knowledge.*

The basic problem with this conclusion is that it presupposes that self-knowledge is independent of all our background empirical beliefs. Those in the grip of the disquotational picture of self-knowledge do not realize that to suspend all our "empirical" beliefs is to undercut any skeptical force to the "possibility" that we are actually on Twin Earth, and that our word 'water' refers to twin-water. For if we suspend all "empirical" beliefs about Twin Earth and twin-water, we literally have no idea what we are talking about, and so we have no reasons for thinking that the "possibility" that we are on Twin Earth raises a *skeptical* threat to our ordinary beliefs. To put it paradoxically, the restricted disquotational picture of self-knowledge leads to the self-defeating conclusion that *to raise and evaluate skeptical hypotheses, we must assume that we do not know what we are talking about.*

To see this, suppose that we are confronted by a skeptic who accepts the restricted disquotational picture of self-knowledge, and challenges us to justify our belief that we are not in a subjectively equivalent world in which our word 'Earth' refers to Twin Earth, and our word 'water' refers to twin-water. Such a person might try to create the impression that this is a *skeptical* possibility by arguing as follows:

Without any question-begging empirical assumptions, you can't rule out the possibility that you are now on Twin Earth, and you have been there long enough to count as a competent speaker of Twin-English. So without empirical investigation you can't know whether or not your word 'water' refers to twin-water.

This rhetoric directs our attention *away* from the question of why the "possibility" is supposed to be *skeptical*. When listening to this challenge, we take for granted our ordinary empirical beliefs that Earth is not Twin Earth and water is not twin-water, so we feel we understand the skeptic's possibility, and feel obliged to say why it is not actual. But when we try to say why the possibility is not actual, we are told we can't assume that Earth is not Twin Earth and water is not twin-water, for that would be "question-begging." Thus at first we feel we understand the skeptic's possibility, but have no resources to rule it out. To succumb to this feeling is to be bamboozled by the skeptic's rhetoric.

A closer look reveals that the skeptic's "possibility" is not *skeptical* at all. The reason is that *to characterize a possibility as "skeptical" we must have some idea of what that possibility is.* Unless we have some idea of what Twin Earth and twin-water are, we have no idea what possibility the skeptic is trying to raise, and so we have no reason for thinking that it is a *skeptical* possibility. If we do as the skeptic requires, and suspend all our background empirical beliefs, we simply have no idea what he is talking about. But if we understand what possibility he is raising well enough to see that it conflicts with our ordinary "empirical" beliefs, then, using arguments like (A1)–(A3) and

(B1)–(B3), we can see that it is not actual.[33] So here's how we should answer
the skeptic:

What are you suggesting?[34] What do you mean by 'Twin Earth' and 'twin-water'? If
Twin Earth is Earth and twin-water is water, then what you are suggesting is not
skeptical at all. But if Twin Earth is not Earth and twin-water is not water, then
I see from your description that the supposedly skeptical possibility is not actual,
since to understand it, I must take for granted that my word 'Earth' refers to Earth
and my word 'water' refers to water. Either way the possibility you are raising is not
a genuine threat to my ordinary beliefs.

At first we felt we *understood* the skeptic's possibility, but had no resources
to rule it out. Now we can see that this feeling was confused. Either we
understand the skeptic's "possibility" well enough to see that it challenges
our ordinary beliefs, in which case we can use arguments like (A1)–(A3) and
(B1)–(B3) to show that it is not actual, or we don't know what the skeptic is
talking about, and so we have no reason to think that his possibility is in
conflict with our "empirical" beliefs.

In this case, the confused feeling that we *understood* the skeptic's possibility
but had no resources to rule it out can be traced to the restricted disquotational
picture of self-knowledge. If we accept this picture, we will assume that we can
know the contents of our beliefs and thoughts even if we suspend all our
empirical beliefs. This assumption fosters the illusion that we can understand
the skeptic's possibility even if we suspend all our empirical beliefs.

---

[33] I do not mean to suggest that we can disarm all skeptical challenges in this way. I am concerned here
with the kinds of possibilities raised in Section 6.5, and disarmed by (A1)–(A3) and (B1)–(B3). Not all
problematic possibilities can be dissolved in this way.

[34] I am alluding here to J. L. Austin's use (1979) of this sentence to make a different (but related) point.
After describing our ordinary procedures for making and evaluating a person's claim to know that
there is a goldfinch in the garden, Austin notes that a traditional skeptic will not be convinced that we
have ruled out all doubts about this claim. Austin argues that the apparently meaningful skeptical
question "Is it a real goldfinch?" does not in fact raise any genuine doubt at all:

The doubt or question "But is it a *real* one?" has always (must have) a special basis, there must be some
"reason for suggesting" that it isn't real, in the sense of some specific way, or limited number of specific
ways, in which it is suggested that this experience or item may be phoney. Sometimes (usually) the context
makes it clear what the suggestion is: the goldfinch might be stuffed but there's no suggestion that it's a
mirage, the oasis might be a mirage but there's no suggestion that it might be stuffed. If the context
doesn't make it clear, then I am entitled to ask "How do you mean? Do you mean it may be stuffed or
what? *What are you suggesting?*" The wile of the metaphysician consists in asking "Is it a real table?" (a kind
of object which has no obvious way of being phoney) and not specifying or limiting what may be wrong
with it, so that I feel at a loss "how to prove" it is a real one. (p. 87)

The question *What are you suggesting?* is especially pressing in the context of an anti-individualistic
approach to belief and thought. We must have some idea of what we are talking about just to see
whether or not a given possibility is in conflict with some of our empirical beliefs. But once we take for
granted empirical beliefs that give content to such possibilities, in many (though not all) cases it is
obvious that they are not actual.

But self-knowledge is not independent of empirical beliefs. I noted in Section 6.3 and Section 6.7 that self-knowledge is an aspect of competence in the use of language. If a speaker has no idea what he is talking about, and suspends all judgments expressed using a term, then he is incompetent in the use of language. He may doubt some (perhaps even most) of his empirical beliefs, but he must rely on other empirical beliefs to give sense to his doubts. To be competent in the use of the word 'water', for example, a speaker must have some background (or other) of empirical beliefs about water, even if he is always revising these beliefs, and most of them are false. If the speaker suspends all his empirical beliefs, in the interests of not begging the question against skepticism, then he has no idea *what* he is talking about, and so we can no longer credit him with any beliefs expressed using the term 'water'.

Once we see that self-knowledge always presupposes some background or other[35] of empirical beliefs, we can see that arguments (A1)–(A3) and (B1)–(B3) do not beg the question against the possibilities that we were born and raised on Twin Earth, or that we were transported there five years ago. For we must take some beliefs for granted if we are to have *any idea* of what these possibilities are. These background beliefs may be revised and criticized almost without limit. But given the way we ordinarily understand the skeptical possibilities that we were born and raised on Twin Earth, or that we were transported there five years ago, we can see that they are not actual. This conclusion rests on empirical assumptions without which those possibilities would not even *appear* to conflict with our ordinary beliefs.

6.10 DOES ANTI-INDIVIDUALISM BEG THE QUESTION AGAINST SKEPTICISM?

One might think that anti-individualism *by itself* begs the question against skepticism, by assuming that we can't know what we think unless we

---

[35] Anthony Brueckner (1994a) considers (what in effect amounts to) the *superficially* similar claim that *there is some background of empirical beliefs (some "pieces of knowledge") which every competent speaker has*. He rightly rejects this claim on the grounds that we can't "isolate those pieces of knowledge which are required in order to understand [our words]" (p. 343, fn. 19). What Brueckner apparently overlooks is that our actual evaluations of competence show that *every competent speaker has some background (or other) of empirical beliefs*. This observation undermines the purely formal conception of self-knowledge without presupposing that we can "isolate those pieces of knowledge which are required in order to understand [our words]," and so it is not vulnerable to Brueckner's objection. Brueckner seems to have missed the importance of the quantifier shift, from *there is some background of empirical beliefs which every competent speaker has*, to *every competent speaker has some background (or other) of empirical beliefs*.

presuppose a background of empirical beliefs. For this feature of anti-individualism undercuts the general skeptical possibility that we may actually be in any one of our subjectively equivalent worlds. In particular, as we have seen, it undercuts the idea that for all we know without special empirical investigation, we may actually be on Twin Earth, and our word 'water' may actually refer to twin-water. If we presuppose that we know enough to see that if we were in that situation, our beliefs would be different from what they actually are, we can also see that we are not in that situation. In the face of these anti-skeptical consequences, the traditional skeptic will charge that *from the start* anti-individualism begs the question against the skeptical possibility that we were born, raised, and now live on Twin Earth, and, more generally, against the skeptical intuition that for all we know without special empirical investigation, we may actually be in any one of our subjectively equivalent worlds.[36]

Before we face this objection directly, it is important to see that even if we accept anti-individualism and presuppose a background of empirical beliefs sufficient for competence and self-knowledge, there remain some far-fetched skeptical hypotheses that we can express and understand even if they are actually true. For example, I may have been transported without my knowledge to Twin Earth, where there is no water. Before I am there long enough to count as a competent speaker of Twin-English, I will naturally think that the liquid I see in the lakes, streams, and oceans is *water*, and so many of my beliefs will be false. It is easy to cook up other far-fetched possibilities of the same kind.[37]

---

[36] Michael Williams (1988) argues in this way. First he sketches the skeptic's problematic:

> The skeptic insists on assessing all our knowledge, or all our knowledge of the world, all at once. This means that the skeptical problem is necessarily addressed from a first-person perspective, since *nothing to do with the world or whatever other people there may be in it can be taken for granted.* (p. 187)

Williams argues that anti-individualism begs the question against skepticism, because anti-individualism depends on assumptions about how things are independent of our subjective first-person perspective:

> [Anti-individualism] ... turns out to involve the idea of unproblematic access to certain causal relations between speakers and objects in the world. If, in the context of the skeptic's question, we grant ourselves this access, the game is over before it begins. (p. 188)

In this passage, Williams is criticizing Donald Davidson's anti-individualistic position in particular, but if his criticism is legitimate, it also applies to Putnam's and Burge's anti-individualism. Thus Williams concludes that anti-individualism begs the question against the skeptic's assumption that for all we know without empirical investigation we are in any one of our subjectively equivalent worlds. In a sense I agree with Williams that if we accept anti-individualism, the skeptical game is over before it begins. But this is because anti-individualism undermines the skeptic's intuitions about what may actually be true, and *not* because anti-individualism begs a coherent skeptical question.

[37] For example, perhaps last night my brain was removed and placed in a vat so that it now receives the same stimulations that it would have received had it not been put into the vat. If so, I have not yet been in the vat long enough to change the contents of my beliefs – I am not yet a "competent" speaker

But of course this won't convince the traditional skeptic that anti-individualism does not beg the question against him. For the possibility that I was born, raised, and now live on Twin Earth looks just as coherent to a traditional skeptic as the possibility that last night I was transported without my knowledge to Twin Earth. And I have argued that if we accept anti-individualism, our very *description* of the "possibility" that we are now and always were on Twin Earth *shows* that this "possibility" is not actual. This seems to beg the question against the traditional skeptic, who assumes that it makes sense to suppose that we are in that situation.

The traditional skeptic supposes from the start that for all we know without special empirical investigation, we may actually be in any one of our subjectively equivalent worlds. Even if we find this supposition compelling, we should be willing to grant that the skeptic's intuitions about what is possible *may* be confused. The skeptic himself will probably refuse to grant that his intuitions may be confused. But if we are to take his challenges seriously, we must be convinced that his intuitions make sense.

The question then arises of how we are to *evaluate* the skeptic's claim that for all we know without special empirical investigation, we may actually be in any one of our subjectively equivalent worlds. In this chapter I have evaluated the skeptic's claim by highlighting aspects of our ordinary practices of attributing and evaluating beliefs and thoughts. Anti-individualists take for granted that our best understanding of belief and thought is expressed in our actual practices of attributing beliefs and thoughts to individuals. They start by taking at face value our actual practices of attributing beliefs and thoughts, and use thought experiments to elucidate aspects of these ordinary practices. The thought experiments show that the proper evaluation of our beliefs and thoughts is settled in part by features of our social and physical environments. I have argued that the same basic approach should be applied to our understanding of self-knowledge. Just as our understanding of belief and thought is expressed in our actual practices of attributing beliefs and thoughts to individuals, so our understanding of self-knowledge is expressed in our actual assessments of whether an

---

of vat-English. Even taking into account all we have said about anti-individualism, it is not immediately incoherent to suppose that I am now a brain in vat. Even though I am confident that I am not actually a brain in a vat, I don't have to suspend *all* my empirical beliefs to think coherently that I may actually be a brain in a vat.

The line between coherent and incoherent possibilities is not clear, however. For example, the supposition that I am actually a brain in a vat would corrode my confidence in my background of empirical beliefs, and ultimately undermine my confidence that I can use my words to make statements and evaluate assertions at all. Thus what appears to be a coherent possibility, given all we have said about anti-individualism, may not be coherent after all.

individual is competent in the use of language. Self-knowledge is an aspect of competence in the use of language: to know the contents of the thoughts we express with our sentences is just to be able to use our sentences to make and evaluate assertions, to ask questions, to describe possibilities, and so on. When we say that a speaker knows the contents of his beliefs without special empirical investigation, we mean that he is in a position to use his words in discourse without first engaging in a special empirical investigation of the "contents" of his thoughts. If a speaker suspends all his background empirical beliefs, then he is incompetent in the use of language. To doubt some of his empirical beliefs he must presuppose others. This shows that unless we presuppose a background of empirical beliefs we can't even *raise* a skeptical challenge to our ordinary beliefs. The inextricability of background empirical beliefs and self-knowledge undermines the traditional skeptic's assumption that for all we know without special empirical investigation, we may actually be in any of our subjectively equivalent worlds.

Faced with this criticism, the skeptic will be inclined to reassert his "intuition" that for all we know without special "empirical" investigation, we may actually be in any one of our subjectively equivalent worlds. He will be inclined to repeat his argument that our first-person experiences would be the same in all these worlds, and that our claims to have self-knowledge must be based solely on these experiences. His reasoning is gripping because we can *picture* ourselves existing in any of our subjectively equivalent worlds. But I have tried to show that such flights of fancy do not give sense to the skeptic's claim that for all we know without special empirical investigation, we may actually be in any one of our subjectively equivalent worlds. I have argued that anti-individualistic elucidations of belief and self-knowledge undermine the skeptic's intuition that for all we know without special empirical investigation, we may actually be in any one of our subjectively equivalent worlds. In this context it is idle to assert that anti-individualism begs the question against the skeptic's intuitions about what is possible.

CHAPTER 7

Is skepticism about self-knowledge incoherent?

Anthony Brueckner

Anti-individualism appears to preclude the possibility of direct, unproblematic knowledge of the contents of one's own intentional mental states. Gary Ebbs argues that such skepticism about the compatibility of anti-individualism and self-knowledge is incoherent (see Chapter 6, Section 6.6, entitled "Why skepticism about self-knowledge is incoherent"). I think that his argument is unsuccessful.

Here is Ebbs's presentation of the self-knowledge skeptic's reasoning:

> Among my subjectively equivalent worlds [worlds in which my sensory surfaces are affected in just the same way they actually are and in which my experiences are as they actually are] is one in which five years ago I was transported without my knowledge from Earth to Twin Earth, and I am now a competent member of the twin-English-speaking community. In that situation my sincere utterances of 'There is water in the basement' do not express the thought that there is *water* in the basement, they express the thought that there is *twin-water* in the basement. I can't tell without empirical investigation whether or not I am in this subjectively equivalent world. So I can't tell without empirical investigation whether my sincere utterances of 'There is water in the basement' express the thought that there is *water* in the basement or the thought that there is *twin-water* in the basement.[1] (Chapter 6, p. 133)

Here is how Ebbs argues that this skeptical reasoning is incoherent:

> This reasoning slips back and forth between taking a "subjective" view of my use of sentences, and using them to describe "objective" possibilities. On the one hand, I am saying that I do not know what "objective" situation I am in, and so I don't know whether my sincere utterances of 'There is water in the basement' express the thought that there is *water* in the basement or the thought that there is *twin-water* in the basement. On the other hand, if I am to *use* my sentence 'There is water in the basement' to *describe* the possible world in which my sincere utterances of 'There is water in the basement' express the thought that there is water in the basement, I must

---

[1] I discuss the reasoning behind skepticism about self-knowledge in the Chapter 1 (this volume) following: Brueckner, 1990, 1992a, 1994a, and Chapter 5 (this volume).

take for granted that, viewed "objectively," my sincere utterances of 'There is water in the basement' express the thought that there is water in the basement. But the attempt to shift back and forth between the "subjective" and "objective" points of view on my use of sentences is deeply confused. For if I can use my sentences to describe possibilities at all, then I in effect undermine the general conclusion that all I know of the "contents" of my thoughts must be based on my "subjective" experiences of using my sentences [experiences that do not enable me to discriminate between *water*-thoughts and *twin-water* thoughts]. (pp. 133–134)

Here is another passage in which Ebbs expresses his objection to the self-knowledge skeptic's reasoning:

When we use our words to express the skeptic's reasoning we in effect undermine the general conclusion that we don't know the contents of our thoughts unless we first find out which of our subjectively equivalent worlds we are in. To use our words to express the various objective possibilities that the skeptic raises is to *show* that we know the contents of our thoughts without special empirical investigation. (p. 134)

I think that Ebbs may have misstated the objection he has in mind. Suppose that I run through the skeptical reasoning sketched by Ebbs. Suppose that in doing so, I use the following sentences about possibilities:

(1) In a possible world in which I am a denizen of water-filled Earth, my sincere utterances of 'There is water in the basement' express the thought that there is water in the basement.
(2) In a possible world in which I am a denizen of twin-water-filled Twin Earth, my sincere utterances of 'There is water in the basement' express the thought that there is twin-water in the basement.

Suppose that I claim, at the end of the Ebbs-style skeptical reasoning, that given the absence of any special empirical investigation on my part, I do not know the contents of the thoughts and beliefs I express when I use the term 'water'. According to Ebbs's objection to the skeptic, it would then follow that (in the absence of special, empirical investigation) I cannot use my words "to express the various objective possibilities that the skeptic raises" (p. 134). In particular, it would follow, according to Ebbs, that (in the absence of any special, empirical investigation) I cannot "*use* my sentence 'There is water in the basement' to *describe* the possible world in which my sincere utterances of 'There is water in the basement' express the thought that there is water in the basement" (pp. 133–134).

  These things do not follow. If I am now on Earth, then my uses of the words 'possible world in which my sincere utterances of 'There is water in the basement' express the thought that there is water in the basement' *do* describe a possible world in which my sincere utterances of 'There is water in the basement' express the thought that there is water in the basement. Even if I am on Twin Earth, it is still true that I can use my sentences to describe various possibilities involving shifting thought content. If I am on Twin Earth, then my uses of (1) describe a possible world in which I am a denizen of twin-water-filled Twin Earth and in which my sincere utterances of 'There is water in the basement' express the thought that there is twin-water in the basement; and if I am on Twin Earth, then my uses of (2) describe a possible world in which my sincere utterances of 'There is water in the basement' do *not* express the thought that there is twin-water in the basement. This is because if I am on Twin Earth, then my uses of (2) describe a possible world in which I am *not* on Twin Earth and in which my sincere utterances of 'There is water in the basement' express a different content from that expressed by my Twin-Earthian utterances of the sentence.[2] Thus, if I am on Twin Earth, then my uses of (1) and (2) successfully describe two subjectively equivalent objective possibilities in which my thought contents differ.

The point that Ebbs may have had in mind does not concern my alleged inability to describe, or express, various possibilities. As I would like to reconstruct Ebbs's objection, the difficulty he has in mind is that if I accept the skeptic's conclusion (and undertake no special empirical investigation), then I cannot claim to *know* which possibilities are described, or expressed, by my uses of (1) and (2). This is because under the foregoing assumptions, I cannot claim to know the content of any thought expressed by any sentence in which I use the term 'water' (and similarly for 'twin-water'). Thus I cannot claim to know which thoughts are expressed by my sincere utterances of (1) and (2). My utterances of (1) may express a thought about a possible world in which I have a *water-* thought, or the utterances may instead express a thought about a possible world in which I have a *twin-water*-thought. (Similar remarks apply to my utterances of (2).) Thus, if I accept the skeptic's conclusion (and undertake no special empirical investigation), then I cannot claim to know which thoughts about possibility are expressed in the course of my reasoning for this conclusion.

---

[2] This can be seen by noting the following points. Just as an Earthian's uses of 'Twin Earth' refer to a (part of a) possible world other than his own world, a Twin Earthian's uses of 'Twin Earth' refer to a (part of a) possible world other than *his* own. Similar points hold for 'twin-water'. Just as an Earthian's uses of that term refer to a possible liquid distinct from his home liquid (H_2O), a Twin Earthian's uses of 'twin-water' refer to a possible liquid distinct from *his* home liquid (XYZ). For a discussion of some difficulties for self-knowledge skepticism arising from these assumptions, see Chapter 5, this volume.

Let us suppose that this is the gist of Ebbs's objection to the skeptical reasoning. Should this give the skeptic cause for worry? I do not see why it should. The skeptic can reply as follows.

Suppose anti-individualism is true. Then of course I do not, in the absence of special empirical investigation, know the content of the thought I express by sincerely uttering (1), since I do not know the content of any thought I express using the term 'water'. But so what? This lack of knowledge does not affect my claim to have presented a sound argument for skepticism about self-knowledge.

The skeptic continues,

On Ebbs's suggestion, we are focusing upon my uses of (1) and (2) in setting up my argument. Even though I do not know which thoughts are expressed by my sincere utterances of those sentences, I *do* know that the thoughts, whatever they are, are thinkings of *true* propositions (given anti-individualism). Consider (1). If I am on Earth, then my sincere utterances of (1) express a *true* thought concerning the nature of my thought contents in a water-filled possible world. If I am on Twin Earth, then my sincere utterances of (1) instead express a different but again *true* thought concerning the nature of my thought contents in a twin-water-filled possible world. Either way, my sincere utterances of (1) express a *true* thought about possibility. Now consider (2). If I am on Earth, then my sincere utterances of (2) express a *true* thought concerning the nature of my thought contents in a twin-water-filled possible world. If I am on Twin Earth, then my sincere utterances of (2) express a *true* thought concerning the nature of my thought contents in a possible world filled with some liquid other than twin-water, a thought to the effect that the contents in question concern some liquid other than twin-water. Either way, my sincere utterances of (2) express a *true* thought about possibility. Therefore, the Ebbs-style considerations do not threaten my claim to have a sound argument for skepticism about self-knowledge. My position has not been shown to be incoherent.

CHAPTER 8

Is skepticism about self-knowledge coherent?

Gary Ebbs

Anti-individualism starts with the observation that speakers of the same natural language typically take each other's words at face value. For example, suppose Oscar is a competent English speaker who has a minimal mastery of the term 'water', but does not know that water is H_2O. If Oscar sincerely utters the sentence 'There is water in the basement' in appropriate circumstances, other English speakers will take Oscar's words at face value – they will take him to have expressed the thought that there is water in the basement. The anti-individualist's thought experiments clarify our understanding of such ordinary thoughts by contrasting them with thoughts attributed to similar individuals who live in different linguistic communities and external environments. For example, an anti-individualist may invite us to consider Twin-Oscar, who has virtually the same physical structure and dispositions to behavior as Oscar, but who lives on Twin Earth, which is similar to Earth except that wherever there is water on Earth, there is twin-water, a liquid with a different molecular structure, on Twin Earth. If we suppose that Twin-Oscar is a competent speaker of Twin-English, the language they use on Twin Earth, even though he does not know the molecular structure of the stuff to which he applies his word 'water', then when Twin-Oscar sincerely utters his sentence 'There is water in the basement' in appropriate circumstances, other Twin-English speakers will take Twin-Oscar's words at face value – they will take him to have expressed the thought that (as we would say it) there is twin-water in the basement. Anti-individualists conclude from such contrasting pairs of thought attributions that an individual's thoughts are not settled solely by his physical structure and dispositions to behavior, described independently of his relationship to his social and physical environments. (For a more

153

thorough and accurate presentation of these points, see Putnam 1975; Burge 1979; Ebbs 1997, Chapters 7 and 8.)

It is natural to generalize from particular thought experiments constructed in this standard way. To begin with, it seems that for each of us, one could describe any number of *subjectively equivalent worlds* in which we (or our twins, as I will call our counterparts in such worlds) receive the same sensory stimulation that we receive in the actual world, but our (or our twins') environments are different from what we take our environment to be in the actual world. If we take this for granted, the crucial generalization can then be stated as follows:

(i) For each of us, there are subjectively equivalent worlds in which our (or our twins') sincere utterances express thoughts that are different from the thoughts that we take our sincere utterances to express in the actual world.

One might think that for all we know without special empirical investigation, we may actually be in any one of our subjectively equivalent worlds, and so (i) leads to skepticism about self-knowledge – the familiar fact that without going through any special empirical investigation, competent speakers know (in some sense yet to be clarified) what thoughts their utterances express. But, as I argue in Chapter 6, Section 6.5, to raise a skeptical challenge to our ordinary assumption that we know without special empirical investigation what thoughts our own utterances express, it is not enough simply to *assert* that for all we know without special empirical investigation, we may actually be in any one of our subjectively equivalent worlds. This assertion simply begs the question against our ordinary assumption that we know without special empirical investigation what thoughts our own utterances express. Hence to raise a serious skeptical challenge, plausible premises must be introduced that are not themselves question-begging, but which, together with (i), imply that we can't know what thoughts our own utterances express without undertaking an empirical investigation.

As I reconstruct the skeptic's reasoning, it rests on two additional premises:

(ii) In all our subjectively equivalent worlds our "first-person experiences" would be the same.

and

(iii) Without empirical investigation, our knowledge of our own thoughts is confined to what we can derive solely from our "first-person experiences."

(Note that in (ii) and (iii) the phrase "first-person experiences" should be understood in such a way that it denotes the greatest common part of our experiences in all our subjectively equivalent worlds. I put quotation marks around the phrase to signal my doubts about this interpretation of it, but my main criticism of the argument (i)–(iii) does not directly depend on these doubts.) From (i)–(iii) the skeptic concludes that without empirical investigation, we cannot know what thoughts our own utterances express.

I find this reasoning initially plausible, but ultimately incoherent. The basic problem, as I will explain below, is that to convince ourselves of premise (i), we must take for granted that we know what thoughts our own utterances express without going through any special empirical investigation, and this requires that we give up premise (iii).

To bring out this incoherence, in Chapter 6 I focus on a particular illustration of the skeptic's argument, as follows:

> Among my subjectively equivalent worlds is one in which five years ago I was transported without my knowledge from Earth to Twin Earth, and I am now a competent member of the twin-English-speaking community. In that situation my sincere utterances of 'There is water in the basement' do not express the thought that there is *water* in the basement, they express the thought that there is *twin-water* in the basement. I can't tell without empirical investigation whether or not I am in this subjectively equivalent world. So I can't tell without empirical investigation whether my sincere utterances of 'There is water in the basement' express the thought that there is *water* in the basement or the thought that there is *twin-water* in the basement. (Chapter 6, p. 133, quoted in Chapter 7, p. 149)

It is important to see that this reasoning *illustrates* the more general reasoning summarized by premises (i)–(iii) above, but does not constitute an independent argument for skepticism about the compatibility of self-knowledge with anti-individualism. As I noted above, it is not enough simply to *assert* that for all I know without special empirical investigation, five years ago I was transported without my knowledge from Earth to Twin Earth, and I am now a competent member of the Twin-English-speaking community. Hence the plausibility of the reasoning just sketched depends on further premises, such as (ii) and (iii).

In Chapter 6, I argue that even though the reasoning illustrated in the passage just quoted *seems* initially plausible, it is ultimately incoherent:

> This reasoning slips back and forth between taking a "subjective" view of my use of sentences, and using them to describe "objective" possibilities. On the one hand, I am saying that I do not know what "objective" situation I am in, and so I don't know whether my sincere utterances of 'There is water in the basement' express the thought that there is water in the basement or the thought that there is twin-water

in the basement. On the other hand, if I am to *use* my sentence 'There is water in the basement' to *describe* the possible world in which my sincere utterances of 'There is water in the basement' express the thought that there is water in the basement, I must take for granted that, viewed "objectively," my sincere utterances of 'There is water in the basement' express the thought that there is water in the basement. But the attempt to shift back and forth between the "subjective" and "objective" points of view on my use of sentences is deeply confused. For if I can use my sentences to describe possibilities at all, then in effect I undermine the general conclusion that all I know of the "contents" of my beliefs must be based in my "subjective" experience of using my sentences. (Chapter 6, pp. 133–134, quoted in Chapter 7, pp. 149–150)

Expanding on this argument later in the chapter, I point out that "To characterize a possibility as 'skeptical' we must have some idea of what that possibility is" (p. 141). More generally, to use my sentences to describe possibilities at all, I must have *some* idea of what possibilities my sentences actually express. But if I accept the argument (i)–(iii), I must admit that I have *no* idea what possibilities my sentences express.

One might think that I could get some idea of what possibilities my sentences express if I engage in empirical investigation. This hope is encouraged by the qualification in premise (iii) that our knowledge of what thoughts our own utterances express is confined to what we can derive solely from our "first-person experiences" *without empirical investigation*. The trouble is that in the context of the skeptical challenge to my self-knowledge presented by premises (i)–(iii), to know that I have some empirical justification for believing, for instance, that water is H_2O, I must have justification for believing that my sincere utterances of the sentence 'water is H_2O' express the *thought* that water is H_2O. But premises (i)–(iii) imply that for all I know I may actually be in a world in which, although I feel justified in uttering the sentence 'water is H_2O' on the basis of "observations" that I express by using other sentences, my utterance of 'water is H_2O' does not express the thought that water is H_2O. For instance, among my subjectively equivalent worlds is a world in which a duplicate of my brain exists in a vat throughout its entire "life," and receives sensory stimulation just like the sensory stimulation that my brain actually receives. In such a world, if my utterances of 'water is H_2O' express any thought at all, they do not express the thought that water is H_2O. Premises (i)–(iii) imply that I can't know that I am not in such a world, *whether or not I engage in what I call empirical investigation*, because *I can't know what thoughts I am actually expressing when I report the results of my investigations.* Brueckner endorses this conclusion in Chapter 1, in which he first argued that self-knowledge is incompatible with the conclusions of Putnam's Twin-Earth thought experiments. He claimed that skepticism about self-knowledge is what skepticism about the external world becomes if we accept the conclusions of the Twin-Earth thought experiments. It should be no surprise, then, that Brueckner's skeptical argument leaves us with no idea what possibilities our sentences express.

As I already noted, however, to use my sentences to describe possibilities at all, I must have some idea of what possibilities my sentences actually express. I therefore cannot *both* take for granted that I can use my sentences to describe possibilities that support premise (i), *and* accept premises (ii) and (iii), which, together with (i), imply that I have no idea what possibilities my sincere utterances of my sentences express. I must therefore give up at least one of these premises. In my view, the problematic premise in the skeptic's argument is (iii). That is why I conclude that "if I can use my sentences to describe possibilities at all, then in effect I undermine the general conclusion that all I know of the 'contents' of my beliefs must be based in my 'subjective' experience of using my sentences." I will expand further on this reasoning in the course of criticizing Brueckner's reply.

8.2 BRUECKNER'S REPLY

Brueckner's reply to my argument begins with a paraphrase of the possibilities involved in my illustration of the skeptic's reasoning. Brueckner imagines that when I raise the skeptic's challenge to my own self-knowledge, I use the following two sentences about possibilities (Chapter 7, p. 150):

(1) In a possible world in which I am a denizen of water-filled Earth, my sincere utterances of 'There is water in the basement' express the thought that there is water in the basement.

(2) In a possible world in which I am a denizen of twin-water-filled Twin Earth, my sincere utterances of 'There is water in the basement' express the thought that there is twin-water in the basement.

Brueckner apparently endorses the skeptical reasoning (i)–(iii), applied to this case. Since my "first-person experiences" don't discriminate between the possibilities described by (1) and (2), I can't know which of these worlds I am in without empirical investigation. Assuming that the thought I express by using my sentence 'There is water in the basement' if I am a denizen of water-filled Earth is different from the thought I express by using my sentence 'There is water in the basement' if I am a denizen of twin-water-filled Twin Earth, Brueckner concludes that without empirical investigation I can't know which of these thoughts I express by using my sentence 'There is water in the basement'.

Brueckner thinks that my argument for the incoherence of skepticism about self-knowledge overlooks an important consequence of anti-individualism: according to Brueckner, I know without empirical investigation that the sentences (1) and (2) that I use to raise the skeptic's challenge to my own self-knowledge are true regardless of whether I am on Earth or Twin Earth. Brueckner's defense of this claim rests on assumptions about what thoughts my sincere utterances of the sentences (1) and (2) *would* express in these two situations. He reasons as follows:

If I am now on Earth, then my uses of the words 'possible world in which my sincere utterances of 'there is water in the basement' express the thought that there is water in the basement' describe a possible world in which my sincere utterances of 'there is water in the basement' express the thought that there is water in the basement. Even if I am on Twin Earth, it is still true that I can use my sentences to describe various possibilities involving shifting thought content. If I am on Twin Earth, then my uses of (1) describe a possible world in which I am a denizen of twin-water-filled Twin Earth and in which my sincere utterances of 'There is water in the basement' express the thought that there is twin-water in the basement; and if I am on Twin Earth, then my uses of (2) describe a possible world in which my sincere utterances of 'There is water in the basement' do *not* express the thought that there is twin-water in the basement. This is because *if I am on Twin Earth, then my uses of* (2) *describe a possible world in which I am not on Twin Earth and in which my sincere utterances of 'There is water in the basement' express a different content from that expressed by my Twin-Earthian utterances of the sentence.* (Chapter 7, pp. 150–151; my emphasis)

The reasoning in this paragraph depends on a number of substantive claims, as Brueckner's defense of the italicized sentence shows. To support this sentence, he reasons as follows:

Just as an Earthian's uses of 'Twin Earth' refer to a (part of a) possible world other than his own, a Twin Earthian's uses of 'Twin Earth' refer to a (part of a) possible world other than *his* own. Similar points hold for 'twin-water'. Just as an Earthian's uses of that term refer to a possible liquid distinct from his home liquid (H_2O), a Twin Earthian's uses of 'twin-water' refer to a possible liquid distinct from *his* home liquid (XYZ). (Chapter 7, p. 151, fn. 2)

Note that if we accept anti-individualism, we cannot regard these claims as true in virtue of Brueckner's stipulation, and hence immune to doubt. (In Chapter 6, pp. 140–141, fn.31), I describe a scenario in which we discover, to our surprise, that Twin Earth is Earth, and twin-water is water. There are many other ways in which Brueckner's claims may be false. I'll consider a different one below.) Nevertheless, I'll assume for now that Brueckner's claims about what thoughts his utterances of sentences (1) and (2) would express if he were on Earth or on Twin Earth are at least *justified*. I'll argue in Section 8.3 that this crucial assumption is incorrect: Brueckner's skepticism about self-knowledge implies that he has *no* justification for his claims about what thoughts his utterances of sentences (1) and (2)would express if he were on Earth or on Twin Earth.

In his criticism of my argument, Brueckner just takes for granted that his claims about what thoughts his utterances of sentences (1) and (2) would express if he were on Earth or on Twin Earth are justified, and concludes that I misstated my objection. As I noted above, in Chapter 6 I concluded that "if I can use my sentences to describe possibilities at all, then in effect I undermine the general conclusion that all I know of the 'contents' of my beliefs must be based in my 'subjective' experience of using my sentences." Brueckner thinks that this is incorrect, because he assumes he is justified in asserting that *whether or not* I am on Twin Earth, I can still use my sentences to describe possibilities that challenge my assumption that I know what I'm thinking without empirical inquiry.

Since Brueckner thinks I *can* use my sentences to describe possibilities even if I don't know what possibilities my sentences express, he reconstructs my argument in a way that does not commit me to denying this:

As I would like to reconstruct Ebbs's objection, the difficulty he has in mind is that if I accept the skeptic's conclusion (and undertake no special empirical investigation), then I cannot claim to *know* which possibilities are described, or expressed, by my uses of (1) and (2) ... I cannot claim to know which thoughts about possibility are expressed in the course of my reasoning for this conclusion. (Chapter 7, p. 151)

Brueckner then replies, in the skeptic's voice, that "This lack of knowledge does not affect my claim to have presented a *sound* argument for skepticism about self-knowledge" (Chapter 7, p. 152; my emphasis). The central claim is that "Even though I do not know which thoughts are expressed by my sincere utterances of those sentences, I *do* know that the thoughts, whatever they are, are thinkings of *true* propositions (given anti-individualism)" (Chapter 7, p. 152).

To defend this claim, Brueckner's skeptic repeats Brueckner's argument that in either of these situations, sentences (1) and (2) express true propositions, as follows:

Consider (1). If I am on Earth, then my sincere utterances of (1) express a true thought concerning the nature of my thought contents in a water-filled possible world. If I am on Twin Earth, then my sincere utterances of (1) instead express a different but true thought concerning the nature of my thought contents in a twin-water-filled possible world. Either way, my sincere utterances of (1) express a *true* thought about possibility. Now consider (2). If I am on Earth, then my sincere utterances of (2) express a *true* thought concerning the nature of my thought contents in a twin-water-filled possible world. If I am on Twin Earth, then my sincere utterances of (2) express a true thought concerning the nature of my thought contents in a possible world filled with some liquid other than twin-water, a thought to the effect that the contents in question concern some liquid other than twin-water. Either way, my sincere utterances of (2) express a *true* thought about possibility. (Chapter 7, p. 152)

8.3 WHY BRUECKNER'S REPLY IS UNSUCCESSFUL

To evaluate the argument in the passage just quoted, one must keep in mind that it is supposed to support the conclusion that my sincere utterances of sentences (1) and (2) are true. To support this conclusion, Brueckner's skeptic tries to establish that

(*) If I am on Earth or on Twin Earth, my sincere utterances of sentences (1) and (2) are true.

But to deduce the conclusion that my sincere utterances of sentences (1) and (2) are true from (*), the skeptic needs to affirm its antecedent:

(**) I am on Earth or I am on Twin Earth.

Hence the skeptic's claim to have presented a *sound* argument for skepticism about self-knowledge is justified only if his acceptance of (**) is justified.

The trouble is that the skeptic's reason for thinking we cannot tell whether we are on Earth or on Twin Earth solely on the basis of our first-person experiences is that no one can distinguish between *any* of his subjectively equivalent worlds solely on the basis of his first-person experiences. But if no one can distinguish between any of his subjectively equivalent worlds solely on the basis of his first-person experiences, then no one is justified in asserting (**) solely on the basis of his first-person experiences. Hence, in particular, the skeptic's acceptance of (**) is not justified. As I just noted, however, the skeptic's claim to have presented a *sound* argument for skepticism about self-knowledge is justified only if his acceptance of (**) is justified. It follows that the skeptic's claim to have presented a sound argument for skepticism about self-knowledge is not justified. In this way, the reasoning Brueckner presents for the conclusion that sentences (1) and (2) express true propositions is self-undermining.

One might think Brueckner can avoid this problem by refusing to offer any argument for his claim that without empirical investigation we can't tell whether we are on Earth or on Twin Earth. As I argued in detail in Chapter 6 and explained briefly in Section 8.1 above, however, simply to assert without argument that for all we know without empirical investigation, we may actually be on Earth or on Twin Earth is to beg the question against our ordinary assumption that we know what thoughts our own utterances express without empirical investigation. The most plausible reconstruction of Brueckner's skeptical reasoning is given by premises (i)–(iii), which together imply that no one can distinguish between any of his subjectively equivalent worlds solely on the basis of his first-person experiences, and thereby show that Brueckner has no justification for asserting (**), on which his argument for the conclusion that sentences (1) and (2) express true propositions depends.

8.4 A WEIRD WORLD

The fact that Brueckner has no justification for asserting (**) points to a deeper problem with his position: if we accept premises (i)–(iii), then for all we know without empirical investigation, we may actually be in a world in which our utterances of (1) and (2) express false propositions. This can be seen in two steps. First, if we accept premises (i)–(iii), then for all we know without empirical investigation, we may actually be in any one of our subjectively equivalent worlds. Second, for each of us there are subjectively equivalent worlds in which our utterances of (1) and (2) express false propositions.

For instance, I can describe a subjectively equivalent world in which (a) my twin's word 'Earth' refers to a water-filled planet on which the word 'water' does not refer to water; (b) my twin believes that on what he calls 'Earth', 'water' refers to water, and (c) my twin does not actually live on what he calls 'Earth', but he *believes* that he does. To make this a bit more vivid we may stipulate that my twin was born, raised, and continues to live on a plant P on which his 'water' refers to water but his word 'Earth' does not refer to P, even though he believes it does. To make sense of the stipulation that my twin's word 'water' refers to water, it is enough to suppose that planet P is water-filled, that on P the word 'water' refers to water, and that my twin learns to use the word 'water' in the same way that I do. To make sense of the stipulation that my twin's word 'Earth' does not refer to P, even though he believes it does, we need only suppose that my twin on P picks up the word 'Earth' from speakers in his linguistic community who *tell* him that he lives on what they call 'Earth', so that he sincerely assents to the sentence 'I live on Earth', thereby expressing his (false) belief that he lives on the planet to which his word 'Earth' refers, even though he does *not* live on that planet. To make sense of (a) in a way that is relevant to my twin's evaluations of his sincere utterances of (1), we can add detail that guarantees that my twin's word 'Earth' refers to a planet Q on which there is one and only one twin of my twin, an individual whose qualitative experiences and brain states are exactly the same as my twin's, but whose word 'water' does not refer to water, even though Q is water-filled. (How could this be? One possibility is that on Q, my twin's twin is and always was a brain in a vat whose sincere applications of 'water' are prompted not by samples of water, even though there is water outside the vat, but by states of a computer that have no semantically significant causal connections with water. Then, according to the principles of anti-individualism, on Q my twin's twin's word 'water' does not refer to water.) By our earlier stipulation, my twin sincerely assents to the sentence 'I live on Earth', thereby expressing his (false) belief that he lives on Q (the planet to which his word 'Earth' refers). He also has the (true) belief that his 'water' refers to water. In effect, therefore, he believes that on Q his twin's word 'water' refers to water. These far-fetched stipulations together specify a world in which (a)–(c) are all true. For reasons I will explain soon, if I were actually in this world, my sincere assertions of (1) would be false.

Suppose also that in this subjectively equivalent world, (d) my twin's word 'Twin Earth' refers to a twin-water-filled planet R, distinct from P and Q, on which there is one and only one twin of my twin, an individual whose qualitative experiences and brain states are exactly the same as my twin's, but whose word 'water' does *not* refer to twin-water. (How could this be? As before, one possibility is that on R, my twin's twin is and always was a brain in a vat whose sincere applications of 'water' are prompted not by samples of twin-water, even though there is twin-water outside the vat, but by states of a computer that have no semantically significant causal connections with twin-water. Then, according to the principles of anti-individualism, on R my twin's twin's word 'water' does not refer to twin-water.) Finally, suppose that in this weird world, (e) my twin believes that on what he calls 'Twin Earth', 'water' refers to twin-water, and (f) my twin's word 'twin-water' refers to twin-water. It turns out that if I were actually in this world, my sincere assertions of (2) would be false.

If, as I argued above, the skeptic's premises imply that without empirical investigation I don't know which of my subjectively equivalent worlds I am in, then in particular, the skeptic's premises imply that without empirical

investigation I don't know whether I am in the strange subjectively equivalent world just described. But then if I accept the skeptic's premises, I must
conclude that for all I know without empirical investigation my sincere
utterances of (1) and (2) are false. Consider, once again, sentence (1):

In a possible world in which I am a denizen of water-filled Earth, my sincere
utterances of 'There is water in the basement' express the thought that there is
water in the basement.

If I am actually in the weird world described above, I am my twin on planet
P, so my words 'possible world in which I am a denizen of water-filled Earth'
denote a possible world in which I am my twin's twin on water-filled planet
Q. Hence when I sincerely utter (1), the claim I thereby express is true if and
only if *in a possible world in which I am my twin's twin on water-filled planet
Q, my sincere utterances of 'There is water in the basement' express the thought
that there is water in the basement.* But Q is a water-filled planet on which my
twin's twin's word 'water' does *not* refer to water. Hence in a possible world
in which I am my twin's twin on water-filled planet Q, my sincere utterances of 'There is water in the basement' do *not* express the thought that
there is water in the basement. Therefore, if I am actually in the weird world
described above, my sincere utterances of (1) are false.

Now consider, once again, sentence (2):

In a possible world in which I am a denizen of twin-water-filled Twin Earth, my
sincere utterances of 'There is water in the basement' express the thought that there
is twin-water in the basement.

If I am actually in the weird world described above, I am my twin on planet
P, so my words 'possible world in which I am a denizen of twin-water-filled
Twin Earth' denote a possible world in which I am my twin's twin on twin-
water-filled planet R. Hence when I sincerely utter (2), the claim I thereby
express is true if and only if *in a possible world in which I am my twin's twin
on water-filled planet R, my sincere utterances of 'There is water in the basement' express the thought that there is twin-water in the basement.* But R is a
water-filled planet on which my twin's twin's word 'water' does *not* refer to
twin-water. Hence in a possible world in which I am my twin's twin on
water-filled planet R, my sincere utterances of 'There is water in the basement' do *not* express the thought that there is twin-water in the basement.
Therefore, if I am actually in the weird world described above, my sincere
utterances of (2) are false.

In fact, if we accept premises (i)–(iii), we are even worse off than this. For
each of us there are countless subjectively equivalent worlds. We cannot

possibly survey or describe *all* the different possible thoughts that we would express by utterances of (1) and (2) in these different worlds. If we accept the skeptic's conclusion that without empirical investigation we can't tell which of these worlds we are in, we must conclude that without empirical investigation we simply have *no idea* what the skeptic's sentences say, whether they are likely to be true, or even whether they express *skeptical* challenges to our ordinary beliefs. That is why I conclude that

the attempt to shift back and forth between the "subjective" and "objective" points of view on my use of sentences is deeply confused. For if I can use my sentences to describe possibilities at all, then in effect I undermine the general conclusion that all I know of the "contents" of my beliefs must be based in my "subjective" experience of using my sentences. (Chapter 6, p. 134)

This is not a misstatement of my conclusion, but a consequence of the fact that if all I know of the 'contents' of my beliefs must be based in my 'subjective' experience of using my sentences, then I have *no idea* what thoughts my sincere utterances of my sentences express, together with the truism that to use my sentences to describe possibilities at all, I must have *some idea* of what thoughts my sincere utterances of my sentences express.

8.5 THE SKEPTIC'S PREDICAMENT

Brueckner apparently accepts this truism, but hopes to contain the damage of the skeptical conclusion by reasoning about what thoughts our utterances of (1) and (2) *would* express if we were on Earth or on Twin Earth. This presupposes, as I explained, that we have some justification for accepting (**). More generally, it presupposes that we can identify a proper subset of our subjectively equivalent worlds such that we are justified in thinking that we are actually in one of the worlds in that subset. The trouble is that if we accept the skeptic's premises (i)–(iii), we cannot be justified in claiming of *any* given proper subset of our subjectively equivalent worlds, that we are actually in one of the worlds in that subset. Premises (i)–(iii) imply that without empirical investigation I don't know whether I am on Earth or on Twin Earth; but they *also* imply that without empirical investigation I don't know (**), and, more generally, that without empirical investigation I don't know, of any given proper subset of my subjectively equivalent worlds, that I am actually in one of the worlds in that subset. If we accept premises (i)–(iii), there is no way to avoid a total skepticism about what thoughts our utterances express that leaves us without any justification for claiming that our sincere utterances of sentences (1) and (2) are true.

Note, finally, that we have justification for premise (i) only if we have justification for particular claims about what thoughts our sincere utterances of our sentences *would* express in different subjectively equivalent worlds. But the kind of reasoning that I used to show that premises (i)–(iii) leave us without any justification for claiming that our sincere utterances of sentences (1) and (2) are true can be used to show that premises (i)–(iii) leave us without any justification for asserting any *other* statements about possibilities that would support premise (i).

Since premise (i) is a consequence of accepting the conclusions of Twin-Earth thought experiments, some might see my argument as a *reductio ad absurdum* of the conclusions of Twin-Earth thought experiments. In my view, however, the incoherence of Brueckner's reasoning shows that we should question his understanding of anti-individualism and self-knowledge. In Chapter 6 and Ebbs 1997, I suggest that the best way to understand both individualism and self-knowledge is to look carefully at our actual practices of attributing thoughts to a person, and of judging whether or not (and in what sense) he "knows" what thoughts his utterances express. Ordinary attributions of "self-knowledge" suggest that to have it is just to be able to use one's words in discourse – to make and evaluate assertions, to ask questions, to describe possibilities, and so on. Although we sometimes entertain second-order thoughts, such as *I am thinking that self-knowledge is puzzling*, we should not force *all* ordinary cases of self-knowledge into this second-order mold. Self-knowledge – the familiar fact that without going through any special empirical investigation, competent speakers "know" (in some sense) what thoughts their utterances express – is much more widespread than the phenomenon of thinking about what one is thinking. It is not best described as a kind of propositional knowledge that requires that one have beliefs about what one is thinking, but as a kind of *know how* – an aspect of our *practical ability* to use language. Seen in this way, self-knowledge is not only *compatible* with the conclusions of the Twin-Earth thought experiments, it is *required* by them. There is typically no gap between the practical abilities that lead us to take a speaker to be expressing a certain thought by uttering a given sentence, and the practical abilities that constitute his "knowing," without any special inquiry, what thought his utterance of that sentence expresses.

This is not the place to provide a detailed description and defense of my view of self-knowledge. My central goal in this paper is to show that Brueckner's reply to my argument that skepticism about self-knowledge is incoherent depends on premises that cannot be justified if, as he believes, our knowledge of our own thoughts is confined to what we can derive solely from our "first-person experiences" of using our sentences. I conclude that despite its initial appearance of plausibility, Brueckner's reply undermines itself. In this unintended way, it provides further support for my argument that skepticism about self-knowledge is incoherent.

ACKNOWLEDGEMENT

For helpful comments I am grateful to Hugh Chandler, Richard Moran, and two anonymous referees for *Philosophical Studies*.

CHAPTER 9

The coherence of skepticism about self-knowledge

Anthony Brueckner

I have argued for the coherence of skepticism about self-knowledge, which, it seems, can be generated from the assumption of anti-individualism about thought-content.[1] Gary Ebbs has responded in Chapter 8. I will attempt to show here that Ebbs has again failed to establish the incoherence in question.

9.1 THE SKEPTICAL ARGUMENT

I will begin by stating Ebbs's formulation of the self-knowledge skeptic's reasoning. Let us assume that anti-individualism about thought-content is true. Consider my claim

(K) I know that I am thinking that there is water in the basement (even assuming the absence of empirical investigation).

The skeptic will try to show that anti-individualism implies the falsity of (K): a paradigmatic failure of self-knowledge. Ebbs says on behalf of the skeptic, "for each of us, one could describe any number of *subjectively equivalent* worlds in which we (or our twins, ... our counterparts in such worlds) receive the same sensory stimulation that we receive in the actual world, but our (or our twins') environments are different from what we take our environment to be in the actual world" (Chapter 8, p. 154). According to Ebbs's skeptic, it follows from anti-individualism that

(i) For each of us, there are subjectively equivalent worlds in which our (or our twins') sincere utterances express thoughts that are different from the thoughts that we take our sincere utterances to express in the actual world. (Chapter 8, p. 154)

I take my sincere utterances of 'There is water in the basement' to express the thought that there is water in the basement. According to (i), Earth and Twin Earth are parts of subjectively equivalent possible worlds in which my

---

[1] See Chapter 7, this volume. This was a reply to Chapter 6. See also Brueckner 1990 and Chapter 5.

utterances of 'There is water in the basement' express different thoughts. Thus we have the following consequences of (i):

(1)   In a possible world in which I am a denizen of water-filled Earth, my sincere utterances of 'There is water in the basement' express the thought that there is water in the basement.
(2)   In a possible world in which I am a denizen of twin-water-filled Twin Earth, my sincere utterances of 'There is water in the basement' express the thought that there is twin-water in the basement.

We will return to these consequences of (i) later.

The skeptical argument proceeds by means of these two further premises:

(ii)   In all our subjectively equivalent worlds our "first-person experiences" would be the same. (Chapter 8, p. 154)
(iii) Without empirical investigation, our knowledge of our own thoughts is confined to what we can derive solely from our "first-person experiences". (Chapter 8, p. 154)

From (i)–(iii), the skeptic draws the conclusion

~(K)   I do not know that I am thinking that there is water in the basement (assuming the absence of empirical investigation).[2]

More generally, "the skeptic concludes that without empirical investigation, we cannot know what thoughts our own utterances express" in cases in which the utterances fall in the purview of (i)–(iii) (Chapter 8, p. 155).

9.2 EBBS'S OBJECTION TO THE COHERENCE OF THE SKEPTICAL ARGUMENT

In Chapter 6, Ebbs objected to the foregoing argument. Consider the skeptic's utterances

(A)   There is a possible world in which my utterances of 'There is water in the basement' express the thought that there is water in the basement.

and

(B)   There is a possible world in which my utterances of 'There is water in the basement' express the thought that there is twin-water in the basement.

---

[2] The argument needs an assumption to the effect that if I know that I am thinking that there is water in the basement, then I know that I am *not* thinking a thought different from that which I take my sincere utterances of 'There is water in the basement' to express (i.e. the thought that there is water in the basement). In the last two papers cited in fn. 1, I present the skeptic's reasoning as involving the foregoing application of a general principle of closure of knowledge under known entailment. This parallels a standard understanding of the Cartesian skeptical argument concerning knowledge of the external world.

These are consequences of (i), in which I attempt to describe two of my subjectively equivalent worlds. According to Ebbs, the skeptic's overall position is incoherent. The skeptic's premises (i)–(iii) imply that I have 'no idea' what possibilities my sincere utterances of (A) and (B) express (Chapter 6, p. 156). This is because his premises imply that the possibility expressed by an utterance of (A), for example, is a function of which of my subjectively equivalent worlds the utterance issues from, and the premises also imply that I cannot know which of my subjectively equivalent worlds I am in. Though he does not put things in this way, it is natural to extend Ebbs's objection as follows: if the skeptic has no idea which possibilities his sincere utterances of (A), (B), (1), and (2) express (these all concern the nature of the subjectively equivalent worlds that (i) treats of), then how can he claim to know that these sincere utterances all express *true propositions about possibility*? So for all he knows, his skeptical argument rests crucially upon falsehoods.

9.3 A RESPONSE TO EBBS'S OBJECTION

Focusing upon (1) and (2), in Chapter 7, I replied in effect that even though the skeptic, in the light of (i)–(iii), does not know which thoughts are expressed by his sincere utterances of (1) and (2), he nevertheless *does* know that they are thinkings of *true* propositions. If the skeptic is on Earth, then both sentences express ordinary, true philosophical thoughts about content. If the skeptic is on Twin Earth, then his sincere utterances of (1) and (2) express different thoughts from the foregoing ordinary ones. Still, the thoughts expressed are true. For example, in uttering (1), the Twin-Earth-located skeptic is correctly saying that in a world in which he is a denizen of twin-water-filled Twin Earth, his sincere utterances of 'There is water in the basement' express the thought that there is twin-water in the basement.[3]

In Ebbs's reconstruction of the logic of my reply, my skeptic reasons as follows:

(*) If I am on Earth or Twin Earth, my sincere utterances of sentences (1) and (2) are true. (Chapter 8, p. 160)

(**) I am on Earth or I am on Twin Earth. (Chapter 8, p. 160)

(***) My sincere utterances of sentences (1) and (2) are true.

---

[3] I leave it to the reader to work out the corresponding reading for the Twin-Earth-located skeptic's utterances of (2).

9.4 EBBS'S COUNTER-RESPONSE

Ebbs's counter-response begins with the point that by the skeptic's lights, 'no one can distinguish between *any* of his subjectively equivalent worlds solely on the basis of his first-person experiences' (Chapter 8, p. 160). Therefore, the skeptic has no justification for (**). So far as the skeptic can tell by his first-person experiences, he could, for example, be in one of his subjectively equivalent worlds that contains some *third liquid*, ABC, distinct from both water (H_2O) and twin-water (XYZ).

But the difficulty for my skeptic is even worse. Ebbs maintains that "for each of us there are subjectively equivalent worlds in which our sincere utterances of (1) and (2) express false propositions" (Chapter 8, p. 161). If this is right, then the skeptic not only has to concede that he has no idea which thoughts are expressed by (1) and (2), but, further, he has no idea whether the thoughts expressed are *true* (contrary to what I had claimed on behalf of my skeptic).

Ebbs's point is well taken. He constructs an ingenious example to illustrate the point. I will spare the reader many of the mind-numbing details and give just the flavor of his effort. Consider one of my subjectively equivalent worlds, a possible world which we will call *the weird world*.[4] In the weird world, my uses of 'Earth' do *not* refer to the water-filled planet *P* I inhabit in that possible world (I have been fooled about 'Earth''s referent by my linguistic community). 'Earth' in my community-deferring uses refers to a *different* water-filled planet from *P*, i.e. *Q*, in a different possible world in which I am a brain in a vat. Call this possible world *the vat world*. In the vat world, my uses of 'water' refer to computer states rather than to the water from which I am causally isolated. This is in contrast to my use of 'water' in the weird world to refer to water. To evaluate my utterance of (1) made in the weird world, we first find a world that makes (1)'s antecedent true, given its weird-world meaning. The vat world is such a world. We then see whether (1)'s consequent is also true of the vat world. No, in the vat world, my sincere utterances of 'There is water in the basement' do *not* express the thought that there is *water* in the basement. So my sincere utterances of (1) in the weird world express a falsehood. So, as Ebbs maintains, in some of my subjectively equivalent worlds, my sincere utterances of (1) express a false proposition.

---

[4] See Chapter 8, Section 8.4.

9.5 THE SKEPTIC TRIES TO HAVE THE LAST LAUGH

The general thrust of Ebbs's counter-response can be put as follows. Suppose that a skeptic puts forward an argument to show that one lacks knowledge of the meanings of the members of a set *S* of sentences (or of the thoughts expressed by sincere uses of them). *Whatever* the argument might be, it will turn out to be incoherent in Ebbs's sense if one or more of the sentences forming the argument is itself in *S*. For then the skeptic cannot justifiably claim to have put forward a sound argument, since by his own reasoning he does not understand part of his own argument.[5]

One worry about this way of showing skeptical incoherence is that it may ignore a legitimate dialectical intention on the part of the skeptic. Suppose he wants to put forward a *reductio ad absurdum* of the assumption that one knows the meanings (and expressed contents) of the sentences in *S*. Assume that one understands the members of *S*, along with the rest of one's language. This assumption, according to the skeptic, leads to the conclusion that one does *not* after all understand the sentences in *S*.

Compare this strategy to the Cartesian skeptical strategy discussed by Harry Frankfurt in Frankfurt 1965. On Frankfurt's interpretation of the *Meditations*,

The sceptic must show that reason can be turned against itself, by showing that there are reasons of the very strongest sort for doubting the reliability of reason. We may say, then, that the sceptic's arguments are designed to provide a *reductio ad absurdum* of the assumption that reason is reliable. (Frankfurt 1965, p. 154)

Frankfurt concludes that the Cartesian skeptic's attempted *reductio* fails for reasons that have nothing to do with any alleged incoherence in his *reductio* procedure. Maybe skepticism about knowledge of meaning and thought content is on a par with skepticism about reason.

However, I would like to set aside these general worries. The issues are extremely difficult and deep. I would like instead to answer Ebbs's counter-response more directly. The skeptic wants to establish

~(K) I do not know that I am thinking that there is water in the basement (assuming the absence of empirical investigation).

---

[5] The response to Ebbs considered in Section 9.3 provides a wrinkle to this dialectic. In the case of the particular skeptical argument we have been discussing, there is a prima facie case to be made for saying that even if the skeptic cannot, by his own lights, claim to understand part of his own argument, he knows that it expresses a truth on any relevant interpretation. Ebbs's counter-response, I think, effectively blocks that skeptical move.

This is to say that I do not know that my sincere utterances of 'There is water in the basement' express the thought I take them to express, i.e. the thought that there is water in the basement. There are two possibilities. Either (I) my sincere utterances of 'There is water in the basement' *do* express the thought I take them to express, or (II) they do *not*, in virtue of my being in one of my subjectively equivalent worlds in which my sincere utterances of 'There is water in the basement' do *not* express the thought I take them to express. According to the skeptic, I do not know which of (I) and (II) is true. Suppose that (I) is true. Then the sorts of worries that Ebbs raised for the soundness of the skeptical argument are unfounded. This is because under our assumption of (I), (1) and (2) express ordinary, true philosophical thoughts about content. So, under our assumption, for all that Ebbs has shown, the skeptic has argued soundly for $\sim$(K). Suppose instead that (II) is true. Then my sincere utterances of 'There is water in the basement' do *not* express the thought I take them to express, in virtue of my being in one of my *tricky* subjectively equivalent worlds (I know not which).[6] In that case, $\sim$(K) is again true: I do not know that I am thinking that there is water in the basement, because I am *not* thinking that thought. Thus, in all of my subjectively equivalent worlds (these are the worlds covered by (I) and II)), the skeptical conclusion $\sim$(K) is true.

Thus, the sort of skepticism about self-knowledge under consideration withstands Ebbs's attempts to impugn its coherence.

9.6 A FINAL WORRY

I would like to end by considering an objection to the skeptical argument that is different from Ebbs's. According to this objection, it turns out that I can rule out the skeptical possibility that I am in a world that is subjectively equivalent to an H_2O-filled world, thinking a thought whose content is a twin of the content I take myself to be thinking via the sentence 'There is water in the basement'. I can rule out this possibility without empirical investigation and without appeal to my 'first-person experiences'. To see this, consider the following constraint on my thoughts: whichever of my subjectively equivalent worlds I inhabit, I am barred from thinking both members of a pair of twin contents. For example, suppose that I have always

---

[6] In some of these worlds, such as the weird world, my utterances of (1) and (2) express false propositions, as Ebbs showed. In others, my utterances of (1) and (2) express true propositions (e.g. worlds in which I inhabit Twin Earth).

resided in an H_2O-world. Then I cannot think the content that would be expressed by a denizen of an XYZ-world when he utters 'There is water in the basement'. In order to think that content, I would need to reside in a liquid environment that is different from that in which I in fact reside. Similarly, that thinker cannot think the content expressed by my utterance of the sentence in question. According to the anti-skeptical objection now under development, these considerations show that it is not possible that I am now thinking a thought whose content is a twin of the content I take myself to be thinking. So my knowledge that I am thinking that there is water in the basement is not threatened by any inability on my part to rule out the skeptical possibility involving twin contents.

The skeptic will reply by invoking the possibility that I am in a switching scenario, in which I *can* think twin contents. In such a scenario, I am unwittingly shuttled between different liquid environments, remaining long enough to acquire and retain various different twin contents. The antiskeptic's objection to the skeptical argument depends upon the assumption that I am not a victim of switching, in so far as the objection depends upon the assumption that I am barred from thinking twin contents. The antiskeptic is surely not entitled to this assumption.

But the foe of the skeptical argument can still raise a connected worry. Let us return to a part of the skeptic's overall position on which Ebbs focused:

(2) In a possible world in which I am a denizen of twin-water-filled Twin Earth, my sincere utterances of 'There is water in the basement' express the thought that there is twin-water in the basement.

If I am not involved in a switching scenario, then 'There is twin-water in the basement' does not express a twin thought which I would think if I were in an XYZ-filled environment. In uttering (2), my intention was to specify and express the thought-content that I would be thinking if I were on Twin Earth. I fail to specify and express such a content, however, if I am not involved in a switching scenario (since in that case I am barred from thinking twin thoughts). So if I am not involved in a switching scenario, then I run into a problem in attempting to state a component of the skeptical position, i.e. (2). Indeed, if I am not involved in a switching scenario, my words 'twin-water' do not even refer to any determinate liquid which is a twin of H_2O.

The skeptic can get around this difficulty by replacing (2) with

(2′) In a possible world in which I am a denizen of an environment containing a twin of H_2O, my sincere utterances of 'There is water in the basement' express a thought whose content is a twin of that which I take my utterances to express.

(2′) is true regardless of whether I am in a normal or, instead, a switching scenario.

Alas, my brain hurts, and I now conclude my defense of the coherence of skepticism about self-knowledge.[7]

---

[7] Thanks to Michael Clark for valuable suggestions.

CHAPTER 10

Why skepticism about self-knowledge is self-undermining

Gary Ebbs

In Chapter 6 and Chapter 8 I explained why I believe that a certain sort of argument that seems to support skepticism about self-knowledge is actually incoherent, or self-undermining. Anthony Brueckner has recently tried to show that even if the central premises of my explanation are true, the skeptical argument in question is not self-undermining. He has also suggested that even if the skeptical argument is self-undermining, it can still serve as a *reductio ad absurdum* of the assumption that we have self-knowledge. My goal here is to explain why I think neither of these responses is successful.

10.1 THE SKEPTICAL ARGUMENT

I will begin by reconstructing the skeptical argument whose coherence is in question. The argument is designed to show that we cannot know without empirical investigation what thoughts our utterances express. Consider our assumption that we each know without empirical investigation that our sincere utterances of 'There is water in the basement' express the thought that there is water in the basement. To begin with, the skeptic relies on standard Twin-Earth thought experiments to support contrasting pairs of sentences about what thoughts our utterances of 'There is water in the basement' would express in different possible worlds. He relies on Twin-Earth thought experiments to show, for instance, that we each must accept the following two sentences:

(1) In a possible world in which I am a denizen of water-filled Earth, my sincere utterances of 'There is water in the basement' express the thought that there is water in the basement.
(2) In a possible world in which I am a denizen of twin-water-filled Twin Earth, my sincere utterances of 'There is water in the basement' express the thought that there is twin-water in the basement.

According to the skeptic, the Twin-Earth thought experiments that support (1) and (2) show that we each must accept that

(3) I know that if my sincere utterances of 'There is water in the basement' express the thought that there is water in the basement, then my sincere utterances of 'There is water in the basement' do not express the thought that there is twin-water in the basement.

The skeptic also assumes that we each accept a general closure principle:

(4) If I know that p and I know that if p then q, then I know that q.[1]

Premises (3) and (4) together imply

(5) If I know that my sincere utterances of 'There is water in the basement' express the thought that there is water in the basement, then I know that my sincere utterances of 'There is water in the basement' do not express the thought that there is twin-water in the basement.

Note that (1)–(5) do not imply that I do not know without empirical investigation that my sincere utterances of 'There is water in the basement' express the thought that there is water in the basement. To get to this conclusion, we need some reason to think that without empirical investigation we cannot rule out that we are in a possible world (such as the one described by (2)) in which our sincere utterances of 'There is water in the basement' do not express the thought that there is water in the basement.

Let us say that a *subjectively equivalent world* for a given person P is one in which P (or a twin of P, as I will call P's counterparts in such worlds) receives the same sensory stimulation that P receives in the actual world, but P's (or P's twin's) environment is different from what P takes his environment to be in the actual world. Generalizing from standard Twin-Earth arguments for (1)–(3), the skeptic accepts that

(6) For each of us, there are subjectively equivalent worlds in which our (or our twins') sincere utterances express thoughts that are different from the thoughts that we take our sincere utterances to express in the actual world.

The skeptic then adds the following initially plausible premises

(7) In all our subjectively equivalent worlds our first-person experiences would be the same.
(8) Without empirical investigation, our knowledge of our own thoughts is confined to what we can derive solely from our first-person experiences.[2]

---

[1] In my previous reconstructions of the skeptic's reasoning I left the Closure Principle unstated. Brueckner points out the need for the Closure Principle in Chapter 9, p. 168, fn. 2. He states a closure principle like (4) in Brueckner 2003, p. 186.
[2] Premises (6)–(8) are numbered (i)–(iii) in Chapter 8.

From (1)–(8), the skeptic concludes that without empirical investigation we cannot know whether our sincere utterances of 'There is water in the basement' express the thought that there is water in the basement or the thought that there is twin-water in the basement, and, more generally, that without empirical investigation, we cannot know what thoughts our utterances express.

10.2 WHY THE SKEPTICAL ARGUMENT IS INCOHERENT

In Chapter 8 I argued in effect that if one accepts premises (7) and (8), then one cannot have justification for accepting premises (1)–(3) and (6) of the skeptical argument. The problem is that one has no justification for accepting premise (6) unless one has justification for accepting particular claims about what thoughts one's own utterances would express in various different subjectively equivalent worlds – claims such as (1) and (2), understood in such a way that (3) is true. But if one accepts premises (7) and (8), then, with or without empirical investigation, one cannot know which subjectively equivalent worlds one is actually in,[3] and so one cannot know what thoughts one's sincere utterances of sentences such as (1) and (2) express. One therefore cannot have justification for accepting such sentences.

Brueckner's counter-response in Chapter 7 was that the skeptic is justified in believing that *whether he is on Earth or on Twin Earth*, his utterances of sentences (1) and (2) express *true* propositions, so he is justified in believing that he has presented a *sound* argument for his skeptical conclusion that he cannot know what thoughts his utterances express. I pointed out in Chapter 8 that this counter-response rests on the premise that the skeptic is either on Earth or on Twin Earth, and the skeptic cannot justify this premise if he accepts premises (7) and (8). I also showed that we can each describe what I call *weird worlds* – subjectively equivalent worlds in which our utterances of sentences (1) and (2) express *false* propositions.[4] But if premises (7) and (8) are true, no one can know which subjectively equivalent world he is actually in, and so no one can know that he is not in one of his weird worlds (worlds in which his utterances of sentences (1) and (2) express *false* propositions).

---

[3] Premises (7)–(8) together imply that I cannot know which subjectively equivalent world I am in even if I *try* to engage in empirical investigation, because I cannot know what thoughts I express when I 'report' the results of my efforts. For a more detailed explanation of this consequence of (7)–(8), see Chapter 8, p. 156.

[4] For a description of one such world, see Chapter 8, Section 8.4. Nathalie Morasch has recently convinced me that the weird world I present in Section 8.4 is under-described. Brueckner accepts my description of it, however, and I will not say more about it here.

Hence no one has any justification for claiming that his utterances of sentences (1) and (2) express *true* propositions. Similar reasoning shows that if premises (7) and (8) are true, then no one is justified in accepting *any* pairs of sentences that support premise (6), and hence no one is justified in accepting premise (6). In short, the skeptical argument (1)–(8) is incoherent, or self-undermining, in the sense that *no one can justifiably accept all of its premises all at once.* I conclude that the skeptic cannot justifiably claim to have put forward a sound argument for his skeptical conclusion.[5]

10.3 BRUECKNER'S ATTEMPT TO DEFEND THE SKEPTIC

Brueckner (Chapter 9, p. 171, fn. 5) concedes that the skeptic cannot have justification for believing that his utterances of sentences (1) and (2) express true propositions and grants that there are weird worlds, but tries to show that the skeptical argument is nevertheless coherent. His new defense has three main parts. In the first part, he notes that

The skeptic wants to establish
~(K) I do not know that I am thinking that there is water in the basement
    (assuming the absence of empirical investigation).
This is to say that I do not know that my sincere utterances of 'There is water in the basement' express the thought I take them to express, i.e. the thought that there is water in the basement. (Chapter 9, pp. 171–172)

In the second part, Brueckner reasons as follows:

There are two possibilities. Either (I) my sincere utterances of 'There is water in the basement' express the thought I take them to express, or (II) they do *not*, in virtue of my being in one of my subjectively equivalent worlds in which my sincere utterances of 'There is water in the basement' do *not* express the thought I take them to express. According to the skeptic, I do not know which of (I) or (II) is true. (Chapter 9, p. 172)

Note that Brueckner's claim that 'according to the skeptic, I do not know which of (I) and (II) is true' is a consequence of premises (7) and (8). The third part of Brueckner's reasoning is supposed to show that there is no incoherence in the skeptic's position – that contrary to what I argued in Chapter 8, the quoted consequence of premises (7) and (8) does not imply that the skeptic cannot justifiably claim to have put forward a sound argument for ~K. Brueckner reasons as follows:

---

[5] This echoes Brueckner's own formulation of my conclusion: "the skeptic cannot justifiably claim to have put forward a sound argument, since by his own reasoning he does not understand part of his argument" (Chapter 9, p. 171).

Suppose that (I) is true. Then the sorts of worries that Ebbs raised for the soundness of the skeptical argument are unfounded. This is because under our assumption of (I), (1) and (2) express ordinary, true philosophical thoughts about content. So, under our assumption, for all that Ebbs has shown, the skeptic has argued soundly for ~(K). Suppose instead that (II) is true. Then my sincere utterances of 'There is water in the basement' do not express the thought I take them to express, in virtue of being in one of my tricky subjectively equivalent worlds (I know not which). In that case, ~(K) is again true: I do not know that I am thinking that there is water in the basement, because I am *not* thinking that thought. Thus, in all of my subjectively equivalent worlds (these are the worlds covered by (I) and (II)), the skeptical conclusion ~(K) is true. (Chapter 9, p. 172)

From this reasoning Brueckner concludes that "the sort of skepticism about self-knowledge under consideration withstands Ebbs's attempts to impugn its coherence" (Chapter 9, p. 172).

10.4 WHY THIS DEFENSE OF THE SKEPTIC FAILS

In the crucial third part of his reasoning, Brueckner needs to show that whether (I) is true or (II) is true, the skeptic can justifiably claim to have put forward a sound argument for ~K. Let us look carefully at what he says about each case.

Brueckner first argues that if (I) is true, then "for all Ebbs has shown, the skeptic has argued soundly for ~K." Note that this is not what Brueckner needs to show to defend the coherence of the skeptic's argument, since an argument may be sound even if we have no justification for accepting its premises. We must therefore check to see whether Brueckner's reasoning shows that the skeptic has justification for accepting the premises of his argument. Brueckner reasons that if (I) is true, then "(1) and (2) express ordinary, true philosophical thoughts about content." But this does not show that the skeptic can justifiably claim to have put forward a sound argument for ~K. Even if (I) is true, the skeptic will not assume that he knows that (I) is true, for that would undermine his conclusion, and imply that his argument is unsound (even if (1) and (2) are true). Therefore, even if (I) is true, the skeptic cannot rule out the possibility that (II) is true. In particular, the skeptic cannot rule out the possibility that he is in one of his weird worlds (in which his utterances of (1) and (2) are false) and so, for the reasons explained above, the skeptic cannot justifiably claim to have put forward a sound argument for ~K.

Brueckner next argues that if (II) is true, then ~K is true, because my belief that my sincere utterances of 'there is water in the basement' express the thought that there is water in the basement is false. But this tells us nothing about whether the skeptic can justifiably claim to have put forward a sound argument for ~K if (II) is true. Here again, however, the reason I sketched above applies: the skeptic cannot rule out the possibility that he is in one of his weird worlds, in which his utterances of (1) and (2) are false, and so the skeptic cannot justifiably claim to have put forward a sound argument for ~K.

I conclude that either way – whether (I) is true or (II) is true – the skeptic cannot justifiably claim to have put forward a sound argument for ~K. Hence Brueckner's reasoning fails to show that the skeptical argument is coherent.

10.5 CAN THE SKEPTICAL ARGUMENT BE VIEWED AS A *REDUCTIO AD ABSURDUM*?

One might grant that Brueckner's reasoning fails to address my criticism of the skeptic's reasoning, but still wonder whether my criticism "ignores a legitimate dialectical intention on the part of the skeptic" (Chapter 9, p. 171). Perhaps the skeptical argument could be viewed as a *reductio ad absurdum* of the assumption that one knows what thoughts one's own utterances express. The *reductio* strategy would be to assume that one knows what thoughts one's own utterances express, and to use the skeptical argument to show that one does *not* know what thoughts one's own utterances express (Chapter 9, p. 171). Viewed in this way, the incoherence of the reasoning could perhaps serve a dialectical purpose by reducing the assumption that one knows what thoughts one's own utterances express to absurdity.

The problem with this suggestion is that the incoherence of the skeptical argument does not by itself tell us which of its premises or assumptions is false. Some philosophers might take the incoherence of the argument to be a *reductio ad absurdum* of premise (6). I cannot reject premise (6), however, because I accept premises (1) and (2), and many similar pairs of sentences that support (6). Some philosophers would reject the closure principle, (4), and, with it, (5). But I see no good reason to reject either one. In my view, the weakest premise of the skeptical argument is (8), which presupposes a controversial *observational model* of self-knowledge.[6] If we want to view the skeptical argument as a *reductio ad absurdum*, we should view it not as a *reductio ad absurdum* of the assumption

---

[6] A number of philosophers reject the observational model of self-knowledge. See, for instance, Burge 1988, Moran 2001, Putnam 1988, and Shoemaker 1988. Brueckner (2003, p. 186) himself acknowledges that the observational model is controversial.

that we know what thoughts our sincere utterances express, as Brueckner suggests, but as a *reductio ad absurdum* of premise (8).[7]

I conclude that the skeptical argument fails for two related reasons. First, it is incoherent, or self-undermining – no one can justifiably accept all of its premises all at once. Second, its incoherence cannot plausibly be viewed as a *reductio ad absurdum* of the assumption that we know what thoughts our sincere utterances express.[8]

---

[7] In Chapter 6, Chapter 8, and Ebbs 2003, I endorse and develop Putnam's sketchy remarks (in Putnam 1988) about self-knowledge. As I see it, ordinary attributions of self-knowledge suggest that to know what thoughts one's utterances express is just to be able to use one's words in discourse – to make and evaluate assertions, to ask questions, to describe possibilities, and so on. In short, self-knowledge is not observational, but *performative*. For a more complete (but still preliminary) sketch of a performative view of self-knowledge, see Chapter 6, Chapter 8, and Ebbs 2003.

[8] My thanks to Anthony Brueckner, whose response to a letter I sent him in November 2004 prompted me to write this paper.

CHAPTER 11

Skepticism about self-knowledge redux

Anthony Brueckner

I would like to take another stab at defending the coherence of skepticism about self-knowledge. A possible world in which I inhabit Twin Earth is, in Gary Ebbs's phrase, a *subjectively equivalent world* for me, in the sense that if I were on Twin Earth, I would receive the same sensory stimulation that I actually receive, though the Twin-Earth environment is different from what I actually take my environment to be.[1] Accordingly, on Twin Earth, my sincere utterances of the sentence 'There is water in the basement' express the thought that there is *twin-water* in the basement, rather than the thought that there is water in the basement. One might maintain that without empirical investigation of my environment, I do *not* know that I am *not* in a world in which I inhabit Twin Earth (or in some other subjectively equivalent world). Thus, in the absence of empirical investigation:

(A) I do *not* know that my sincere utterances of 'There is water in the basement' do *not* express the thought that there is twin-water in the basement.

The idea behind A is that without empirical investigation, the only way to know that I am not in some subjectively equivalent world such as a Twin-Earth world is to appeal to my experiences. But those experiences are indistinguishable from those I would have if I were on Twin Earth (or in some *other* subjectively equivalent world).

Given that I know that if I am thinking a water-thought, then I am *not* thinking a twin-water-thought, and given an appropriate closure principle,[2] we have

(B) If I know that my sincere utterances of 'There is water in the basement' express the thought that there is water in the basement, then I know that my sincere utterances of 'There is water in the basement' do *not* express the thought that there is twin-water in the basement.

---

[1] See Chapter 10. Ebbs's definition is consistent with the possibility that in the actual world, I inhabit Twin Earth.

[2] That is: if I know that *p*, and I know that if *p* then *q*, then I know that *q*.

From A and B we have

(~K) I do not know that my sincere utterances of 'There is water in the basement' express the thought that there is water in the basement.

~K is a skeptical conclusion about self-knowledge. Ebbs maintains that there is something incoherent, or self-undermining, about the foregoing skeptical argument for ~K.[3]

I argued, in effect, in Chapter 7 that regardless of whether I am on Earth or Twin Earth, (i) A and B express true propositions, and (ii) the argument expressed by the set S of sentences A– ~K is sound (and, in general, all the self-knowledge skeptic's philosophical claims about content come out true). Ebbs's reply in Chapter 8 is that in some *weird* subjectively equivalent worlds, S does *not* express a sound argument.[4] So by the reasoning given above in support of A, I do not know that S expresses a sound argument, since I do *not* know that I am *not* in some subjectively equivalent weird world.

I replied as follows (Chapter 9). Either (I) my sincere utterances of 'There is water in the basement' express the thought I take them to express, or (II) they do *not*, in virtue of my being in one of my subjectively equivalent worlds in which my utterances do *not* express the thought I take them to express. If (I) holds, then I can take the sentences in S at face value, and S *does* express a sound argument. So we have ~K. If (II) holds, then whatever argument is expressed by S – sound or not – we nevertheless have ~K. This is because I take my utterances to express the thought that there is water in the basement. If my utterances do *not* express that thought, then by the factivity of knowledge, I do *not* know that they *do*: that is ~K.

---

[3] The argument is a streamlined version of the one formulated in Chapter 10, pp. 175–177.

[4] Ebbs's weird world example concerns the sentence

(1) In a possible world in which I am a denizen of water-filled Earth, my sincere utterances of 'There is water in the basement' express the thought that there is water in the basement.

Ebbs holds that (1) comes out false in some of my subjectively equivalent worlds. His example of such a weird world turns on the assumption that in the world in question, my term 'Earth' does not refer to the water-filled planet I inhabit in that possible world. In that weird world, my term 'Earth' instead refers to a planet in a possible world W distinct from the weird world. In W, my term 'water' does not refer to water, though in the weird world, my term 'water' *does* so refer. The upshot is then when we evaluate the truth value of (1) as uttered by me in the weird world, the sentence comes out false. None of the sentences in S, however, contains the term 'Earth'. So it is not obvious how to extend Ebbs's point about his weird world so as to show that in some of my subjectively equivalent worlds, S does not express a sound argument. However, let us assume for the sake of argument that Ebbs can justifiably maintain that somewhere in the logical space of my subjectively equivalent worlds, there is a world in which S fails to express a sound argument.

Ebbs (Chapter 10) replies, in effect, as follows. Given the skeptical conclusion ∼K, I do not know which of (I) and (II) is true. This means that I do not know whether or not S expresses a sound argument for ∼K: if (II) holds, then S *could fail* to express a sound argument in virtue of my being in one of the *weird* subjectively equivalent worlds described by Ebbs. Thus he says, "the skeptic cannot justifiably claim to have put forward a sound argument for ∼K" (Chapter 10, p. 178).

It is not obvious that this is a terrible problem for the self-knowledge skeptic. Consider the following example. I find what appear to be some English sentences written on a blackboard – call the set of sentences S′. I am told that the writer may well be using a language that is superficially similar to English but nevertheless *not* English (call it *Twenglish*). The sentences S′ are these:

(A′)　If you know that I am speaking English, then you know which language I am speaking.
(B′)　You do not know which language I am speaking.
(∼K′)　You do not know that I am speaking English.

Either (I′) the writer is speaking English, or (II′) the writer is not speaking English. If (I′) holds, then S′ expresses a sound argument. Premise A′ is obviously true under its English interpretation. Further, as a matter of fact, I, the reader, do not know which language the writer is speaking – it could be English, and it could be Twenglish. So B′ is true. So if (I′) holds, then the argument is sound. We then have ∼K′. On the other hand, if (II′) holds, then the writer is *not* speaking English. By the factivity of knowledge, I do *not* know that the writer *is* speaking English. We then again have ∼K′.

So it seems that we can establish ∼K′ in the foregoing manner even though I do not know whether or not the writer's sentences S′, with the meanings he attaches to them, express a sound argument. If he is speaking English, then they do; if he is speaking Twenglish, then they may or may not. But either way, we have ∼K′.

Returning to the self-knowledge skeptic's argument, we similarly have ∼K even though I do not know whether or not my sentences S express a sound argument. It seems that this situation is no more problematic for the proponent of ∼K than is the situation in which the proponent of ∼K′ finds himself.

I will conclude by briefly drawing a parallel with the skeptic about knowledge of the external world. In the Good Case, I am a normal human in a normal world; I have hands. In the Bad Case, I am in a subjectively equivalent world; I have no hands (in virtue of being a brain in a vat, or a victim of Evil Genius deception, or . . .). The skeptic argues as follows. 'Either (I'') I am in the Good Case, or (II'') I am in the Bad Case. If I am in the Good Case, then we have

($\sim$K'') I do not know that I have hands.

This is because my experiences do not enable me to rule out the possibility that I am in the subjectively equivalent Bad Case. Therefore I do *not* know that I am *not* in the Bad Case. By the same sort of closure considerations as those discussed above, I do not know that I *am* in the Good Case in which, as I believe, I have hands. So we have $\sim$K''.' Call the sentences in the quotes marks S''.

Now suppose that in some of the Bad Case no-hands worlds, some arguments that appear to me to be obviously sound are in fact *un*sound. This is a version of Descartes's full-bore Evil Genius scenario. Since I cannot rule out the possibility that I am in that *sort* of Bad Case, I do not know whether or not S'' expresses a sound argument. Still, if I am somehow, some way in the Bad Case, then I do *not* have hands. By the factivity of knowledge, I do *not* know that I *do* have hands. Either way, Good Case or Bad Case, we have $\sim$K'' even though I do not know whether or not S'' expresses a sound argument. That seems to be a fairly nasty skeptical result.

In each piece of skeptical reasoning that we have considered (self-knowledge, knowledge of the blackboard writer's language, knowledge of hands), Ebbs's complaint is in force, at least to a degree: I do not know whether or not the sentences S, the sentences S', and the sentences S'' express a sound argument. However, in each case there is a larger argument that, it seems, I *do* know to be sound: (a) the argument proceeding from the assumption that either (I) or (II) holds, whose conclusion is $\sim$K (skepticism about self-knowledge), (b) the argument proceeding from the assumption that either (I') or (II') holds, whose conclusion is $\sim$K' (skepticism about knowledge of the blackboard writer's language), and (c) the argument proceeding from the assumption that either (I'') or (II'') holds, whose conclusion is $\sim$K'' (skepticism about knowledge of hands).

CHAPTER 12

Self-knowledge in doubt

Gary Ebbs

To have what I call *minimal self-knowledge* is to know without empirical investigation what thoughts one's own utterances express. Although we each ordinarily take for granted that we have minimal self-knowledge, there is no consensus among philosophers about whether we have it, or even about what it is. As with other sorts of knowledge, one way to investigate and clarify minimal self-knowledge is to examine skeptical arguments that purport to show that we do not have it. With this aim in mind, I shall (first) summarize and develop my previous criticisms of Brueckner's attempts to raise a skeptical doubt about whether we have minimal self-knowledge, (second) propose that we reject the conception of minimal self-knowledge on which Brueckner's skeptical arguments rely, and adopt instead the minimal conception of minimal self-knowledge that I have sketched in previous work, and (third) sketch a methodological framework within which our failure to be able to raise a coherent doubt about whether we have minimal self-knowledge helps us to see both what it is and that we have it.

12.1 HOW TO RAISE A SKEPTICAL CHALLENGE: THREE CONDITIONS

Brueckner's attempts to raise doubts about minimal self-knowledge are modeled on more familiar skeptical arguments that introduce skeptical hypotheses and challenge us to rule them out. To set the framework for my reconstruction and evaluation of Brueckner's arguments, in this section I shall state and defend three conditions that any successful skeptical challenge of this kind should meet. To simplify the formulations, I shall focus on skeptical arguments that purport to show that we do not know that S, for some significant domain of statements S that we ordinarily take ourselves to know, and I shall call this domain of statements the *domain* of the skeptical argument. I assume, also, that the domains of skeptical arguments of the kind in question are *limited* in the sense that they do not contain statements that express the rules of reasoning that one takes to license the inferences from their premises to their conclusions.

Condition 1. The argument specifies an hypothesis H about how things may actually be for us such that (a) we grant that H is possibly actually true, (b) we grant that if H is actually true, we do not know that S, for any S in the domain of the argument.

It is not difficult to see why a skeptical argument of a kind that introduces skeptical hypotheses and challenges us to rule them out is successful only if it satisfies Condition 1. If a skeptical argument fails to specify any skeptical hypothesis at all, then it is clearly not a skeptical argument of the relevant kind. And if an argument A specifies a skeptical hypothesis H, then there are just two ways in which A could fail to satisfy Condition 1 – (first) A could fail to satisfy clause (a) of Condition 1 or (second) A could fail to satisfy clause (b) of Condition 1. Suppose A fails to satisfy clause (a) of Condition 1. In this case, even if A satisfies condition (b) of Condition 1, we do not regard H as a challenge to our assumption that we are justified in believing S, for any S in A's domain. Since we do not grant that H is possibly actually true, we do not grant that H specifies a possibility that is incompatible with our actually knowing that S, for any S in A's domain, and so A does not get off the ground. Alternatively, suppose A fails to satisfy clause (b) of Condition 1. In this case, even if A satisfies condition (a) of Condition 1, we do not take A's hypothesis H to conflict with, and hence to challenge, our assumption that we know that S, for any S in A's domain, and hence we are not obliged to try to rule out H if we are to take ourselves to know that S, for any S in A's domain.

In contexts of skepticism about ordinary justification for perceptual and other "empirical" beliefs, Condition 1 is not usually emphasized, because most philosophers believe it is easy to satisfy. Even in these contexts, however, Condition 1 may be more difficult to satisfy than it seems.

To see why, let us consider a standard way of trying to satisfy Condition 1. Let S be the statement that *I am now seated before my computer*, and suppose that I take myself to know that S. Let H be the hypothesis that *I am now dreaming*. Most philosophers would grant that this H satisfies Condition 1, if the domain of the skeptical argument is all statements S that specify contents of our perceptual beliefs. But let us look at each clause of Condition 1, and see whether, and, if so, how, it is satisfied.

Consider, first, clause (b) of Condition 1. As Barry Stroud, among others, has argued, if I am now dreaming that I am now seated before my computer, then I do not now know that I am now seated before my computer, whether or not I am, in fact, seated before my computer. I find this convincing, and shall not question it.

Clause (a) of Condition 1 is more difficult to assess, since it is not clear what it is to grant that an hypothesis H is "possibly actually true." A first step toward clarifying this phrase is to see that to grant that H is "possibly actually true" is not to grant that H is epistemically possible for us, where epistemic possibility is understood as what is compatible with what we take ourselves know. For suppose, again, that H is the hypothesis that *I am now dreaming.* Then to grant that H is epistemically possible for me would be to grant that H is compatible with what I now take myself to know. Before I encounter the skeptical argument, I take myself to know that I am now awake, not dreaming, and hence H is not compatible with what I take myself to know. But a skeptical argument must move me from my starting, ordinary assumptions about what I know. It cannot reasonably move me from these assumptions by begging the question against them. If the dreaming hypothesis, H, is to satisfy clause (a) of Condition 1, then, in a way that could be part of a successful skeptical argument, we must find a sense in which we grant that H is possibly actually true, even though H is not now epistemically possible for us. What sense could that be?

Many philosophers are inclined to reason as follows.

"Even though I believe that I am not now dreaming, I can suspend this belief, and suppose that I am now dreaming. Moreover, the supposition that I am now dreaming is coherent, and hence also logically consistent. To say that it is 'possibly actually true' that I am now dreaming is just to say that the supposition that I am now dreaming is coherent, and hence also logically consistent."

It is unclear what the relevant senses of "coherent" and "logically consistent" are, and I shall not try to elucidate them until later in this chapter, when I focus on the question of whether it is logically consistent for us to suppose that we lack minimal self-knowledge. In the meantime, to get my inquiry going, I shall simply accept (first) that to say that it is "possibly actually true" that I am now dreaming is just to say that the supposition that I am now dreaming is coherent, and hence also logically consistent, in some relevant senses of "coherent" and "logically consistent," and (second) that in those relevant senses of "coherent" and "logically consistent," the supposition that I am now dreaming is coherent, and hence also logically consistent. More generally, I shall accept the standard view that there are skeptical hypotheses that satisfy Condition 1(a) without begging the question against our ordinary assumptions about what we know.

Condition 2. The argument convinces us, in a series of steps each of which we can accept without begging the question against the beliefs we start with, to give up our starting, ordinary assumption that for some statements S in its domain, we know that S.

In this context, again, it is not legitimate simply to assert that it is epistemically possible for us that the skeptical hypothesis is true. Such an assertion would beg the question against our starting assumption that for some statements S in its domain, we know that S. The skeptic must provide an argument A for the initially unacceptable conclusion that we do not know any statement S in A's domain.

In the case of the dream argument, for instance, the skeptic must convince us that it is epistemically possible for us that we are now dreaming, and hence, by Condition 1(b), that we do not know S, for any statement S that specifies the content of one of our perceptual beliefs. In Barry Stroud's presentation of the dream argument, a key premise is that there are no certain indications by which to determine whether or not I am dreaming. This challenges us to defend our ordinary assumption that we know that we are not now dreaming, where it is assumed that the hypothesis that we are now dreaming satisfies Condition 1. And, according to Stroud, we find that we are unable to do so: anything in our experience to which we may appeal in an attempt to answer this challenge could itself be dreamt, and hence cannot serve to defend our ordinary assumption that we know that we are not now dreaming. If we find this reasoning convincing, we must retract any claim to know that we are not now dreaming, and even suspend our belief that we are not dreaming. We thereby change our minds about what is epistemically possible for us. We conclude that it is epistemically possible for us that we are now dreaming, and hence, by Condition 1(b), that we do not know S, for any S that specifies the content of one of our previous perceptual beliefs.

I shall not endorse or reject this familiar line of reasoning. My point in rehearsing it here is to illustrate one might try to develop a dream argument that satisfies Condition 2 if one supposes that the hypothesis that we are now dreaming satisfies Condition 1.

Condition 3. It is reasonable for us to take ourselves to be justified in accepting all of the premises of the argument, all at once.

We can derive Condition 3 from two appealing premises:

(i) We seek to accept only sound arguments – i.e. valid arguments whose premises are all true.

and

(ii) It is reasonable for us to accept a premise P of an argument (or any other statement, for that matter), and hence to regard P as true, only if we have justification for accepting P.

From (i) and (ii), it follows that it is reasonable for us to accept an argument only if we have justification for accepting all of its premises, all at once.

There are two ways an argument could *fail* to satisfy Condition 3. First, we may have good reasons that are independent of the argument itself for rejecting some of its premises, and hence do not take ourselves to be justified in accepting all of its premises. Second, we may find that the argument's premises, taken together, or its conclusion, undercut our justification for accepting some of its premises, so that we cannot take ourselves to be justified in accepting all of its premises, and its conclusion, all at once. If we don't find anything wrong with any of the premises, but realize that we cannot take ourselves to have justification for accepting all of them, as well as the conclusion of the argument, all at once, then I shall say that the argument is *self-undermining* – something is wrong with it, even if we cannot specify what. A skeptical argument that fails in either of these ways is unsuccessful.

One might worry that *reductio ad absurdum* arguments fail to satisfy Condition 3. But such arguments can be viewed as having *as premises* only those assumptions that the argument does not show to be contradictory or absurd. Thus viewed, *reductio ad absurdum* arguments satisfy Condition 3.

On some reconstructions of Descartes's dream argument, it is self-undermining, and hence fails to satisfy Condition 3. For instance, suppose we take Descartes's dream argument to rest on the following two premises (among others):

(P) There are no certain indications by which to determine whether or not one is dreaming.

and

(Q) One is justified in accepting (P) only if one is justified in believing that one has had dreams that were qualitatively indistinguishable from experiences that one has had while awake.

Suppose, also, that we accept (P), (Q), and other premises that together commit us to the skeptical conclusion that we don't know, and have no justification for accepting, any of our perceptual (or, more broadly, empirical) beliefs. Then, given (Q), one must conclude that one has no justification for accepting (P). Thus construed, the dream argument is self-undermining in the sense I explained above – one cannot take oneself to be justified in accepting all of its premises, all at once.

To avoid this problem, Barry Stroud rejects (Q). Stroud claims that we are justified in accepting (P) even if we have no justification for accepting any of our empirical beliefs, including our belief that in the past we have had dreams that were qualitatively indistinguishable from experiences that we have had while awake (Stroud 1984, p. 17). This reformulation makes it much more difficult to see why it is reasonable to accept (P), but it is required if the dream argument is to satisfy Condition 3.

One might object to Condition 3 on the grounds that some powerful and legitimate skeptical arguments introduce hypotheses (such as the hypothesis that an evil demon is now deceiving us about *everything*) that call into question all one's rules of reasoning, including the rules of reasoning that one takes to license (a) the inferences from their premises to their conclusions and (b) the inferences on which one's justification for accepting their premises relies.[1] Recall, however, that my goal in this section is to state conditions on the success of skeptical arguments, such as the dream argument, whose conclusions do not call into question all one's rules of reasoning. I believe that such *limited domain* skeptical arguments are successful only if they satisfy Condition 3.[2]

Putting these points together, I conclude that a limited domain skeptical argument is successful only if it satisfies Conditions 1–3:

Condition 1. The argument specifies an hypothesis H about how things may actually be for us such that (a) we grant that H is possibly actually true, (b) we grant that if H is actually true, we do not know that S, for any S in the domain of the argument.

Condition 2. The argument convinces us, in a series of steps each of which we can accept without begging the question against the beliefs we start with,

---

[1] Such an argument would be an (SU2) (ii) argument, according to Brueckner's classification in Chapter 13 of this volume.

[2] Suppose a given limited domain skeptical argument is self-undermining, but we take ourselves to have strong *prima facie* justifications for accepting each of its premises, and we are (so far) unable to identify any dubious premises in the argument. (Such an argument would be an (SU2) (i) argument, according to Brueckner's classification in Chapter 13 of this volume.) We should then be puzzled about what to believe, but we should not take the argument to establish its skeptical conclusion. Perhaps we could nevertheless take such an argument to yield a different sort of skeptical conclusion – roughly, that we are unable to arrive at a stable view about whether its conclusion is true. By confusing us about whether we know that S, for some S in its domain, such an argument might be taken to raise doubts about whether we know that S. In this chapter, I shall neither endorse nor reject this view, since it is not relevant to my criticisms of Brueckner's skeptical reasoning. If I am right, some of Brueckner's premises are much less plausible than the others, and so his argument does not present us with a puzzle that undermines our minimal self-knowledge.

to give up our starting, ordinary assumption that for some statements S in its domain, we know that S.

Condition 3. It is reasonable for us to take ourselves to be justified in accepting all of the premises of the argument, all at once.

12.2 BRUECKNER'S MAIN ARGUMENT

In this section I reconstruct what I take to be Brueckner's main argument for skepticism about minimal self-knowledge, and in the process consider, in a preliminary way, whether it satisfies Conditions 1 and 2. (The premises of my reconstruction here are the same as the ones I present in Chapter 10, Section 10.1.)

Brueckner's argument is designed to show that we cannot know without empirical investigation what thoughts our utterances express. To support this claim, Brueckner focuses on particular, representative statements about what thoughts our utterances express, statements our knowledge of which is in question. If the reasoning is sound, we should be able to generalize it to a large number of statements of that kind.

For instance, I ordinarily assume that I know without empirical investigation that my sincere utterances of 'There is water in the basement' express the thought that there is water in the basement. Bruckner starts by trying to specify an hypothesis H that satisfies Condition 1, where S is the statement that *my sincere utterances of 'There is water in the basement' express the thought that there is water in the basement*. For this purpose, he relies on standard Twin-Earth arguments to establish that we must each accept the following two sentences:

(1) In a possible world in which I live on water-filled Earth, my sincere utterances of 'There is water in the basement' express the thought that there is water in the basement.
(2) In a possible world in which I live on twin-water-filled Twin Earth, my sincere utterances of 'There is water in the basement' express the thought that there is twin-water in the basement.

Note that we are justified in accepting (1) and (2) only if we are justified in accepting standard anti-individualist arguments for them. Such thought experiments describe various possible worlds in which behavioral, functional twins of ours exist, and evoke our judgments about what thoughts our twins' utterances express in those possible worlds.

Note also that strictly speaking, it may be that I now live on twin-water-filled Twin Earth, but my sincere utterances of 'There is water in the basement' do not express the thought that there is twin-water in the basement. This could happen if, for instance, I was transported to twin-water-filled Twin Earth without my knowledge yesterday. In such a situation, most anti-individualists agree, I would remain an English speaker today, and speakers on Twin Earth who take my utterances of 'There is water in the basement' to express the thought that there is twin-water in the basement would be wrong. Similarly for premise (1). To accept Brueckner's premises (1) and (2), we must understand them to mean, in effect,

(1′) In a possible world in which I live on water-filled Earth, and speak English, the language used by members of the Earth community with which I interact, my sincere utterances of 'There is water in the basement' express the thought that there is water in the basement.

(2′) In a possible world in which I live on twin-water-filled Twin Earth and speak Twin-English, the language used by members of the Twin-Earth community with which I interact, my sincere utterances of 'There is water in the basement' express the thought that there is twin-water in the basement.

This clarification of premises (1) and (2) is important to my reasoning in Section 12.7 below. To save words I shall simply use "I live on twin-water-filled Twin Earth" as short for "I live on twin-water-filled Twin Earth, and speak Twin-English, the language used by members of the Twin-Earth community with which I interact", and similarly for "I live on water-filled Earth".

According to Brueckner's skeptic, the Twin-Earth thought experiments that establish (1) and (2) also show that we must each accept

(3) I know that if my sincere utterances of 'There is water in the basement' express the thought that there is water in the basement, then my sincere utterances of 'There is water in the basement' do not express the thought that there is twin-water in the basement.

The skeptic adds that we should each accept a general closure principle:

(4) If I know that p and I know that if p then q, then I know that q.

Premises (3) and (4) together imply

(5) If I know that my sincere utterances of 'There is water in the basement' express the thought that there is water in basement, then I know that my sincere utterances of 'There is water in basement' do not express the thought that there is twin-water in the basement.

Premises (1)–(5) constitute the heart of Brueckner's attempt to satisfy Condition 1, where S is the statement that *my sincere utterances of 'There is water in the basement' express the thought that there is water in the basement*, and H is the hypothesis that *I live on twin-water-filled Twin Earth*, understood in such a way that it implies, by (2), that my sincere utterances of 'There is water in the basement' express the thought that there is twin-water in the basement.

Let us now pause to check whether, given premises (1)–(5), the hypothesis H and statement S just specified satisfy Condition 1.

Consider Condition 1(b). Suppose I know that my sincere utterances of 'There is water in the basement' express the thought that there is water in the basement. Then, by (5), I know that my sincere utterances of 'There is water in basement' do not express the thought that there is twin-water in the basement. But the hypothesis that I now live on twin-water-filled Twin-Earth implies, by (2), that my sincere utterances of 'There is water in the basement' express the thought that there is twin-water in the basement, and hence that my sincere utterances of 'There is water in the basement' do not express the thought that there is water in the basement. But if my sincere utterances of 'There is water in the basement' do not express the thought that there is water in the basement, then I do not know that my sincere utterances of 'There is water in the basement' express the thought that there is water in the basement. Hence premises (1)–(5) satisfy Condition 1(b), where H is the hypothesis that I now live on twin-water-filled Twin Earth, and S is the statement that my sincere utterances of 'There is water in the basement' express the thought that there is water in the basement.

Now consider Condition 1(a), with the hypothesis H as just specified. Suppose I am considering the skeptical argument. I assume at the start that H is not true – that I do not live on twin-water-filled Twin Earth. I therefore do not regard it as epistemically possible for me that I now live on twin-water-filled Twin Earth. The question is whether I (and others who reflect about the above premises, as uttered by them) nevertheless grant that H is possibly actually true, in the sense I discussed above.

This is an obscure and difficult question. To get clearer about it, it helps to think more about the standard Twin-Earth thought experiments of the sort that support Premises (1) and (2). Such thought experiments presuppose that some person on Earth and his physical, behavioral, and phenomenological twin on Twin Earth are in the same subjective state, in some sense of "same" and "subjective," even if the thoughts they express by their respective utterances are different. Such thought experiments therefore suggest that for each person we can describe what I call *subjectively equivalent worlds*, in which everything that is relevant to the person's subjective assessment of her situation *seems the same* to her as it does in the actual world, in some sense of "seems the same," but in which her social or physical environments may, but need not, differ from her social and physical environment in the actual world. (Note that on this characterization of a subjectively equivalent world, the actual world is one of my subjectively equivalent worlds.)

It is not easy to articulate the relevant senses of "same" and "subjective" here, but I think many philosophers are initially inclined to accept that the assumption that the possible world in which I now live on twin-water-filled Twin Earth is subjectively equivalent for me, and that this implies that the hypothesis that I now live on twin-water-filled Twin Earth satisfies Condition 1(a). The idea is that just as it is possibly actually true that I am now dreaming, even though it is not epistemically possible for me that I am now dreaming (since I assume that I know that I am not now dreaming), so it is possibly actually true that I now live on twin-water-filled Twin Earth, even though it is not epistemically possible for me that I now live on twin-water-filled Twin Earth (since I assume that I know that I now live on water-filled Earth).

It is always problematic in philosophy to rely on analogies, and this one, in particular, raises many difficult questions about how to specify the sense of "seems the same" that is relevant to the hypothesis that I now live on twin-water-filled Twin Earth. Nevertheless, I shall grant, provisionally, that this hypothesis satisfies Condition 1(a). (I return to this crucial assumption in Sections 12.7–12.8 below.) More generally, for reasons I shall articulate in in Section 12.3, Brueckner's method for coming up with his H suggests that for a large number of statements S of the form

My sincere utterances of '_____' express the thought that _____.

where the blanks are filled by sentences of my language, we can find a skeptical hypothesis H that satisfies Condition 1.

Let us turn now to Condition 2. Can premises (1)–(5) by themselves convince me, in a series of steps each of which I can accept without begging the question against the beliefs I start with, to give up my starting assumption that I know without empirical investigation that my sincere utterances of 'There is water in the basement' express the thought that there is water in the basement? The answer is "No." I can accept all these premises without thereby having any reason to give up my assumption that I know without empirical investigation that my sincere utterances of 'There is water in the basement' express the thought that there is water in the basement. To get us to the skeptical conclusion that I do not know without empirical investigation that my sincere utterances of 'There is water in the basement' express the thought that there is water in the basement, Breuckner's argument must go beyond premises (1)–(5). Hence to satisfy Condition 2, we have to add premises that provide some reason to think that without empirical investigation we cannot rule out that we are in a possible world (such as the one described by premise (2)) in which our sincere utterances of 'There is water in the basement' express the thought that there is twin-water in the basement.

One might be inclined to think that it is enough to assert that

(0) Either I live on water-filled Earth or I live on twin-water-filled Twin Earth.

But if (0) is understood to imply that I don't know that we live on water-filled Earth, then it begs the question against my starting assumption that I know that I live on water-filled Earth, and the argument consisting of (1)–(5) and (0) therefore fails to satisfy Condition 2.

Brueckner does not explicitly address this problem, or acknowledge the importance of satisfying something like Condition 2. He often writes as if we must grant a premise such as (0) at the start, without deriving it from premises we ordinarily take ourselves to know. In my previous reconstructions (in Chapters 8 and 10) of Brueckner's skeptical argument, however, I formulate additional premises that, together with premises (1)–(5), seem to satisfy Condition 2 in a way that fits with Brueckner's attempts to establish a skeptical conclusion about minimal self-knowledge. In his replies to my criticisms of his argument, Brueckner has not objected to my reconstructions of it, and in Chapter 11, p. 182, he tacitly endorses it. I shall accordingly once again present these additional premises as part of a satisfactory reconstruction of his reasoning.

The first of these premises is a consequence of my above characterization of subjectively equivalent worlds. Generalizing from standard anti-individualist arguments for (1)–(3), the skeptic accepts that

(6) For each of us, there are subjectively equivalent worlds in which our (or our twins') sincere utterances express thoughts that are different from the thoughts that we take our sincere utterances to express in the actual world.

This premise does not move us beyond our starting assumption that we live on water-filled Earth, not on twin-water-filled Twin Earth. By highlighting the notion of subjective equivalence, however, this premise sets us up for reasoning about minimal self-knowledge in way that leads to a skeptical conclusion. As I reconstruct it, the reasoning has two additional steps:

(7) In all of our subjectively equivalent worlds our first-person experiences are the same.
(8) Without empirical investigation, our knowledge of our thoughts is confined to what we can derive solely from our first-person experiences.

These two premises in effect present a particular conception of self-knowledge, according to which it is based on our first-person experiences. This conception of self-knowledge, especially premise (8), suggests that minimal self-knowledge is rooted in a kind of introspection that involves scanning one's inner subjective experiences, and aiming to base one's beliefs about what one's utterances express on what one thereby learns of one's subjective experiences.

If one grants these additional premises (6)–(8), the resulting argument, (1)–(8), satisfies Condition 2. The key idea behind the argument is that without empirical investigation we do not know that we do not live on twin-water-filled Twin Earth, since the possible world in which we live on that planet is subjectively equivalent for us to the world we take ourselves to be in. In other words, without empirical investigation we cannot rule out the skeptical hypothesis that we live on twin-water-filled Twin Earth. Since, as we saw above, this hypothesis satisfies Condition 1(b), we must conclude that we do not know that our utterances of 'There is water in the basement' express the thought that there is water in the basement. Moreover, for reasons I shall explain in the next section, the same sort of reasoning that supports premises (1)–(5) may be used to generate a wide range of very similar premises that, together with premises (6)–(8), imply skeptical conclusions of the form "I do not know without empirical investigation that my sincere utterances of '_____' express the thought that _____," where the blanks are filled by sentences of my language.

12.3 BRUECKNER'S MAIN ARGUMENT AND CONDITION 3

I shall now argue that even if we grant that (1)–(8) satisfies Conditions 1 and 2 for the reasons explained in the previous section, it does not satisfy Condition 3 – we cannot reasonably take ourselves to be justified in accepting all of the premises of the argument, all at once.

To see the problem, it helps to recall that to construct the kinds of hypotheses that Brueckner takes to challenge our minimal self-knowledge, he relies on standard Twin Earth thought experiments that describe various possible worlds in which behavioral, functional twins of ours exist, and evoke our judgments about what thoughts our twins' utterances express in those possible worlds. In particular, Brueckner relies on one such thought experiment to establish that we must each accept sentences (1) and (2):

(1) In a possible world in which I live on water-filled Earth, my sincere utterances of 'There is water in the basement' express the thought that there is water in the basement.

(2) In a possible world in which I live on twin-water-filled Twin Earth, my sincere utterances of 'There is water in the basement' express the thought that there is twin-water in the basement.

Note, however, that my acceptance of these sentences does not alone guarantee that I can construct an hypothesis that conflicts with my assumption that I know that my sincere utterances of 'There is water in the basement' express the thought that there is water in the basement, and thereby satisfies Condition 1(b). Suppose, for instance, that Twin Earth is identical to Earth, and twin-water is identical to water. Then the hypothesis that I live on twin-water-filled Twin Earth does not conflict with my assumption that I know that my sincere utterances of 'There is water in the basement' express the thought that there is water in the basement. One might think we can somehow guarantee the truth of the statement that *Twin Earth is not identical to Earth, and twin water is not identical to water* by a special act of stipulation. As I argue in Chapter 6, note 31, however, if we accept anti-individualism, we are committed to the possibility, in principle, of discovering that Twin Earth is identical to Earth, and twin-water is identical to water.

Brueckner's skeptic must therefore make the case that the particular Twin-Earth thought experiments that establish (1) and (2) also show that we should each accept

(3) I know that if my sincere utterances of 'There is water in the basement' express the thought that there is water in the basement, then my sincere utterances of 'There is water in the basement' do not express the thought that there is twin-water in the basement.

For if we are persuaded by a particular Twin-Earth thought experiment to accept (1) and (2), understood in such a way that (3) is true, then we should each accept that the hypothesis that we live on twin-water-filled Twin Earth conflicts with our assumption that we know that our sincere utterances of 'There is water in the basement' express the thought that there is water in the basement.[3]

As I suggested above, this reasoning can be generalized. For there are bound to be convincing Twin-Earth thought experiments that support other triples of sentences of the forms

(F1) In subjectively equivalent world w, my sincere utterances of '_____' express the thought that _____,

---

[3] Strictly speaking, for reasons explained in Section 12.2 above, we should use formulations (1′) and (2′), and a corresponding (3′). Following Brueckner, I take a shortcut here by using the simpler formulations, (1)–(3).

(F2) In subjectively equivalent world w', my sincere utterances of '_____'
     express the thought that _ _ _ _ _ _,

(F3) I know that if my sincere utterances of '_____' express the thought that
    _____, then my sincere utterances of '_____' do not express the
    thought that _ _ _ _ _ _.

where the solid lines in (F1)–(F3) are uniformly replaced by a given sentence
S of one's language, the dashed lines in (F2) and (F3) are uniformly replaced
by a sentence S' of one's language that is different from S, and 'w' and 'w''
are assigned two of one's subjectively equivalent worlds, x and y, respectively, such that $x \neq y$. Such alternative premises would enable us to
construct an hypothesis H' that satisfies Condition 1(b), where the knowledge claim that H' undermines is of the form

I know that my sincere utterances of '_____' express the thought that

_____,

with the blanks filled by sentence S.

    Like (1)–(3), any triple of sentences obtained from the forms (F1)–(F3) in
the way I just described would support premise (6) of Brueckner's argument:

(6) For each of us, there are subjectively equivalent worlds in which our (or our
    twins') sincere utterances express thoughts that are different from the thoughts
    that we take our sincere utterances to express in the actual world.

This brings us to the heart of the matter. As I understand Brueckner's
argument, the role of premise (6) is not to provide any independent support
for anti-individualism, but

(i) To express a general truth that may be inferred by existential generalization
    from the particular Twin-Earth thought experiments that support premises
    (1)–(3), or from similar Twin-Earth thought experiments that support prem-
    ises of the forms (F1)–(F3) that are structurally similar to (1)–(3),

and

(ii) To relate the results of the particular Twin-Earth thought experiments that
    support premises (1)–(3), or similar ones, to premises (7) and (8), which reflect
    a certain conception of what is required for minimal self-knowledge.

In particular, as I understand Brueckner's argument,

(*) One is justified in accepting premise (6) only if one is justified in accepting
    particular, contrasting statements about what thoughts one's utterances would
    express in certain specified subjectively equivalent worlds – statements such as
    (1) and (2), understood in such a way that (3) is true.

And now we can see why Brueckner's argument is self-undermining. For if one accepts premises (6), (7), and (8), then one cannot know what thoughts one's sincere utterances of sentences (1)–(3) express. More generally, if one accepts premises (6), (7), and (8), then one cannot know what thoughts one's sincere utterances of any three sentences of the respective forms (F1)–(F3) express. One therefore cannot know without empirical investigation any particular triple of premises of the forms (F1), (F2), and (F3), respectively, from which one could infer (6). By (*), then, one is not justified in accepting (6).[4]

One might nevertheless think that (as Brueckner in effect[5] claims in Chapter 7) even if one accepts premises (6), (7), and (8), one is justified in believing that *whether or not one lives on water-filled Earth or on twin-water-filled Twin Earth, one's sincere utterances of sentences* (1)–(3) *express true propositions*. The problem is that even if one is justified in believing this, if one accepts premises (6)–(8), one has no justification for believing

(o) Either I live on water-filled Earth or I live on twin-water-filled Twin Earth.

One therefore cannot infer from the italicized claim that one's sincere utterances of sentences (1)–(3) express true propositions. In fact, as I showed in Chapter 8, the standardly accepted principles of anti-individualism imply that we can each describe what I call *weird worlds* – subjectively equivalent worlds in which our utterances of sentences (1) and (2) express false propositions. The method I used to construct weird worlds in Chapter 8 could also be used to construct similarly weird worlds for any pairs of sentences that are obtained from the forms (F1) and (F2) in the way I described above. Hence the method could be used to show that if one accepts premises (6)–(8), then for any two such sentences, one has no

---

[4] The situation is even worse that this, however, since, as I argued, in effect, in Chapter 8 (p. 156), if one accepts premises (6)–(8), then *with or without empirical investigation*, one cannot know what thoughts one's sincere utterances of any two sentences of the forms (F1) and (F3) express, and hence *with or without empirical investigation*, one is not justified in accepting (6). I qualify this with "in effect," because in Chapter 8 I did not specify the forms (F1)–(F3), but focused on particular instances of them.

[5] I write "in effect" here because in Chapter 7 Brueckner makes a weaker claim, namely, that even if one accepts premises (6)–(8), one is justified in believing that *whether or not one lives on water-filled Earth or on twin-water-filled Twin Earth, one's sincere utterances of sentences* (1)–(2) *express true propositions*. He does not focus on premise (3), but just assumes that if (1) and (2) are true, (3) is also true. As I noted above, however, this conditional is not guaranteed to be true and Brueckner must support each of (1)–(3) in order to show that his skeptical hypothesis satisfies Condition 1(b). I therefore take Brueckner to assume in Chapter 7 the stronger claim that even if one accepts premises (6)–(8), one is justified in believing that *whether or not one lives on water-filled Earth or on twin-water-filled Twin Earth, one's sincere utterances of sentences* (1)–(3) *express true propositions*.

justification for believing that they express true propositions. Given (*), then, if one accepts premises (6)–(8), one has no justification for accepting premise (6). In short, the argument (1)–(8), and any other argument sufficiently like it, but with different premises in place of (1)–(5), is *self-undermining* in the sense I described above: no one can justifiably accept all of its premises, all at once.

In this explanation of why Brueckner's argument is self-undermining, (6) and (*) are analogous, respectively, to (P) and (Q) of the self-undermining version of the dream argument that I discussed above in Section 12.1. In particular, just as

(P), together with certain familiar premises about what is required for perceptual knowledge, implies that
    (a) one is not justified in believing that one has had dreams that were qualitatively indistinguishable from experiences that one has had while awake, and hence, by (Q), that
    (b) one is not justified in accepting (P);

so

(6), together with premises (7) and (8), which partly characterize Brueckner's conception of minimal self-knowledge, implies that
    (a′) one is not justified in accepting any particular contrasting statements about what thoughts one's utterances would express in certain specified subjectively equivalent worlds – statements such as (1) and (2), understood in such a way that (3) is true, and hence, by (*), that
    (b′) one is not justified in accepting (6).

Recall that Stroud tries to save the dream argument from undermining itself by claiming that we are justified in accepting (P) even if we have no justification for accepting any of our empirical beliefs, including our belief that in the past we have had dreams that were qualitatively indistinguishable from experiences that we have had while awake. In short, according to Stroud, we are justified in accepting (P) even if we suppose that (Q) is false. Suppose Stroud is right about this. Could we save Brueckner's argument (1)–(8) from undermining itself by claiming, analogously, that we are justified in accepting (6) even if we suppose that (*) is false?

The answer, I believe, is "no." The problem is that no one has yet given any plausible justification for accepting (6), or for accepting anti-individualism more generally, that does not rest on particular claims of the sort exemplified by (1)–(3), and we have no idea how it could be reasonable to accept (6) without relying on such claims.[6] We therefore cannot reject (*) and still take ourselves to be justified in accepting (6).

I conclude that the argument (1)–(8), and any other argument sufficiently like it, but with different premises in place of (1)–(5), is *self-undermining* and therefore fails to satisfy Condition 3.

12.4 BRUECKNER'S (I)–(II)–(~K) ARGUMENT

Brueckner's response to this criticism of his argument (1)–(8) was to argue as follows (where '~K' is short for "I do not know that my sincere utterances of 'There is water in the basement' express the thought that there is water in the basement."):

> Either (I) my sincere utterances of 'There is water in the basement' express the thought that there is water in the basement, or (II) they do *not*, in virtue of my being in one of my subjectively equivalent worlds in which my utterances do *not* express the thought I take them to express. If (I) holds, then I can take the sentences in [(1)–(8)] at face value, and [(1)–(8)] *does* express a sound argument. So we have ~K. If (II) holds, then whatever argument is expressed by [(1)–(8)] – sound or not – we nevertheless have ~K. This is because I take my utterances to express the thought that there is water in the basement. If my utterances do *not* express that thought, then by the factivity of knowledge, I do *not* know that they *do*: that is ~K. (Chapter 11, p. 183)

I shall call this Brueckner's (I)–(II)–(~K) argument. One problem with the argument is that it presupposes that I do not know which of (I) and (II) is true, and therefore that I do not know whether I am in one of my weird subjectively equivalent worlds in which in (1)–(8) does not express a sound argument. The problem is that when the skeptic asserts the argument he expresses by using sentences (1)–(8), he cannot justifiably claim to have put

---

[6] Tyler Burge writes, "The celebrated twin-earth thought experiments are just illustrative. No one such experiment provides general grounds for anti-individualism" (Burge 2010, p. 80). This may appear to suggest that according to Burge we can have grounds for accepting (6) that are completely independent of any and all Twin-Earth thought experiments of the sort that support premises such as Brueckner's (1) and (2), understood in the way I explained in the text above. In fact, however, Burge does not claim in the above passage that we would have reasons to accept (6) even if we did not accept *any* particular Twin-Earth thought experiment. What he says is, "No *one* such experiment provides general grounds for anti-individualism." (My emphasis.) His point, I think, is that particular Twin-Earth thought experiments do not by themselves guide us in forming *explanatory* generalizations about how our mental contents, or the contents of the sentences we utter, are related to our social and physical environments. To formulate such generalization, we need to engage in another kind of reflection, a sort he sketches in Burge 2010, pp. 80–82. This is not a challenge to my claim that we have no idea how it could be reasonable to accept (6) without relying on particular claims of the sort exemplified by (1) and (2), understood in such a way that they imply (3).

forward a sound argument for ~K, and the skeptic's reasoning therefore does not satisfy Condition 3. (See Chapter 10, pp. 179–180.)

In Chapter 11, Brueckner grants this point, but nevertheless tries to show that we are justified in taking his (I)–(II)–(~K) argument to be sound. He presents two arguments that he believes we are justified in taking to be sound, and that are analogous to his (I)–(II)–(~K) argument. The first of these he presents as follows:

Consider the following example. I find what appear to be some English sentences written on the blackboard – call the set of sentences S′. I am told that the writer may well be using the language that is superficially similar to English but nevertheless *not* English (call it *Twenglish*). The sentences S′ are these:
  (A′) If you know that I am speaking English, then you know which language I am speaking.
  (B′) You do not know which language I'm speaking.
  (~K′) You do not know that I speak English.
Either (I′) the writer is speaking English, or (II′) the writer is not speaking English. If (I′) holds, then S′ expresses a sound argument. Premise A is obviously true under its English interpretation. Further, as matter of fact, I, the reader, do not know which language the writer is speaking – it could be English, and it could be Twenglish. So B′ is true. So if (I′) holds, then the argument is sound. We then have ~K′. On the other hand, if (II′) holds, then the writer is *not* speaking English. By the factivity of knowledge, I do not know the writer *is* speaking English. We then again have ~K′. (Chapter 11, p. 184)

Brueckner concludes that in this case we can established a skeptical conclusion by reasoning about an argument – the one expressed by S′ – that we do not know to be sound. Analogously, he believes, the skeptic about self-knowledge can establish his conclusion without knowing that the argument (1)–(8) is sound. He claims, in addition, that "in each case there is a larger argument that, it seems, I *do* know to be sound: (a) the argument proceeding from the assumption that either (I) or (II) holds, whose conclusion is ~K (skepticism about self-knowledge), [or] (b) the argument proceeding from the assumption that either (I′) or (II′) holds, whose conclusion is ~K′ (skepticism about knowledge of the blackboard writer's language)..." (Chapter 11, p. 185).

There is a problem with Brueckner's reasoning about the blackboard example, however. In this example, we are given only that "the writer may well be using the language that is superficially similar to English but nevertheless *not* English (call it *Twenglish*)." From this and the assumption that the writer is not speaking English (II′) we should conclude that we do not know what the sentences in the set S′ mean. Since ~K′ is in the set S′, we should therefore conclude that we do not know what ∼K′ means. (It does not help to be told that ∼K′ is part of Twenglish, which is superficially similar to English, since we do not know what the similarities are.) But since we do not know what ∼K′ means, we do not know, in particular, that ∼K′ has the same meaning as the English sentence 'You do not know that I speak English'. Hence we cannot conclude that ∼K′ is true. In short, if (II′), we have no basis for concluding ∼K, as Brueckner does. We therefore have no basis for concluding that there is a sound argument proceeding from the assumption that either (I′) or (II′) holds, whose conclusion is ∼K (skepticism about knowledge of the blackboard writer's language).

Another argument that Brueckner takes to be analogous to his (I)–(II)–(∼K) argument rests on the premise that either (I″) I am a normal human being in a normal world who has hands, or (II″) I am in a subjectively equivalent world in which I have no hands (in virtue of being a brain in a vat, or a victim of Evil Genius deception, or . . .). (Chapter 11, pp. 184–185) The problem with this premise is similar to the problem I raised for (0) above: the disjunction (I′) or (II″) only covers a proper subset of my subjectively equivalent worlds, and hence we cannot take ourselves to be justified in accepting this premise without empirical investigation if, as Brueckner supposes, we do not know without empirical investigation which of our subjectively equivalent worlds we are actually in.

But perhaps Brueckner does not need to provide analogous arguments, such as the blackboard argument, in order to support his claim that his (I)–(II)–(∼K) argument is sound. Perhaps it is enough for his skeptic to assert (6)–(8) of argument (1)–(8), and then argue that he can derive ∼K from either (I) or (II), which together exhaust all the alternatives.

This reply may at first seem plausible, but, in fact, it highlights the deepest problem with Brueckner's (I)–(II)–(∼K) argument, namely, that it overlooks (*), the central premise in my argument that Brueckner's argument (1)–(8) is self-undermining. Brueckner's skeptic apparently ignores (*) and asserts (6) without providing any justification for it. As I explained above, however, we know of no plausible justification for accepting (6), or for accepting anti-individualism more generally, that does not rest on particular claims of the sort exemplified by (1) and (2), understood in such a way that they imply (3), and we therefore have no idea how it could be reasonable to accept (6) without relying on such claims. We therefore cannot reject (*) and still take ourselves to be justified in accepting (6). This shows, I think, that we have no justification for believing that Brueckner's (I)–(II)–(∼K) argument is sound. We have reason for believing it is sound only if his argument (1)–(8), or a similar argument, with different but structurally similar premises in place of

(1)–(5), satisfies Condition 3. I conclude that Brueckner's (I)–(II)–(∼K) argument fails to satisfy Condition 3 for essentially the same reasons that his (1)–(8) argument fails to satisfy Condition 3 – it overlooks (*).

12.5 ON THE RELATIVE PLAUSIBILITY OF BRUECKNER'S PREMISES

Let us return, then, to our evaluation of Brueckner's argument (1)–(8). The fact that this argument is self-undermining, and therefore fails to satisfy Condition 3, does not tell us which of its premises is implausible or false. With the goal of finding and diagnosing the mistakes in Brueckner's argument (1)–(8), let us now try to determine which of its premises are the least plausible.

I begin with premise (6). Some might be inclined to reject this premise, and thereby, in effect, to reject anti-individualism. As we saw above, however, (6) is supported by premises (1)–(3), and premises (1)–(3) are themselves supported by standard Twin-Earth thought experiments. We therefore cannot reject (6) without also rejecting premises (1)–(3), and any other, similar premises that imply (6). And since our acceptance of premises of this kind that imply (6) are themselves justified by standard Twin Earth thought experiments, to reject the premises that support (6), such as (1)–(3), is thereby to reject standard Twin-Earth thought experiments. I accept these arguments, however, and so does Brueckner. Neither one of us regards it as a serious option to reject the standard Twin-Earth thought experiments that support such premises as (1)–(3), which imply (6). Hence neither one of us regards it as a serious option to give up premise (6).

The remaining premises to consider are (4), (5), (7), and (8). Premise (5) follows from (3) and (4). We have already vetted premise (3). So let's look at (4). This is a closure principle of a sort that is familiar from many discussions in epistemology. Although some philosophers reject such principles, Brueckner and I both accept (4). For me this comes down to a judgment of comparative plausibility. For reasons I explain in the next paragraph, I believe that the puzzles generated by Brueckner's argument (1)–(8) highlight the implausibility of (7) and (8). We can avoid the puzzles by rejecting those premises (7) and (8), hence without rejecting (4).

As I noted above, premises (7) and (8) in effect present a particular *conception* of minimal self-knowledge, according to which if one has such knowledge at all, it must be based on one's introspective awareness of one's inner subjective experiences. The idea is that if *u* is one of one's utterances, then to know what thought *u* expresses, one must form a true belief about what *u* expresses, a belief that is also *justified* by the relevant inner subjective experiences that one has while uttering *u*. This conception of minimal self-knowledge is central to Brueckner's skeptical reasoning. For if *u* is one of one's utterances of 'There is water in the basement', for instance, then, given (1)–(6), together with (7) and (8), no belief about what thought *u* expresses that I can arrive at without empirical investigation is justified, and hence I cannot have minimal self-knowledge of what thought *u* expresses.

Conceptions of minimal self-knowledge that imply (7) and (8) are at best controversial, however. Tyler Burge, for instance, rejects them. According to Burge 1988a, we know what thoughts we are presently thinking not by examining our subjective first-person experiences of thinking, but by *thinking the thoughts self-ascriptively*, as when I judge that *I am now thinking, with this very thought, that Burge's account of minimal self-knowledge is different from Brueckner's account of minimal self-knowledge*. It may be that standard ways of constructing Twin-Earth thought experiments strongly suggest a conception of self-knowledge that implies (7) and (8), by tempting us to believe that it is coherent to worry about which of our subjectively equivalent worlds we are actually in. But the fact that Brueckner's argument is self-undermining shows, I think, that we should resist this temptation. I conclude that premises (7) and (8) are the least plausible of Brueckner's premises (1)–(8).

12.6 A MINIMALIST CONCEPTION OF MINIMAL SELF-KNOWLEDGE

To resist the temptation to accept (7) and (8), we need to articulate a conception of minimal self-knowledge that does not imply (7) and (8), and that is more plausible than any conception of minimal self-knowledge that does imply (7) and (8). In Chapters 6, 8, and 10 of this volume, and in Ebbs 2009, Sections 9.4–9.8, I sketch a minimalist conception of minimal self-knowledge that satisfies these conditions, but differs from most standard conceptions, including Burge's, in that it does not imply that all self-knowledge is metalinguistic, second-order, or reflexive. The key idea behind my minimalist conception is that

(C1) To take a speaker to use words of her language to express thoughts, make claims, raise questions, and so on is also to take her to have minimal self-knowledge of the thoughts she thereby expresses.[7]

---

[7] Principle (C1) is designed to accommodate and explain Putnam's observation (in Putnam 1981, Chapter 1, and Putnam 1988, p. 32) that the only sense in which most speakers know what they are thinking when they utter their own words and sentences is that they are able to *use* those words and sentences in discourse and inquiry.

Recall, for instance, the thought experiment we used to support (1) and (2). When Oscar utters the sentence, 'There is water in the basement', in the situation described in the thought experiment, we take Oscar to have said that there is water in the basement. By (C1), to take Oscar to have said that there is water in the basement by uttering the sentence 'There is water in the basement' is *also* to take Oscar to have minimal self-knowledge of the thoughts that he thereby expresses – the thought that there is water in the basement. Similarly, when Twin-Oscar utters the sentence, 'There is water in the basement', in the situation described in the thought experiment, we take Twin-Oscar to have said that there is twin-water in the basement. By (C1), to take Twin-Oscar to have said that there is twin-water in the basement by uttering the sentence 'There is water in the basement' is *also* to take Twin-Oscar to have minimal self-knowledge of the thoughts that he thereby expresses – the thought (as we express it) that there is twin-water in the basement.

If we adopt a conception of minimal self-knowledge that implies (C1), we will conclude that minimal self-knowledge goes hand-in-hand with minimal linguistic competence – the sort of competence in the use of words that we take to license particular attributions of thoughts and beliefs to a speaker. To elucidate minimal self-knowledge, we must therefore elucidate minimal linguistic competence.

Let me begin with two preliminary observations about minimal linguistic competence. First, to be minimally linguistically competent in the use of given word w or sentence s, one must do more than simply write or utter a word or sentence that has the same spelling as w or s. We will not take a person to be minimally competent in the use of the English word 'elm', for instance, if the only sentences with occurrences of 'E-l-m' in them that she accepts are, 'Elms are geese', and 'Elms fly south in the winter', and she refuses to accept any attempts to correct the judgments she express by her utterances of these sentences. Second, as Hilary Putnam emphasizes (in Putnam 1975), not much is required for minimal linguistic competence in the use of the English word 'elm'. One does not need to be able to distinguish elm trees from beech trees to be in a position to use 'elm' or 'beech' in utterances that are taken at face value by other English speakers, and evaluated accordingly, and thereby to be judged minimally competent in the use of either 'elm' or 'beech'. Beyond these observations, however, is not easy to say what *is* required for minimal competence in the use of 'elm', or of any other word. Such requirements can only be discovered by investigating our actual practices of identifying another speaker's words or sentences with words or sentences that we can directly use to specify the thoughts that his utterances express.

There are three additional observations about minimal linguistic competence that are especially important for our understanding of minimal self-knowledge, given (C1). First, although it may be that there is no single belief that every speaker whom we take to be minimally competent in the use of given word w expresses by using w, a careful look at our practices of taking other speakers to be using words of English shows that for each speaker who is taken to be minimally competent in the use of a given word w there is some belief or other that she expresses by using w. Together with (C1), this observation implies that

(C2) A speaker has minimal competence in the use of w only if there are some beliefs or other that she expresses by using w.

Second, the beliefs that a speaker expresses by using w are part of her present *understanding* of the truth conditions of the thoughts she uses w to express. Such beliefs do not *determine* the truth conditions of the thoughts she uses w to express, however, since the beliefs may be false or misleading. A speaker may have minimal competence in the use of a given word w even if her understanding of the truth conditions of thoughts that she expresses by using w is partial, confused, or incorrect. Together with (C1), this observation commits us to the conclusion that a speaker may also have minimal self-knowledge of the thoughts she expresses by using w even if her understanding of those thoughts is partial, confused, or incorrect. In short, and contrary to what many philosophers are tempted to believe,

(C3) A speaker may have minimal self-knowledge even if she does not have accurate beliefs about the truth conditions of the thoughts her utterances express.

Third, we typically acquire our minimal competence in the first instance through testimony from others (Austin 1979, p. 83 n. 1). When we learn the word 'elm', for example, we are told that elms are trees, and perhaps are shown an example of an elm. Either we trust what we are told, or we ask others to corroborate it. In the first instance, then, our competence in the use of the word 'elm' is typically not based on our own empirical investigations into how others use the word, but in their telling us how it is used. Moreover, for many words, including 'water', and other natural kind terms, our minimal linguistic competence typically rests on substantive, empirical beliefs that we express by using the words and that we learned from the testimony of others. Nevertheless, there is a perfectly ordinary sense in which, even in the early stages of language learning, to be minimally competent in the use of a given word w, we do not need to go through any special empirical investigations of our own. Given (C1), this observation shows that we may have minimal self-knowledge of what thoughts our uses of a given word *w* express even if we do not know this *a priori* – i.e. without relying on anything but reasoning and introspection. More generally,

(C4) To know "without empirical investigation" what thoughts one's uses of a given word *w* express is not to know *a priori* (i.e. without relying on anything but reasoning and introspection) what thoughts one's uses of *w* express, but, instead, to know it *without going through any special empirical investigation of one's own*.

If we accept (C1)–(C4), as I propose, then we will conclude that a person may have minimal self-knowledge even if she does not actually entertain any metalinguistic beliefs about what thoughts her utterances express. Our use of words to express our own thoughts is therefore practically and conceptually prior to any metalinguistic reflections about what thoughts we thereby express. We are nevertheless each in a position to formulate and accept metalinguistic beliefs about what thoughts our utterances express if we understand disquotation. For instance, a person who knows how to use the English sentence 'There is water in the basement' and understands disquotation is thereby in a position to assert the sentence, "My utterances of 'There is water in the basement' in the language I now actually speak as I now use it express the thought that there is water in the basement." When I assert this sentence, for instance, I thereby express my disquotational metalinguistic belief that my utterances of 'There is water in the basement' in the language I now actually speak as I now use it express the thought that there is water in the basement.

In short, to have minimal self-knowledge of what thoughts one's utterances express is to just be able to use those words to express those thoughts. If, in addition, one understands disquotation, then one is in a position to express a disquotational metalinguistic sentence of the form:

(D) My utterances of '_____' in the language I now actually speak as I now use it express the thought that _____.

Given (C1)–(C4), however, our minimal self-knowledge goes hand in hand with our use of words to express our own thoughts, and is therefore both practically and conceptually prior to our acceptance of particular instances of (D). It is also practically and conceptually prior to our explicit acceptance of particular instances of:

(B) I judge by this very thought that I am thinking that _____.

Judgments that we express by affirming particular instances of (B) are *reflexive*, to use Burge's terminology – they involve explicit self-ascriptions of thoughts, or particular acts of thinking. One might think that the minimalist conception of self-knowledge is unacceptable because it has the consequence that the speaker has minimal self-knowledge even when she does not explicitly self-ascribe the thoughts she is expressing. In fact, however, this consequence of the minimalist conception fits well with our actual practices of ascribing minimal self-knowledge to ourselves and others. It is not the minimalist conception that fails to fit with such practices, but the requirements that minimal self-knowledge be explicitly reflexive. Burge in effect concedes this point when he asserts (as he should, given his view) that

> Many cases of self-aware conscious thoughts that *p* – that is, self-aware propositional attitudes that do not explicitly formulate a self-attribution of the propositional attitude – are nevertheless reflexive self-attributions of the relevant attitude toward the content that *p*. The self-awareness often involves an unarticulated reflexive self-attribution. (Burge 2003, p. 430)

In my view, however, it is less artificial to adopt the minimalist conception of minimal self-knowledge characterized by (C1)–(C4) above, and to add that in some cases speakers also self-attribute such knowledge.

12.7 WHY BRUECKNER'S HYPOTHESIS DOES NOT SATISFY CONDITION 1(A)

Let us now return to the question of whether Brueckner's skeptical hypothesis that *I now live on twin-water-filled Twin Earth* is "possibly actually true" in a way that satisfies Conditions 1(a). Suppose, again, that I am considering Brueckner's skeptical argument, but without premises (7) and (8), which we've now seen to be implausible. I assume at the start that I do not live on twin-water-filled Twin Earth, and I take myself to have minimal self-knowledge – I take myself to know without empirical investigation that my sincere utterances of 'There is water in the basement' express the thought that there is water in the basement. I therefore do not regard it as epistemically possible for me that I now live on twin-water-filled Twin Earth. Can I coherently grant that Brueckner's skeptical hypothesis that *I now live on twin-water-filled Twin Earth* is "possibly actually true" in a way that satisfies Conditions 1(a)?

In Section 12.2, I accepted, provisionally, that the answer is "yes." The standard ways of constructing Twin-Earth thought experiments tempt us to believe that it is coherent to worry about which of our subjectively equivalent worlds we are actually in. The idea is that just as it is possibly actually true that I am now dreaming, even though it is not epistemically possible for me that I am now dreaming (since I assume that I know that I am not now dreaming), so it is possibly actually true that I live on twin-water-filled Twin Earth, even though it is not epistemically possible for me that I now live on twin-water-filled Twin Earth (since I assume that I know that I now live on water-filled Earth).

If we adopt the minimal conception of minimal self-knowledge sketched in the previous section, however, then we can show that Brueckner's skeptical hypothesis that we are actually on twin-water-filled Twin Earth is contradictory, and hence that it cannot satisfy Condition 1(a). Recall first, however, that Brueckner's skeptical hypothesis that I live on twin-water-filled Twin Earth is short for the hypothesis that I live on twin-water-filled Twin Earth, and speak Twin-English, the language used by members of the Twin-Earth community with whom I interact. We can now add that I speak Twin-English only if I am minimally competent in the uses of Twin-English words. Together, these points support the following lemma:

Lemma. It is built into Brueckner's skeptical hypothesis that I now live on twin-water-filled Twin Earth that I am minimally competent in the uses of my words 'There is water in the basement', as I now use them, and that these are the Twin-English words 'There is water in the basement'.

We may now reason as follows. Suppose (toward contradiction) that Brueckner's skeptical hypothesis that I now live on twin-water-filled Twin Earth is true. Then, by the Lemma,

(M) I am minimally competent in the uses of my words 'There is water in the basement', as I now use them.

But, also by the Lemma, my words 'There is water in the basement', as I now use them are the Twin-English words 'There is water in the basement'. My utterances of them therefore do not express the thought that there is water in the basement. This conflicts with at least one thing that I take myself to know without empirical investigation, namely, that my sincere utterances of 'There is water in the basement' express the thought that there is water in the basement. I must infer that in this respect, at least, I do not have minimal self-knowledge. From (C1), I can then infer that

(~M) I am not minimally competent in the use of my words 'There is water in the basement', as I now use them.

The conjunction of (M) and (~M) is a contradiction. Hence Brueckner's skeptical hypothesis that I now live on twin-water-filled Twin Earth cannot be true.

If one reads this argument too quickly, it might appear that it begs the question against Brueckner's skeptical hypothesis that I now live on twin-water-filled Twin Earth by assuming that I know without empirical investigation that my sincere utterances of 'There is water in the basement' express the thought that there is water in the basement, and inferring from this premise that I do not live on twin-water-filled Twin Earth. But this is not how the argument works. The argument shows, instead, that if we adopt the miminalist conception of self-knowledge, then to suppose that we do not have minimal self-knowledge of what thoughts our utterances of 'There is water in the basement' express is thereby *also* to suppose that we do not have minimal linguistic competence in the use of the words 'There is water in the basement' – a supposition that conflicts with Brueckner's hypothesis that I now live on twin-water-filled Twin Earth, as understood in accordance with the Lemma. The reasoning exploits the fact that if we adopt the minimal conception of minimal self-knowledge, we cannot separate our assumption that we have minimal self-knowledge from our acceptance of the empirical, substantive beliefs that (by (C1)–(C4)) partly constitute our minimal linguistic competence. To adopt the minimalist conception of self-knowledge is therefore to commit oneself to principles from which it follows that Brueckner's skeptical hypothesis cannot actually be true. His skeptical hypothesis therefore fails to satisfy Condition 1(a).

12.8 BIPOLARITY, UNIPOLARITY, AND ENTITLEMENT

I began my investigation of Brueckner's skeptical argument by granting, provisionally, that his skeptical hypothesis satisfies Condition 1, but have now arrived at the conclusion that Brueckner's skeptical hypothesis (understood without assuming premises (7) and (8)) cannot actually be true, and hence fails to satisfy Condition 1. If my reasoning is successful, it should convince us that Brueckner's skeptical hypothesis does not describe how things may actually be. But how could an argument change our minds about whether a given statement describes how things may actually be? This is a deep and difficult question to which I shall now only briefly sketch an answer.

My sketch relies on the following terminology:

Bipolarity: Person P takes statement S to be bipolar (at t) if and only if P can make sense of S's being true (at t) and P can make sense of S's being not true (at t).

Example: As I write this (at 10:48 a.m. on July 12, 2011) I take the statement that *President Obama is now in Washington, D.C.* to be bipolar. I believe that President Obama is now in Washington, D.C. but I can make sense of its being not true that President Obama is now in Washington, D.C.

Unipolarity: P takes S to be unipolar (at t) if and only if P can make sense of S's being true (at t) or P can make sense of S's being not true (at t), but not both.

Example: I take the statement that *water is wet and water is not wet* to be unipolar, since I cannot make sense of its being true, but I can make sense of its being not true – indeed, I accept the negation of the statement.

Note that the sentences that we use to express false, unipolar statements are meaningful.

Note also that the phrase "make sense of S's being true" is schematic. What it takes to make sense of S's being true may vary from statement to statement, and even, perhaps, from context to context.

The crucial methodological point is that *we may change our minds about whether a statement is bipolar*. To see how, let us start with a simple case in which we learn that a statement we (briefly) took to be bipolar is (we now think) unipolar (this sort of example is taken from Chapter 4 in this volume):

(Δ) There is a barber who lives in Tisbury, Massachusetts and who shaves all and only those who live in Tisbury, Massachusetts but who do not shave themselves.

This statement follows a familiar form that is known to be contradictory, and hence we know that the statement is not true. When one first encounters a statement of this form, however, one might very well suppose that it may actually be true, and hence that it is bipolar. It takes some reasoning to see that it is inconsistent, hence unipolar, and not true. Without yet knowing whether the statement is consistent, we may try to get clearer about the conditions under which it would be true, if it were consistent. We may at first have supposed that (Δ) is bipolar, and may actually be true, but on further reflection we find that it is inconsistent, and hence unipolar – we cannot make sense of its being true.

Let us now apply this same pattern to the more complicated case in which we initially regard Bruckner's hypothesis that we live on twin-water-filled Twin Earth as bipolar, and possibly actually true, and later come to believe that it is inconsistent, and hence unipolar – we cannot make sense of its being true. When one first encounters Bruckner's hypothesis that we live on twin-water-filled Twin Earth, one might very well suppose that it is possibly actually true, and hence that it is bipolar. As we saw above, it takes a longer train of reasoning to see that it is inconsistent, hence unipolar, and not true. Without yet knowing whether the hypothesis is consistent, we may try to get clearer about the conditions under which it would be true, if it were consistent.

This was my strategy above. I assumed provisionally that the hypothesis is bipolar and hence consistent, and that it satisfies Condition 1. I then reconstructed Brueckner's reasoning in a way that satisfies Condition 2, and argued that it fails to satisfy Condition 3, because it is self-undermining. I diagnosed the problem as due to Brueckner's tacit conception of minimal self-knowledge, a conception that commits him to the implausible premises (7) and (8). I proposed that we adopt, instead, a minimalist conception of self-knowledge that implies (C1)–(C4). Finally, I argued that if we adopt this conception, then we cannot accept that Brueckner's hypothesis that we actually live on twin-water-filled Twin Earth is bipolar, and hence possibly actually true, in the sense relevant to Condition 1(a). The problem, as we saw above, is that if I adopt the minimalist conception of minimal self-knowledge, then Brueckner's hypothesis that I actually live on twin-water-filled Twin Earth implies both (M) and (~M). We may at first have supposed that Brueckner's hypothesis is bipolar, and may actually be true, but on further reflection we find that it is inconsistent, and hence unipolar – we cannot make sense of its being true.

This reasoning depends on my proposal that we adopt the minimalist conception of minimal self-knowledge. One might think that this proposal unfairly begs the question against the coherence of Brueckner's skeptical hypothesis that we are on twin-water-filled Twin Earth. But what does fairness require here? A skeptical challenge to our ordinary and scientific beliefs can succeed only if it relies solely on principles and premises that we cannot reasonably reject. We are therefore fully within our rights to respond to Brueckner's skeptical argument by rejecting his problematic conception of minimal self-knowledge and adopting the minimalist conception of minimal self-knowledge, from which it follows, as we have seen, that his skeptical hypothesis is unipolar and false. Similar reasoning can be used to show that we are entitled to accept the negations of any other hypotheses that tempt us to suppose that we can be minimally linguistically competent in the use of our words, yet fail to know without going through any special empirical investigation (recall (C4)) what thoughts our utterances express.

Finally, let us briefly consider how these reflections bear on the question of whether we are entitled to believe that we have minimal self-knowledge. Our failure to be able to raise a coherent skeptical doubt about whether we have minimal self-knowledge does not show that we can say why we believe that we have minimal self-knowledge without presupposing that we have minimal self-knowledge. To keep track of this point, it is useful to use the ordinary term 'reason' in a restricted way that is partly fixed by the following constraint:

(T1) A person has a *reason* for believing that S only if she can say *why* she believes that S without presupposing that S.

We can then express the above observation as follows: our failure to be able to raise a coherent skeptical doubt about whether we have minimal self-knowledge is not a reason, in the sense of 'reason' constrained by (T1), to believe that we have minimal self-knowledge.

Our failure to be able to raise a coherent skeptical doubt about whether we have minimal self-knowledge may nevertheless have positive epistemic significance. For it is plausible to suppose that there are some statements, such as the statement that *it is not the case that water is wet and water is not wet*, that it is epistemically reasonable for us to believe, despite the fact that we have no *reason* for believing them, in the sense of "reason" constrained by (T1). We need a word to describe the epistemological standing of such beliefs. I propose that we use 'entitlement', subject to the following constraint:

(T2) A person has an *entitlement* (or is entitled) to believe that S if and only if she has no reason (in the sense of 'reason' constrained by (T1)) for believing that S – she cannot say *why* she believes that S without relying on S – but it is *epistemically reasonable* for her to believe that S.

To relate (T2) to statements that we take to be unipolar and true, such as *it is not the case that water is wet and water is not wet*, I propose that we adopt the following principle:

(T3) If a person understands a statement S well enough to raise the question of whether or not S is to be believed, she tries to specify a way in which S may actually be false, exercises due diligence in this effort, but finds she is unable to specify a way in which S may actually be false, then it is *epistemically reasonable* for her to believe that S.

If we accept (T1)–(T3), as I propose,[8] then if we regard a statement S as unipolar and true, we are thereby also committed to regarding ourselves as entitled to accept S. In particular, if we accept (T1)–(T3), we may take

---

[8] For a more detailed defense and application of principles similar to (T1)–(T3), see Ebbs 2009, Section 4.9.

ourselves to be entitled to accept that there is no barber of the sort described by (Δ), that water is not both wet and not wet, and that we have minimal self-knowledge.

Brueckner's skeptical reasoning pushes our understanding of minimal self-knowledge to its limits and beyond. Despite the apparent plausibility of Brueckner's reasoning, I have found I cannot reconstruct it in a way that satisfies Conditions 1–3. One main problem is that it presupposes an implausible, observational conception of self-knowledge. If we adopt the minimalist conception of self-knowledge, as I propose, we simultaneously avoid the problems with Brueckner's reasoning, and commit ourselves to principles that imply that we cannot make sense of doubting that we have minimal self-knowledge. Finally, if we adopt the methodological framework that I just sketched, we are in a position to see that our failure to make sense of doubting that we have minimal self-knowledge entitles us to believe that we have it.[9]

[9] My thinking about self-knowledge and anti-individualism was shaped early on by many stimulating discussions with Hilary Putnam, whose views about minimal self-knowledge and the methodology of inquiry are the main inspiration for my account of why we are entitled to believe that we have minimal self-knowledge. The details of my account have been slow in coming, however, and hard won. I thank all those whose comments on Chapters 2, 4, 6, 8, and 10 of this volume helped me to develop and clarify the views I summarize here. I also thank Mark Kaplan for comments that led to improvements in Section 12.1. If I have made progress in my effort to show that we cannot make sense of doubting that we have minimal self-knowledge, however, it is largely due to Tony Brueckner's challenging and resourceful responses to my criticisms of his attempts to raise a skeptical problem for minimal self-knowledge. I thank Tony for his willingness to debate these issues with me in detail and to collaborate with me on this volume, and for his excellent comments about previous drafts of this chapter.

CHAPTER 13

Looking back

Anthony Brueckner

13.1 INTRODUCTION

As I originally saw it, the central issue that is debated in this volume is this: assume externalism about mental content, on the one hand, and about meaning, reference, and truth conditions, on the other (i.e., assume Burgean anti-individualism and Putnamian semantic externalism); does it then follow that one can generate a coherent, prima facie powerful argument for skepticism about knowledge of (1) one's contents, and (2) the semantic properties of one's own language? I originally answered this question in the affirmative, and Gary Ebbs answered in the negative. The real bone of contention between us, I think, concerns the *grounds* for his *negative* answer. Ebbs holds that arguments for skepticism about knowledge of content are somehow *incoherent* or *self-undermining*. He also holds that skepticism about knowledge of the semantic properties of one's own language rests upon a mistaken conception of the dialectical situation regarding the Putnamian semantic framework that allegedly powers such skepticism: Ebbs maintains that we cannot make sense of the putative possibility behind such skepticism. Let us lump these claims of Ebbs together under the rubric of *the incoherence charge*. The bulk of the Ebbs–Brueckner debate concerns the question of whether the incoherence charge against skepticism about knowledge of (1) one's contents, and (2) the semantic properties of one's own language, can be made good *and* can be shown to be significant. I argued in the negative, but this does not mean that I embrace the skepticism in question. After struggling with these issues for many years – going back to my 1986 Chapter 1, which, I think, is the first paper in which Putnam-fueled skepticism about knowledge of the semantic properties of one's own language was bruited – I am agnostic on the question of whether the prima facie skeptical worries generated by anti-individualism and semantic externalism are well-founded. However, I do still think that these genuine worries cannot be clearly answered by adverting to the incoherence charge. But that view is compatible with the view that there is some *other* sort of answer. As emerges below, however, in looking back, I realize that there is some convergence between Ebbs and me on the incoherence charge, but there remains disagreement about its significance.

As the reader who has made it this far well knows, Ebbs and I have gone round and round on a byzantine set of issues. But that is what happens in philosophy. You start with relatively well-defined theses (e.g., anti-individualism), and some natural questions about them arise. Resolving the questions requires examination of a number of consequences of the theses in question, and you eventually find that that resolution in turn depends upon examination of complex, detailed, tricky considerations involving those consequences. As they say, the devil is in the details! This is especially true in philosophy, where it is often the case that a lot hangs on the arcane details.

In the case of the debate recorded in this volume, the pertinent details are extremely delicate. At one point in an exchange between Ebbs and myself, I said, in a homage to *Monty Python*'s John Cleese, "Alas, my brain hurts." Looking back on the debate, I would now like to make some observations.

13.2 THE PUTNAMIAN DIALECTICAL SITUATION

A theme in my Chapter 1 is that the conclusion of my reconstructed Putnamian anti-skeptical argument is *metalinguistic* in nature:

(C) My utterances of 'I am a BIV' are false.

In order to reach the desired *non*-metalinguistic conclusion

(C*) I am not a BIV

I need to appeal to reasoning involving the interaction between negation and the device of quotation, from (C) to

(C′) My utterances of 'I am not a BIV' are true

and then I need to use a disquotational principle in order to derive (C*) from (C′):

(DQ) My utterances of 'I am not a BIV' are true iff I am not a BIV.

But the dialectical situation, on my understanding of it, *blocks* such an appeal. I enter into the argument lacking knowledge of whether or not I am a BIV. The point of the argument is to prove (C*), that is, that I am not a BIV. Putnam holds that (A) if I *am* a BIV, then my sentences do *not* have disquotational truth conditions, and (B) if I am *not* a BIV, then my sentences *do* have disquotational truth conditions. These Putnamian semantic claims constitute the backbone of the reconstructed anti-skeptical argument. So in the course of proving (C*) I need to assume, at the last step, that the antecedent of (B) is true. But that antecedent is what the argument is supposed to prove.

Ebbs's considered response to this objection to the reconstructed argument is found in Chapter 4. He grants that in the Putnamian argument, as in other anti-skeptical arguments, I must begin with an attitude of agnosticism about whether I am in a vat world or a normal world. He objects, though, that

Brueckner's understanding of agnosticism rules out an important kind of response to skepticism, one that begins by entertaining the possibility that a given skeptical hypothesis is coherent, and may actually be true, and ends by concluding that the hypothesis, while meaningful, cannot actually be true.

I do not see the force of this remark. I do begin by entertaining the possibility that the vat hypothesis is coherent and may actually be true. I would like to end up with the conclusion that the hypothesis is not actually true – the conclusion (C*). I guess I could put this by saying that *given* the success of the reasoning, the hypothesis *cannot* actually be true. So my understanding of agnosticism is perfectly compatible with acknowledging an anti-skeptical argument of the kind Ebbs describes. My objection to the reconstructed argument was just that in order to reach its desired conclusion that the skeptical hypothesis is actually false, I need to first know that conclusion: I need to know it in order to make the necessary disquotational step.

In Chapter 4, Ebbs goes on to say that on Putnam's view, though the vat hypothesis

may at first *seem* to be a coherent possibility, we discover after further semantic reflection that it is not coherent and that we cannot make sense of actually being a brain that is always in a vat.

I do not understand what Ebbs means here by 'coherent possiblity'. It seems to me that *if* I can successfully reach my desired conclusion, *then* I can rightly describe my position as follows: 'There is a coherent possibility that I was initially worried about, but I have now ruled out that coherent possibility as being non-actual'. It's just that I can't successfully reach that desired conclusion without assuming its truth. Regarding 'cannot make sense of actually being a BIV': it seems to me that *if* I can successfully reach my desired conclusion, *then* I can rightly describe my position as follows. 'I can make sense of actually being a BIV, but I have just proved that that hypothesis, though it makes sense, is actually false, just as I can prove that the hypothesis that my BMW actually has a VW engine, though it makes sense, is actually false'. It's just that I can't successfully reach the desired conclusion without assuming its truth.

13.3 INCOHERENCE AS *BEING SELF-UNDERMINING*

What does it mean to say that an argument is *incoherent*, such as an argument for skepticism about knowledge of the contents of one's own mental states – skepticism about self-knowledge? Let us start by considering a defect that an *argument* – viewed as a set of sentences expressing propositions – can suffer from. An argument is *formally circular* when it has the following structure:

P1
P2
.
.
C
.
.
Pn
So, C

You can tell that an argument is formally circular just by inspecting its premises and conclusion.

There are also epistemic defects that attach to cases of *reasoning*, where this is viewed as a psychological process in which a particular thinker reasons from the premises of an argument to the conclusion of the argument. Consider *epistemic circularity*. S's reasoning from some premises to a conclusion exhibits epistemic circularity just in case the justification that S has for some premises involves or requires his belief of the conclusion. You cannot tell whether a thinker's reasoning from premises to conclusion is epistemically circular just by inspecting the premises and conclusion. You have to know what is *his justification* for the premises. Consider the following *track record argument* TR:

Vision says that P on occasion 1 & P
Vision says that Q on occasion 2 & Q
.
.
.
Vision says that Z on occasion n & Z
So, Vision is reliable.

If S reasons using TR, is his reasoning epistemically circular? It all depends upon S's reasons for, justifications for, the premises. If S believes the second conjuncts of his premises on the basis of a belief of his conclusion – that vision is reliable – then his reasoning is epistemically circular. But if S believes the second conjuncts on the basis of divine revelation, or on the basis of testimony, or on the basis of the use of touch, then whatever are the merits of the reasoning, it cannot be criticized as being epistemically circular. So epistemic circularity of reasoning, unlike formal circularity of arguments, is not "inspectable."[1]

So, again, what does it mean to say that an argument, or maybe a piece of reasoning, is *incoherent*? Ebbs's writings in our exchange about skepticism about knowledge of content in Chapters 6–11 suggest that being incoherent is a matter of being somehow *self-undermining* or *self-defeating*. Let us consider several formulations of the notion of *being self-undermining* that emerged during our exchange. Consider

(SU1) A piece of reasoning by S is *self-undermining 1* just in case: if S's conclusion is true, then S does not know what his premises mean.

A model "skepticism about knowledge of content" argument that Ebbs and I discussed at length – call it S-K – is, I agreed, self-undermining 1.

(A) I do *not* know that my sincere utterances of 'There is water in the basement' do *not* express the thought that there is twin-water in the basement.
(B) If I know that my sincere utterances of 'There is water in the basement' express the thought that there is water in the basement, then I know that my sincere utterances of 'There is water in the basement' do *not* express the thought that there is twin-water in the basement.

So,

(~K) I do not know that my sincere utterances of 'There is water in the basement' express the thought that there is water in the basement.

If I reason through S-K, then I arrive at a conclusion which satisfies SU1: if the conclusion (~K) is true, then I do not know what my premises mean, since I do not know which language they are in (English vs. Twin-English). But I did not regard this as being a major problem for the reasoning. I *in effect* replied that the potentially *nasty* sort of self-underminingness is captured in the following formulation:

---

[1] Similar remarks about an epistemic defect of a piece of reasoning not being inspectable apply to Crispin Wright's *transmission failure* and to Jonathan Vogel's *bootstrapping*. See Wright 2004 and Vogel 2000.

(SU2) A piece of reasoning by S is *self-undermining 2* just in case: if S's conclusion is true, then either (i) S does not know his premises to be true, and hence does not know that his reasoning is sound – S does not know that he reasons validly from true premises to a true conclusion, or else (ii) S does not know that his reasoning is sound in virtue of not knowing his reasoning to be valid.[2]

I in effect maintained in Chapter 7 that if I reason through S-K, then my reasoning is *not* self-undermining 2. This is because I know that my reasoning *is* sound in the sense of SU2 no matter whether I am reasoning in English or instead in Twin-English (and hence do not know the meanings of my premises and conclusion).

Ebbs replied in Chapter 8 that there are certain conditions, which I cannot knowledgeably rule out without empirical investigation, under which my reasoning using S-K *is* unsound (see his "weird world" example). Thus my reasoning using S-K *is* self-undermining 2: given the truth of my conclusion, I do *not* know my premises to be true and hence do *not* know my reasoning to be sound.

I in effect replied as follows in Chapter 9. Maybe being self-undermining 2 is not a terrible sin. I reason through S-K to my skeptical conclusion ∼K. I can agree that given Ebbs's "weird world" gambit, it looks as if my S-K reasoning is self-undermining 2. But my counter-gambit was as follows. We can "embed" S-K within a larger argument by cases. We have two possibilities: (I) My sentences express the contents I take them to express; in this case I can take my sentences at face value, and thus my S-K reasoning for ∼K is sound; (II) My sentences do *not* express the contents I take them to express (say, I am on Twin Earth, or, worse, in the "weird world"); in this case, we again have my conclusion ∼K, in virtue of the factivity of knowledge – if my thoughts do *not* express the contents I take them to express (such as that there is water in the basement), then I do not know that they *do*.

In Chapter 10, Ebbs replied, in effect, that being self-undermining 2 *is* indeed a sin. I, in the role of the skeptic, reason through S-K to my conclusion ∼K, but, on my admission, I do not know whether my reasoning for ∼K is sound. Is this a problem?

13.4 FRENCH CONNECTION I

The question of whether a stretch of reasoning's being self-undermining 2 is clearly a bad thing is revisited in my Chapter 11. One of the examples of

---

[2] When I say "in effect" above and in the text that follows, my point is that Ebbs and I never explicitly formulated principles SU1 and SU2.

self-undermining 2 reasoning I discussed there concerned the full-bore Cartesian Evil Genius hypothesis and thus takes us all the way back to Meditation I. I will leave it to the reader to, again, peruse my use of the Evil Genius in that example, but I will now proceed to take a bit broader of a look at how the Evil Genius hypothesis bears on the alleged defect of being self-undermining 2. Descartes clearly engages in such reasoning in Meditation I. He eventually repudiates the reasoning, but *not* on the grounds that it is somehow incoherent because self-undermining 2.

This is a bit of a long story, but let me start by saying that as a graduate student teaching assistant for a course taught by Keith Donnellan, I first encountered the question (from Donnellan): "Hasn't Descartes made the Evil Genius too strong?" This is a question that is echoed in a way in a famous paper by my former colleague Harry Frankfurt: "Descartes on the Validation of Reason."[3] I will return to Frankfurt's Descartes below. The issue is this: in the full-bore unrestricted Evil Genius skeptical hypothesis of Meditation I, I am asked to conceive of an apparently metaphysically possible world in which all that exists is (1) me, a non-physical mind with mental states exactly like those I actually possess over time, and (2) a God-like Evil Genius who directly causes my sense-experiences and non-experientially based beliefs. My experientially based beliefs are all mistaken (because there is no physical world to make them true), and my seemingly a priori known, non-experientially based beliefs (about mathematics, logic, pure geometry, conceptual matters, etc.) are also all mistaken. That's just how *le malin genie* rolls! We have the following *Evil Genius Argument Schema* which will apply to *every* φ which I claim to know ('EG' denotes the foregoing Evil Genius Hypothesis):

$$K\varphi \to K{\sim}EG$$
$${\sim}K{\sim}EG$$
$$\text{So, } {\sim}K\varphi$$

The first premise is justified by the principle that knowledge is closed under known entailment, and the second by familiar considerations concerning the experiential indiscriminability of normal worlds and EG worlds.

Doesn't the Evil Genius Agument somehow undermine itself? (I think that this was what Donnellan had in mind.) That is, when I reason through some instances of the above schema, isn't my reasoning self-undermining 2? Suppose, for example, that for 'φ' we put 'Modus Tollens is a valid rule of inference'. Then if the resulting argument's conclusion is true, I do not

---

[3] Frankfurt 1965, pp. 149–156.

know that my reasoning to that conclusion is sound, because I do not know that Modus Tollens is a valid rule of inference. I do not know that the reasoning is sound *not* because I fail to know whether the premises are true; rather, it is because I do not know that the reasoning is valid. So the reasoning is self-undermining 2 in virtue of the violation of clause (ii), not clause (i).[4]

A bit of digression follows. Consider the notion of *rule circularity*: a piece of reasoning by S for the conclusion that *an epistemic rule R is reliable* is *rule circular* just in case R is used in the reasoning. Jonathan Vogel, for one, holds that rule circularity is an epistemic sin.[5] Suppose rule R is of the form: 'If you have evidence Ei, then you are justified in believing Hi'. Consider the argument schema

(A) Ei
(B) Hi (using the rule R).
(C) Rule R generates the conclusion Hi.
(D) Rule R generates the conclusion Hi & Hi.
(E) Repeat many times.
(F) Therefore, the use of rule R is reliable.

If the (B)-like premises can be supported on grounds that do *not* involve the use of R, then the reasoning would be acceptable. But as it stands in the represented reasoning (see (B)), this is not so. Hence the represented reasoning is rule circular and therefore objectionable, according to Vogel. This is because there is a *defeater* of the justification which the premises of the form on display would otherwise provide for the conclusion if they were independently supported:

(RC) The represented reasoning for (F) is rule circular.

Let us return to the 'Modus Tollens is a valid principle of inference' instantiation of the Evil Genius Argument Schema. The situation there is close to being the *inverse* of rule circular reasoning. The reliability of Modus Tollens is assumed *in practice* in the reasoning (though not as a *premise*), and then Modus Tollens is shown to be *not known* to be valid by *using* Modus Tollens. This is not a *reductio ad absurdum*, in which

Modus Tollens is a valid principle of inference

is assumed as a premise in reasoning in the course of which a contradiction is deduced using other unimpeachable premises. But the reasoning is in the

---

[4] One might countenance the possibility that reasoning can be legitimately self-undermining in this second way but not in the first. See Ebbs's Chapter 12, fn. 2.
[5] See Vogel 2008, pp. 518–539.

ballpark of *reductio* reasoning: you could call it *rule reductio ad absurdum* (*RRAA*). In an RRAA argument, a rule of reasoning is used in the reasoning to show that the rule's validity is not known (as opposed to rule circular reasoning's showing that a rule under consideration is reliable by using the rule).

13.5 FRENCH CONNECTION II

On Frankfurt's reading of Descartes, Descartes embarks upon the *Meditations* while being open to the possibility that the strictest use of reason will undermine reason itself: it will lead to the conclusion that reason is unreliable. Such a use of reason would be self-undermining 2, as is the foregoing 'Modus Tollens is valid' instance of the Evil Genius Argument Schema. Descartes, on this reading of him, did not rule out of court the possibility of a self-undermining 2 outcome for his investigation of the consistency of reason. On Frankfurt's interpretation, though, Descartes thought in the end that when reason examines its own powers, when reason is used in the strictest possible way, the feared outcome does not in fact eventuate, though it clearly seemed at the outset that it *could have*. This is because the strictest possible use of reason leads to proofs of the existence of a non-deceiving God who ensures that whatever is clearly and distinctly perceived is true. This is what Frankfurt calls "Descartes's validation of reason."

However, Frankfurt, in a footnote, raises the following worry.[6] Let us grant that the strictest use of reason leads to the conclusion that (1) reason is reliable because a veracious God exists. Frankfurt wonders:

> may it not also lead to the conclusion that [2] there is an omnipotent demon whose existence renders reason unreliable? Of course, these conclusions [(1) and (2)] are incompatible, and if the proper use of reason established both of them it would mean that reason is unreliable.

Frankfurt is chiefly worried in his paper about the circularity charge that has been leveled against Descartes's overall procedure in the *Meditations*, and he argues at length that this charge is misplaced. This is not our concern here, but it is worth noting that having raised the bleak possibility of the foregoing double outcome – reason is proved to be both reliable and unreliable by the strictest use of reason – Frankfurt says that Descartes surely "cannot take for granted" that the bleak possibility is *not* realized. In other words, Descartes surely "cannot take for granted" that the strictest use

---

[6] Frankfurt 1965, p. 155, fn. 22.

of reason is *not* self-undermining 2. Taking this for granted would beg the question of the consistency of reason, reopening the charge of circularity (albeit a *different* sort of circularity charge, says Frankfurt, from that which has traditionally been laid at Descartes's door).

Thus, worries about the genuine possibility of successful self-undermining 2 reasoning seem to have an historical pedigree. This is not exactly a validation of the kosher character of such reasoning, but it is at least worth noting that the father of modern skepticism seemed to countenance the possibility that skeptical reasoning in its most radical form is self-undermining 2 (and is an instance of RRAA). Much of the work of the *Meditations*, at least on Frankfurt's reading, consists in ruling out this apparently genuine possibility.

In the end, I think that RRAA reasoning and self-undermining 2 reasoning are as legitimate as regular reductio ad absurdum reasoning. I think that the incoherence charge has not been made good in the following sense. Assume that the charge "Skeptical reasoning about knowledge of one's thought-contents is incoherent" is understood to mean that such reasoning is self-undermining 2. I grant that this charge is well-founded, as explained in the foregoing synopsis. But I think that it has not been established that if a piece of reasoning is self-undermining 2, then it can be rejected on *that* ground alone.[7] Some other problem with the reasoning must be elucidated.[8]

---

[7] For support for Ebbs's side of the debate on the incoherence charge, see Wright 1991.

[8] I would like to thank Tyler Burge for many discussions of anti-individualism over the years, starting from when he first introduced his views in graduate seminars at UCLA in the 70s. I would also like to thank Michael Clark for helpful discussions in his capacity as editor of *Analysis*. My greatest debt, of course, is to Gary Ebbs for engaging in these stimulating exchanges and for collaboration on this volume.

Bibliography

Papers by Brueckner and Ebbs that appear in this volume cite other papers of theirs that appear in the volume. These are listed in the Acknowledgements, and are not also included in the following list.

Austin, J. L. 1979. Other minds. In J. O. Urmson and G. J. Warnock, eds., *Philosophical Papers*, 3rd edn., Oxford University Press, pp. 76–116.

Bilgrami, Akeel. 1992. Can externalism be reconciled with self-knowledge?, *Philosophical Topics* 20: 223–267.

Boghossian, Paul. 1989. Content and self-knowledge. *Philosophical Topics* 17: 5–26.

    1992. Externalism and inference. In E. Villanueva, ed., *Rationality in Epistemology*, Atascadero, Calif.: Ridgeview Publishing Co., pp. 11–28.

Brueckner, Anthony. 1984. Putnam's model-theoretic argument against metaphysical realism. *Analysis* 44: 134–140.

    1985. Skepticism and epistemic closure. *Philosophical Topics* 13: 89–117. Reprinted in *Essays on Skepticism*.

    1990. Scepticism about knowledge of content. *Mind* 99: 447–451. Reprinted in *Essays on Skepticism*.

    1992a. Semantic answers to skepticism. *Pacific Philosophical Quarterly* 73: 200–219. Reprinted in *Essays on Skepticism*.

    1992b. Genova, Davidson, and content scepticism. *Analysis* 52: 228–231.

    1994a. Knowledge of content and knowledge of the world. *Philosophical Review* 103: 327–343. Reprinted in *Essays on Skepticism*.

    1994b. The structure of the skeptical argument. *Philosophy and Phenomenological Research* 54: 827–35. Reprinted in *Essays on Skepticism*.

    2003. Two transcendental arguments concerning self-knowledge. In S. Nuccetelli, ed., *New Essays on Semantic Externalism and Self-Knowledge*, Cambridge, Mass.: MIT Press, pp. 185–200.

    2010. *Essays on Skepticism*. Oxford University Press.

Burge, Tyler. 1979. Individualism and the mental. In P. A. French, T. E. Uehling, and H. K. Wettstein, eds., *Midwest Studies in Philosophy* Volume IV, Minneapolis: University of Minnesota Press, pp. 73–122.

    1982a. Two thought experiments reviewed. *Notre Dame Journal of Formal Logic* 32: 284–293.

    1982b. Other bodies. In A. Woodfield, ed., *Thought and Object: Essays on Intentionality*, Oxford University Press, pp. 97–120.

1986. Cartesian error and the objectivity of perception. In P. Pettit and J. McDowell, eds., *Subject, Thought, and Context*, Oxford University Press.

1988a. Individualism and self-knowledge. *Journal of Philosophy* 85: 649–663.

1988b. Reply: authoritative self-knowledge and perceptual individualism. In R. Grim and D. Merril, eds., *Contents of Thought*, Tucson: University of Arizona Press.

2003. Mental agency in authoritative self-knowledge: Reply to Kobes. In M. Hahn and B. Ramberg, eds., *Reflections and Replies: Essays on the Philosophy of Tyler Burge*, Cambridge, Mass.: MIT Press, pp. 417–433.

2010. *Origins of Objectivity*. Oxford: Clarendon Press.

Christensen, David. 1993. Skeptical problems, semantic solutions. *Philosophy and Phenomenological Research* 53: 301–321.

Davidson, Donald. 1974. On the very idea of a conceptual scheme. In Donald Davidson, *Inquiries into Truth and Interpretation*, Oxford: Clarendon Press, pp. 183–198.

1984a. The method of truth metaphysics. In Donald Davidson, *Inquiries into Truth and Interpretation*, Oxford: Clarendon Press, pp. 199–214.

1984b. First-person authority. *Dialectica* 38: 101–111.

1986. A coherence theory of truth and interpretation. In *Truth and Interpretation*. Oxford: Blackwell.

1987. Knowing one's own mind. *Proceedings and Addresses of the American Philosophical Association* 60: 441–458.

1988. Reply to Burge. *Journal of Philosophy* 85: 664–665.

1991. Three varieties of knowledge. In A. Phillips Griffith, ed., *A. J. Ayer: Memorial Essays*, Cambridge University Press, pp. 153–166.

Dretske, Fred. 1970. Epistemic operators. *Journal of Philosophy* 67: 1007–1023.

Ebbs, Gary. 1992. Realism and rational inquiry. *Philosophical Topics* 20: 1–33.

1997. *Rule-Following and Realism*. Cambridge: Mass., Harvard University Press.

2003. A puzzle about doubt. In S. Nuccetelli, ed., *New Essays on Semantic Externalism and Self-Knowledge*, Cambridge, Mass.: MIT Press, pp. 143–168.

2009. *Truth and Words*. Oxford University Press.

Eliot, T. S. 1963. Fragment of an agon. In *Collected Poems: 1909–1962*, 130–136. London: Faber and Faber Ltd.

Evans, Gareth. 1982. *Varieties of Reference*. Oxford: Clarendon Press.

Falvey, Kevin and Owens, Joseph. 1994. Externalism, self-knowledge, and skepticism. *Philosophical Review* 103: 107–137.

Fodor, Jerry. Narrow meaning and content holism. Unpublished.

1982. Cognitive science and the twin-earth problem. *Notre Dame Journal of Formal Logic* 32: 98–118.

Frankfurt, Harry. 1965. Descartes' validation of reason. *American Philosophical Quarterly* 2: 149–156.

Gallois, André. 1992. Putnam, brains in vats, and arguments for skepticism. *Mind* 101: 273–286.

Genova, A. C. 1991. Craig on Davidson: a thumbnail refutation. *Analysis* 51: 195–198.

Heil, John. 1988. Privileged access. *Mind* 1988: 238–251.

Hill, Christopher S. 1990. Review of *Subject, Thought, and Context*, ed. P. Pettit and J. McDowell. *Journal of Philosophy* 87: 106–112.

Horwich, Paul. 1982. How to choose between empirically indistinguishable theories. *Journal of Philosophy* 79: 61–77.

Hylton, Peter. 1991–2. Translation, meaning, and self-knowledge. *Proceedings of the Aristotelian Society* 91: 269–290.

Kaplan, David. 1989. Demonstratives. In J. Almog, J. Perry, and H. Wettstein, eds., *Themes from Kaplan*, Oxford University Press, pp. 481–569.

Kripke, Saul. 1982. *Wittgenstein on Rules and Private Language*. Cambridge, Mass.: Harvard University Press.

Loar, Brian. 1988. Social content and pscyhological content. In R. Grimm and D. Merrill, eds., *Contents of Thought*, Tuscon: University of Arizona Press, pp. 99–110.

Malcolm, Norman. 1949. Defending common sense. *Philosophical Review* 58: 201–220.

Moore, G. E. 1959a. Four forms of skepticism. In G. E. Moore, *Philosophical Papers*, London: Allen and Unwin, pp. 196–225.

  1959b. Certainty. In G. E. Moore, *Philosophical Papers*, London: Allen and Unwin, pp. 226–251.

Moran, Richard. 2001. *Authority and Estrangement: an Essay on Self-Knowledge*. Cambridge, Mass., Harvard University Press.

McIntyre, Jane. 1984. Putnam's brains. *Analysis* 44: 59–61.

Nagel, Thomas. 1986. *The View from Nowhere*. Oxford University Press.

Nozick, Robert. 1981. *Philosophical Explanations*. Cambridge, Mass.: Harvard University Press.

Putnam, Hilary. 1962. The analytic and the synthetic. Reprinted in Hilary Putnam, *Mind, Language, and Reality: Philosophical Papers*, Vol. II, Cambridge University Press, 1975, pp. 33–69. Originally published in Herber Feigl and Grover Maxwell, eds., *Minnesota Studies in the Philosophy of Science*, Vol. III, Minneapolis: University of Minnesota Press, 1962.

  1975. The meaning of 'meaning'. In Hilary Putnam, *Mind, Language, and Reality: Philosophical Papers*, Vol. II, Cambridge University Press, 1975, pp. 215–271.

  1978. Realism and reason. In Hilary Putnam, *Meaning and the Moral Sciences*. Boston: Routledge and Kegan Paul.

  1980. Models and reality. *Journal of Symbolic Logic* 44: 464–482.

  1981. *Reason, Truth, and History*. Cambridge University Press.

  1987. Truth and convention: on Davidson's refutation of conceptual relativism. *Dialectica* 41: 69–77.

  1988. *Representation and Reality*. Cambridge, Mass.: MIT Press.

  1989. Why is a Philosopher? In A. Cohen, and M. Dascal, eds., *The Institution of Philosophy*, La Salle, Ill.: Open Court.

Quine, W. V. 1940. *Mathematical Logic*. Cambridge, Mass.: Harvard University Press.

1960. *Word and Object*. Cambridge, Mass.: MIT Press.

Searle, John R. 1987. Indeterminacy, empiricism, and the first person. *Journal of Philosophy* 84: 123–146.

Shoemaker, Sydney. 1988. On knowing one's own mind. *Philosophical Perspectives* 2: 183–209.

　　1994. Self-knowledge and "inner sense." *Philosophy and Phenomenological Research* 54: 249–314.

Stalnaker, Robert. 1990. Narrow Content. In C. A. Anderson and J. Owens, eds., *Propositional Attitudes*, Chicago: CSLI Lecture Notes, pp. 131–145.

Stroud, Barry. 1984. *The Significance of Philosophical Scepticism*. Oxford: Clarendon Press.

Tymoczko, Thomas. 1989. In defense of Putnam's brains. *Philosophical Studies* 57: 281–297.

Vogel, Jonathan. 2000. Reliabilism leveled. *Journal of Philosophy* 97: 602–623.

　　2008. Epistemic bootstrapping. *Journal of Philosophy* 105: 518–39.

Williams, Bernard. 1978. *Descartes: the Project of Pure Enquiry*. Harmondsworth: Penguin.

Williams, Michael. 1984. Review of *Reason, Truth and History* by Hilary Putnam. *Journal of Philosophy* 81: 257–261.

　　1988. Skepticism and charity, *Ratio* 12: 176–194.

Wright, Crispin. 1991. Scepticism and dreaming: imploding the demon. *Mind* 397: 87–116.

　　2004. Warrant for nothing. *Supplement to the Proceedings of the Aristotelian Society* 78: 167–212.

Index

var